Theorizing Race in the Americas

Theorizing Race in the Americas

Douglass, Sarmiento, Du Bois, and Vasconcelos

JULIET HOOKER

Oxford University Press is a department of the University of Oxford. It furthers
the University's objective of excellence in research, scholarship, and education
by publishing worldwide. Oxford is a registered trade mark of Oxford University
Press in the UK and certain other countries.

Published in the United States of America by Oxford University Press
198 Madison Avenue, New York, NY 10016, United States of America.

Library of Congress Cataloging-in-Publication Data
Names: Hooker, Juliet, author.
Title: Theorizing Race in the Americas : Douglass, Sarmiento, Du Bois, and
Vasconcelos / Juliet Hooker.
Description: New York, NY : Oxford University Press, 2017. | Includes bibliographical
references and index.
Identifiers: LCCN 2016038306 (print) | LCCN 2017003616 (ebook) |
ISBN 9780190633691 (hardcover) |
ISBN 9780190055868 (paperback) |
ISBN 9780190633707 (Updf) | ISBN 9780190671273 (Epub)
Subjects: LCSH: Douglass, Frederick, 1818–1895—Political and social views. |
Sarmiento, Domingo Faustino, 1811–1888—Political and social views. |
Du Bois, W. E. B. (William Edward Burghardt), 1868–1963—Political and social views. |
Vasconcelos, José, 1881–1959—Political and social views. | Race relations—Philosophy. |
United States—Race relations—History. | Latin America—Race relations—History. |
United States—Intellectual life. | Latin America—Intellectual life. |
BISAC: POLITICAL SCIENCE / History & Theory.
Classification: LCC E449.D75 H66 2017 (print) | LCC E449.D75 (ebook) |
DDC 305.800973—dc23
LC record available at https://lccn.loc.gov/2016038306

To my mother, Thalia Coe

Contents

Acknowledgments

WRITING ABOUT FOUR such iconic thinkers as Douglass, Sarmiento, Du Bois, and Vasconcelos could have been a daunting task, but working on this book has been a pleasure and extremely rewarding. I am eternally grateful for the enthusiasm with which this project has been met whenever I have presented it, and for the many suggestions about texts, events, ideas, and arguments from so many colleagues who are experts in Latin American and African American political thought, or those who work in other fields but have also generously engaged with the book. Their contributions have enormously enriched this book. My deepest thanks to all of them, and as always any errors or omissions that remain are entirely my own.

In particular, I wish to thank the following individuals who made suggestions, read drafts, commented on various chapters or generally nurtured the project. Kate Gordy generously commented on the introduction and various other parts of the book. She has been a key interlocutor on Sarmiento and Latin American political thought in general going back to graduate school, and her encouragement and advice throughout have been invaluable. Likewise, conversations and co-teaching with Stephen Marshall over many years have deepened and informed my thinking on African American political thought. Our disagreements about Douglass pushed me to develop the arguments about black fugitivity in the book. Neil Roberts has been an enthusiastic supporter of the project and encouraged me to highlight the hemispheric dimension of Douglass's political thought. Lawrie Balfour, Inés Valdez, and Minkah Makalani provided key suggestions and feedback on Du Bois. My thanks to Lawrie, in particular, who provided extensive and extremely helpful comments on the entire manuscript. Alejandro de la Fuente pushed me to foreground the shared intellectual context of scientific racism and to sharpen my discussion of mestizaje. Jossianna Arroyo and Emiko Saldivar helped me think through key arguments about mestizaje that sharpened my analysis of Vasconcelos. Christina Beltrán encouraged me to publish an article on the connections between Vasconcelos and Anzaldúa much earlier than I normally would have, and my thinking about Latino politics has benefited enormously from conversations with her. Jimmy Causas Klausen provided critical feedback on an early version of chapter 2 that forced me to rethink my reading of Sarmiento in key ways. Adam Dahl, Maya Berry, and Tony Lucero provided valuable suggestions that helped me more fully develop the concept of juxtaposition as an alternative to comparison. Charlie Hale and Jeff Tulis gave important feedback on structure and argumentation as I began to conceptualize the book, and Jeff was a generous source of advice at various stages of the publication process.

Audiences at conferences, workshops, and talks at the following venues and institutions provided valuable comments and suggestions on draft chapters and the ideas of the book in general: the annual meetings of the American Political Science Association, the Western Political Science Association, and the Latin American Studies Association, the Working Group on Racisms in Comparative Perspective at New York University, the Reproduction of Race and Racial Ideologies Workshop at the University of Chicago, the Afro-Latino Working Group in the Department of African American Studies at Northwestern University, the Faculty Seminar of the Center for African and African-American Studies at the University of Texas at Austin, the Political Theory Workshop at Texas A&M University, the Political Theory Workshop at the University of Connecticut, the Conference on "Citizens, Constitutions, and Democracy in Post-Neoliberal Latin America" at the University of Pennsylvania, Williams College, the University of Washington, the University of California-Merced, Ohio State University, and the Graduate Center of the City University of New York.

This book could not have been completed without the generous financial support of various institutions. A Summer Stipend Award from the National Endowment for the Humanities and a Humanities Research Award from the College of Liberal Arts at the University of Texas at Austin were invaluable in funding trips to various archives and giving me time to write, and a University of Texas at Austin Subvention Grant awarded by the Office of the President that supported indexing costs. I am also deeply grateful for the various research leaves supported by the College of Liberal Arts at the University of Texas at Austin, without which the manuscript would have taken much longer to complete, including a College Research Fellowship, a Faculty Research Assignment, and a Supplemental College Research Fellowship. I also received a Faculty Research Leave from the

Teresa Lozano Long Institute of Latin American Studies at the University of Texas at Austin, which helped fund a semester of leave. The process of writing and revision was made much more amenable by two semesters spent as a Visiting Fellow in the extremely collegial and productive settings of the W. E. B. Du Bois Institute for African American Research at Harvard University and the Advanced Research Collaborative at the Graduate Center of the City University of New York. The faculty, graduate students, and staff at the Du Bois Institute and ARC were generous and supportive hosts, and I benefited tremendously from the interdisciplinary conversations and convivial company of Nigel Hatton, Celia Cussen, Henry Louis Gates Jr., Don Robotham, Veronica Benet-Martinez, Kim Potowski, Janet Johnson, and many others. At a crucial stage in the process, Tom Pangle, the Joe R. Long Chair in Democratic Studies, and the Teresa Lozano Long Institute of Latin American Studies generously funded a book manuscript workshop in which I received valuable feedback from colleagues and graduate students, including Lawrie Balfour, Alejandro de la Fuente, Stephen Marshall, and Minkah Makalani, who generously agreed to serve as discussants.

I received invaluable research assistance on this book from various archives and individuals. The holdings at the Schomburg Center for Research in Black Culture in New York City and the Benson Latin American Collection at the University of Texas at Austin were essential to the completion of the book. I especially want to thank the staff at the Museo Histórico Sarmiento in Buenos Aires, especially Adriana de Muro in the Archivo Histórico and Vilma Perez. Over the course of writing the book I benefited immensely from the energy and enthusiasm of various graduate research assistants; at Harvard: Layla Bermeo, at UT-Austin: Courtney Morris, Alysia Mann Carey, David Hutchinson, and Pablo Lopez Oro. I am especially indebted to Courtney, who helped with the initial research as I was still conceiving the book. At a key moment Marianela Muñoz gathered materials for me at the Benson while I was away from Austin. The arguments in this book have also been propelled by discussions and debates over the years with students in my graduate seminars on Latin American and African American political thought. I am grateful for their insight and enthusiasm. Cambridge University Press graciously allowed me to reuse: " 'A Black Sister to Massachusetts': Latin America and the Fugitive Democratic Ethos of Frederick Douglass," *American Political Science Review* 109, no. 4 (November 2015): 690–702; and portions of "Hybrid Subjectivities, Latin American Mestizaje, and Latino Political Thought on Race," *Politics, Groups, and Identities* 2, no. 2 (2014): 188–201, are reprinted with the permission of Taylor & Francis

Ltd., on behalf of the Western Political Science Association. I am grateful to the anonymous reviewers for both journals for their helpful feedback.

While this book was being written I was fortunate to be surrounded by smart, supportive colleagues in the Departments of African and African Diaspora Studies and Government at the University of Texas at Austin. I am also thankful for the friends and colleagues in Austin and beyond who provided community and fellowship while I was in the process of writing this book, especially Jossianna Arroyo, Lyndon Gill, Xavier Livermon, Simone Browne, Ted Gordon, Jennifer Wilks, Charlie Hale, Melissa Smith, Luis Cárcamo, Lorraine Leu, Carlos Ramos-Scharron, Alfonso Gonzalez, Sean Theriault, Megan Thomas, Tianna Paschel, Shatema Threadcraft, Al Tillery, Leith Mullings, Frank Guridy, Jafari Allen, Dalizza Rodriguez, and Carla López.

I would be remiss not to thank Angela Chnapko at Oxford University Press, who has been a pleasure to work with. I would also like to thank the anonymous reviewers for the press, whose enthusiastic response to the initial manuscript and insightful suggestions were enormously encouraging. The final version of the book has benefited significantly from their input.

The map that became the cover artwork is one of over 60 charts, graphs, and maps that visualize data on the state of black life in the United States, produced under the direction of W. E. B. Du Bois for the "Exhibit of American Negroes" that he co-curated for the *Exposition Universelle* held in Paris in 1900. The hand-drawn illustrations, and the exhibit in general, were meant to represent black contributions to the United States since emancipation. It is an apt reminder that the work of all the thinkers in this book transcended national boundaries.

Finally, I need to thank my family for their love and support. My maternal family, the Coes, including my aunts, uncles, cousins, and my sister Thalia, have been a constant source of encouragement and good times. I particularly want to thank my parents, Thalia Coe and Ray Hooker. This book is dedicated to my mom, who has helped make me the woman I am today. My dad, whose life's work as a teacher and public servant has been an inspiration, has been attentive to the book's progress, and was the one who suggested that I include photographs of each thinker. My grandmother Lilia is no longer with us in body, but her spirit lives on. I have now lived half my life in the United States, but growing up as a part of Bluefields's creole community on Nicaragua's Caribbean Coast shaped my outlook on Latin America and the African Diaspora, and made me attuned to the way people and ideas travel across the hemisphere. This book is an homage to those linkages.

J.H.

Theorizing Race in the Americas

Introduction

RACE THEORY AND HEMISPHERIC JUXTAPOSITION

IN 1845 TWO thinkers from the American hemisphere—the Argentinean *pensador* and statesman Domingo Faustino Sarmiento, and the fugitive ex-slave, abolitionist leader, and brilliant black thinker and orator from the United States Frederick Douglass—both published their first books. *Facundo: Civilization and Barbarism* and *Narrative of the Life of Frederick Douglass, an American Slave, Written by Himself* would become the most famous and enduring texts in what were both prolific careers. *Facundo* and the *Narrative* also ensured Sarmiento and Douglass's positions as leading figures in the canon of Latin American and US African American political thought, respectively.[1] *Facundo* has been described as "the most important book written by a Latin American in any discipline or genre," while Douglass's thought is said to have "influenced nearly every [subsequent] text in African-American philosophy."[2] Despite the fact that *Facundo* and the *Narrative* both deal directly with key political and philosophical questions in the Americas—such as the character of the post-independence *criollo* republics of the hemisphere and slavery's constitutive impact on these experiments in popular sovereignty—Douglass and Sarmiento are never read alongside each other. This could be attributed to the fact that they are seen as very different thinkers, both in terms of the social positions from which they approached the political problems of their respective nations and also in terms of their dominant philosophical preoccupations. Douglass was principally concerned first with slavery, and later racism's, distorting effects on democracy and republicanism, while Sarmiento wrote about the causes of post-independence political conflicts in Latin America and espoused a virulent form of anti-indigenous racism.

Yet their divergent political ideas are not the only, or even primary, reason that they are never read alongside each other. Rather, it is symptomatic of the fact that African American and Latin American political thought are rarely analyzed in conjunction.[3] There are several explanations for this aporia, from the differences between the thematic preoccupations that predominate in each tradition to the more practical obstacle posed by the fact that political theorists that specialize in one tradition are usually unfamiliar with the other. Yet there is much to be learned by reading US African American and Latin American political thought alongside each other, particularly where race is concerned. This book bridges this gap by developing a hemispheric conceptual frame that reveals the intellectual connections and political genealogies of racial thought within the Americas.

This is an account of dialogically formed racial discourses and political projects that intersect and bind (in its multiple meanings) the Americas to each other and to scientific discourses about race that comprise the shared intellectual backdrop of the hemispheric juxtapositions traced here. It is thus also a book about how ideas travel. It analyzes the ideas about race of four prominent nineteenth- and twentieth-century US African American and Latin American thinkers—Frederick Douglass, Domingo F. Sarmiento, W. E. B. Du Bois, and José Vasconcelos—in order to chart a hemispheric intellectual genealogy of race theory produced in the Americas at key historical moments. Tracing these links shows how leading ideas about race across the hemisphere were conceived in relation to the "other" America: the United States for Latin American thinkers, and Latin America for African American thinkers. I thus approach Douglass, Sarmiento, Du Bois, and Vasconcelos as hemispheric thinkers. They are hemispheric thinkers because they (to differing degrees) looked to the other America as a source of inspiration or contrast, and engaged with political or philosophical problems central to the Americas, such as the legacy of slavery, mestizaje (racial mixture), multiracial democracy, and so on.[4]

Dominant readings of all four thinkers have often suffered from a kind of unthinking nationalism. To read Douglass, Sarmiento, Du Bois, and Vasconcelos as hemispheric thinkers is to dislocate them from the purely national frames in which their political ideas are usually analyzed.[5] It highlights elements of their political thought that have been dismissed as anomalous or ignored altogether. For Latin American thinkers, for example, the United States functioned not only as a foil in a comparative trope that served to vindicate Latin America. Because these thinkers (not just their ideas) also traveled, we see that Sarmiento and Vasconcelos actually developed some of their more radical and progressive ideas about race while living in the United States or in their writings about US racial politics. Meanwhile, in Douglass's case, we see the extent to which he and other African Americans in the pre–Civil War era engaged with what they viewed as sites of black freedom and multiracial democracy in the Caribbean and Central America, thereby revealing a heretofore underappreciated hemispheric dimension of his political ideas. Racial mixing or mestizaje likewise emerges as a key theme in Du Bois's political thought. Adopting a hemispheric intellectual frame thus allows us to better understand how African American and Latin American thinkers, who wrote and lived side by side, theorized race.

I trace the links between US African American and Latin American ideas about race and demonstrate the centrality of those ideas for anti-racist political projects in both contexts. For thinkers in both traditions mythologies of race were formed in relation to an American other.[6] Hemispheric comparison has been central to the formulation of both African American and Latin American ideas about race. This is a well-known feature of Latin American political thought, but is much less recognized in the case of US thinkers. Latin American thinkers were forced to grapple with the United States as both a model and imperial threat. Reading both traditions side by side allows us to see that US thinkers also at times looked to Latin America for political models, however, particularly where race was concerned. Latin American thinkers, meanwhile, set themselves against both scientific racial thought produced in the United States and US racial politics. Or rather (more often) Latin American thinkers positioned their region as an alternative to their own creative misreading of US race relations. African American thinkers, meanwhile, also drew on their own (often romanticized) perceptions of Latin American race relations to intervene in US debates about race. For each tradition the other therefore functions at different moments as antithesis, object lesson, model, and aspiration.

This is a concurrent reading of two subaltern traditions that are generally viewed as disparate. Both African American and Latin American political thought are geographically Western, but not fully European. Yet characterizing elite thinkers such as Sarmiento and Vasconcelos as "subaltern" might seem surprising, as they were not marginal figures within Latin America. African American thinkers also occupy a complex, if more clearly marginal, position. While they are doubtless not the dominant voices within US political thought, they are nevertheless (geo-graphically at least) situated in the "Global North."[7] Yet these two tra-ditions are subaltern insofar as they are both situated at the margins of Western political thought; simultaneously of it, but not at its cen-ter. Sarmiento and Vasconcelos may be central figures in the canon of Latin American political thought, but the position of the tradition as a whole is marginal. Latin American and African American thinkers have drawn substantially on Western thinkers and ideas, but they incorpo-rate European ideas and sources in the service of exploring political and philosophical problems and experiences distinctive to the Americas. Douglass's political thought, for instance, is marked by the experi-ence of enslavement and fugitivity in ways that reshape and challenge typical understandings of freedom in Western political thought, while Sarmiento's preoccupation with American questions overtakes and dis-places Europe in his texts, even as he ostensibly embraces European ideas and rejects indigenous American sources.[8] Rather than engaging in the reflexive gesture in political theory to invoke or reject Europe, therefore, this book stages a South-to-South juxtaposition instead.[9] Instead of approaching African American and Latin American political thought as stable and discrete traditions, it shows how both ideas and thinkers traveled across the hemisphere.

Some of the constitutive elements of a political theory of race in the Americas revealed by adopting a hemispheric frame include an expanded concept of democratic fugitivity and the notion of mestizo futurism.[10] The question of multiracial democracy was a central preoccupation of both Douglass and Sarmiento, but my analysis of Douglass in particular revises the concept of democratic fugitivity. It shows how incorporating an account of slave fugitivity enriches contemporary democratic theory. Similarly, futu-rity in service of contemporaneous political projects is a theme throughout the book, but it is especially salient in Du Bois and Vasconcelos's accounts of the politics of mestizaje or racial mixing. I thus develop the concept of mestizo futurism to describe the way in which utopian fantasies of mixture allowed thinkers in the Americas in the first half of the twentieth century to formulate "a prehistory of . . . the third world," to envision a post-racist, decolonized Global South that was yet-to-be.[11] During historical eras when the dominance of scientific racism shaped rigid racial orders and political imaginations such that interracial intimacy was viewed as dangerous, Du Bois and Vasconcelos imagined different racial futures in order to bolster contemporaneous struggles against global white supremacy.

The questions that Douglass, Sarmiento, Du Bois, and Vasconcelos grappled with—immigration, multiracial democracy, racial violence, and the politics of mixture—are not just problems of the past. They endure, like a palimpsest of racial master codes that has never been fully erased or superseded. For instance, we see traces of Vasconcelos's theory of mestizaje, formulated in the first half of the twentieth century to counter US imperialism, in the contrast between Latin American and US processes of racial formation that undergirds contemporary accounts of Latino racial exceptionalism.[12] The intellectual hemispheric genealogy performed in this book urges us to move beyond such facile narratives about one region's superior approach to race. Tracing the use of strategies of racial comparison back to nineteenth-century US and Latin American thinkers who looked to political models in the "other" America to advance racial projects in their own countries, we can instead historicize the deployment of similar arguments in contemporary debates about race. These traces of the presence of the past are signaled throughout the book via brief, suggestive allusions to contemporary events, such as contemporary debates about immigration and the emergence of movements such as the DREAMers and Black Lives Matter in the United States, or the way Sarmiento "lives on" in Latin America in the form of repressive state policies toward indigenous peoples. References to the present are textual reminders of the complex entanglement of past, present, and future. The robust afterlife of previous hemispheric racial thought speaks to the continued salience of the ideas explored in this book. It is a reminder, as David Scott has observed, that political presents are always understood and theorized in relation to "reconstructed pasts and anticipated futures."[13]

A Shared Albatross: Scientific Racism

The US African American and Latin American thinkers examined here were operating within a common discursive field, which was the scientific racism that dominated US and European intellectual circles from the second half of the nineteenth through the first half of the twentieth century. Despite the divergence between US and Latin American racial formations, for Douglass, Sarmiento, Du Bois, and Vasconcelos, the racial science of their time functioned as a shared grammar of race, as they grappled with the same hegemonic racist ideas. Scientific racism was the leading science of the time, articulated by the best minds of the West and disseminated in its most illustrious centers of higher learning (such as Harvard, where

Louis Agassiz, a leading member of the American School of Ethnology with whose ideas both Douglass and Sarmiento engaged, was a distinguished faculty member). It was a corpus of knowledge, meanings, and truths that anyone thinking about race had to contend with, and which framed each of these thinkers's ideas in fundamental ways. This corpus was common to both pairs of authors. The ideological landscape within which their ideas about race emerged was thus constrained to an extent that is easy to miss today, when scientific racism has largely been debunked, by notions of biological racial difference and innate racial hierarchy that had the imprimatur of science.

The field of scientific racism changed over time during the two eras within which these thinkers formulated their ideas. In order to understand the broader transnational intellectual context within which Douglass, Sarmiento, Du Bois, and Vasconcelos operated it is thus necessary to map the different varieties of scientific racism that dominated intellectual production in the Americas and Europe between 1850 and 1890 in the case of the first pairing, and between 1890 and 1940 in the case of the second. The arguments of the American school of ethnology were a shared intellectual albatross hovering over both Douglass and Sarmiento, as was eugenics for Du Bois and Vasconcelos. At the same time, the pervasiveness of scientific racism did not mean that these thinkers had no agency in how they chose to understand and apply these ideas, which were themselves deeply contradictory and unsystematic. Douglass, Sarmiento, Du Bois, and Vasconcelos at times uncritically reproduced certain claims of scientific racism and selectively borrowed from racial science, but for the most part (albeit to varying degrees) they creatively reformulated and resisted it in the service of anti-racist and anti-colonial ends. Indeed, it is only against the backdrop of scientific racism that we can fully appreciate the revolutionary effects of their ideas, how subversive the mestizo futurisms of Du Bois and Vasconcelos were at the time.

Over the course of the nineteenth century, dominant Western ideas about race shifted from the (relatively) short-term explanations of human difference based on climate and environment that dominated Enlightenment thought, to full-fledged scientific theories of race as heredity and fixed notions of biological racial inferiority and "natural" racial hierarchy. Scientific racism is understood here to mean racial theories with the credence and backing of science that posited the innate and permanent inferiority of nonwhites.[14] Three principal strands of racist science emerged in the second half of the nineteenth century: the "ethnological-biological" school, the "historical school," and social Darwinism.[15] As George M. Fredrickson has shown, in the United States the ascendance of scientific racism began with the emergence of the American school of ethnology in the 1840s and 1850s, which "affirmed . . . that the races of mankind had been separately created as distinct and unequal species."[16] As polygenesis (the theory that different racial groups were created separately as distinct species endowed with unequal aptitudes) supplanted monogenesis (the theory that all humans were descended from a common origin and that different rates of degeneration accounted for subsequent differences between racial groups), explanations for racial difference shifted from external factors, such as climate and geography, to permanent inherited characteristics. Other elements of the scientific racism propounded by the American school of ethnology were the notion that there were separate climate zones destined for habitation by different racial groups, and that racial mixing led to degeneration.[17] Outside the United States, the American school of ethnology was also influential in Latin America. Their ideas were spread by European converts and the influence of one of its members, Louis Agassiz, who visited Brazil and was widely cited by Latin American intellectuals.[18]

Two other influential strands of scientific racism during the second half of the nineteenth century were racially deterministic theories of history that purported to establish the superiority of Aryans or Anglo-Saxons and social Darwinism. As exemplified by Count Joseph Arthur de Gobineau's writings, especially his *Essay on the Inequality of the Human Races* (1853–1855), the historical school argued that race was the central factor in historical development, that Aryans or Anglo-Saxons had reached the most advanced level of civilization, and that racial mixing led to degeneration.[19] Unlike the American ethnologists, de Gobineau accepted monogenesis, but the two strands coincided in presenting nonwhite inferiority as a predetermined historical fact. Usage of the term "race" during this era reflected the historical strand's restriction of its racially deterministic arguments about "white" superiority to Nordic or Northern European populations. Within racist science race was used to refer to both human groupings identified in terms of phenotype (such as blacks, whites, etc.) and to refer to distinctions between "Latins" and "Saxons." Latin Americans who accepted the premise of white supremacy but who believed that their populations could be "whitened" via racial mixing with European immigrants tended to gloss over the distinction between Latins and Anglo-Saxons, as most European immigrants to Latin America were from Southern Europe (i.e., Latins).

The third major strand of scientific racism during this era was social Darwinism (the application of biological concepts of natural selection and survival of the fittest to human society), which was very influential in Latin America.[20] Despite the fact that the premises of social Darwinism differed from the polygenist arguments of the American school of ethnology (because Darwin's arguments about evolution were based on the idea of mutations that began from a single species), adherents of racist science nevertheless managed to reconcile them.[21] Proponents of social Darwinism argued that different races exhibited different levels of aptitude, including the ability to survive and become dominant, and as a result some were destined to rule over others; their conclusions were thus the same as those of the other strands of racist science, it was the details of the explanations that differed. The ideas of the American school of ethnology, historical racial determinists/proponents of Aryan superiority, and social Darwinists formed the varied toolkit of scientific racism, despite the fact that some of the details of their various arguments supporting white supremacy contradicted each other. As Thomas Skidmore has observed about Brazil, in a characterization that is equally applicable to thinkers throughout the hemisphere, "these three schools of racist thought influenced all . . . who bothered to think seriously about race."[22]

Douglass and Sarmiento had to engage with racial science because its claims influenced key policy debates about slavery and US expansionism in the second half of the nineteenth century. For instance, in the United States, prior to the Civil War, the conclusions of the American school of ethnology were marshaled by defenders of slavery to buttress various arguments against abolition. Pro-slavery thinkers argued that enslavement benefited people of African descent by placing them in contact with a superior race, that blacks were destined to servitude because they were an inferior race that had never developed an advanced civilization, and that emancipation was unwise because it would lead to intermarriage and racial degeneration.[23] The claims of racial science were also used to argue against US expansionism to Latin America, and to justify black removal from the United States via colonization schemes. Opponents of expansionism argued that the United States should avoid incorporating Latin American countries composed mostly of inferior nonwhite races. At the same time, white advocates of the establishment of black colonies in Latin America also drew on the "new climatic racial determinism" to argue for black removal. Blacks and whites were supposedly destined to live in separate climate zones, they argued, and blacks should therefore be relocated to tropical regions.[24] For Latin Americans, meanwhile, racist science posed "a difficult intellectual dilemma."[25] On the one hand, many of the region's most influential thinkers embraced scientific racism because it provided a convenient explanation for the region's post-independence turmoil (which could be attributed to Latin American racial deficiencies), and because it justified the dominance of a white Europeanized elite over a large nonwhite or mixed-race population. Yet, on the other hand, the idea of Anglo-Saxon superiority was also problematic for Latin Americans as it served as a justification for US imperial expansion to the region.[26] Scientific racism was thus deployed in service of both promoting and resisting US expansionism to Latin America at different points in time.

Du Bois and Vasconcelos also had a shared intellectual foe in racist science, particularly the ideas of US eugenicist Madison Grant. In addition to the continued influence of some of the earlier strands of scientific racism, especially historical accounts of Aryan superiority and social Darwinism, the early decades of the twentieth century were the high point of eugenics, which was widely adopted and reformulated in various Latin American countries. According to Nancy Leys Stepan: "As a science, eugenics was based on supposedly new understanding of the laws of human heredity. As a social movement, it involved proposals that society ensure the constant improvement of its hereditary makeup by encouraging 'fit' individuals and groups to reproduce themselves and ... by discouraging or preventing the 'unfit' from contributing their unfitness to future generations."[27] Eugenics, as was the case with other strands of scientific racism, rather than a fringe or marginal movement, was highly respectable and embraced as the leading science of the day. In the United States (among other applications), it translated into legislation that mandated forced sterilization of "the poor (and often black) inmates of institutions for the feeble minded."[28] In Latin America, where it was so popular that "hardly a single area in ... [the region] remained completely untouched by eugenics by the 1930s," it took a somewhat different form. Latin Americans tended to selectively borrow from, and reassemble, race science.[29] The result was "a 'preventive' eugenics directed to improving the nation by cleansing ... [it of] those factors considered to be damaging to people's hereditary health."[30] Eugenics also played an important role in debates about the consolidation of national identity in Latin America, as hereditary science came to be seen as something that could assist in the biological homogenization of various national types. "Thus the Mexicans praised racial hybridization as itself a form of eugenization that would help consolidate the nation around the mestizo; [while] the Argentinians condemned racial and cultural intermixture as threats to the unity of an Argentine nationality."[31] Eugenics was thus widely influential throughout the Americas during this era.

In the United States, eugenics directly shaped official state policy in the decades prior to World War II. Eugenicists such as Madison Grant combined the racial determinism of the historical school with new notions of racial hygiene to argue for racial purity, racial segregation, bans on nonwhite immigration, and reductions in the flow of Southern European immigrants. Grant's *The Passing of the Great Race or The Racial Basis of European History*, which was first published in 1916, was immensely popular. It went through multiple printings and was translated into various languages, including French, in 1926, the edition that Vasconcelos read and commented on. Grant argued that the superior "Nordic" race needed to be defended against the threat of mixing with inferior races. Drawing on eugenics, he advocated for the separation and eventual removal (via sterilization) of undesirables, defectives, and inferior race types. Grant's ideas were influential on public policy in the United States. He advocated restricting immigration to the United States from Southern and Eastern Europe and banning it completely from Asia, prescriptions that were effectively encoded in the Immigration Act of 1924 with its national origin quotas. Grant was also a proponent of racial classification and anti-miscegenation laws that helped codify the "one-drop rule" and segregation in Virginia in the 1920s. Demonstrating the influence of eugenic ideas on various areas of public policy at the time, the Virginia "Racial Integrity Act" of 1924, which became a model for other racial segregation statutes in the US South, was passed at the same time as a forced sterilization act for the "feebleminded." Indeed, the resurgence and expansion (to include all nonwhites, not just blacks) of anti-miscegenation law in the first decades of the twentieth century in the United States found strong support in the dictates of the racial science of the day. Older and newer forms of scientific racism thus provided support for the encoding of white supremacy in public policy.

Vasconcelos and Du Bois, like other Latin American and African American thinkers writing about race in the first half of the twentieth century, therefore had to engage directly with eugenics, and other strands of racist science, if they wanted to counter theories of white supremacy. Important strands of thinking about international relations in the early twentieth century, for example, envisioned worldwide

Anglo-Saxon domination as a means of securing peace and order.[32] In the Americas, calcifying notions of Anglo-Saxon racial superiority served to legitimize US intervention in Latin America, with its large mixed-raced population and political turmoil that could be attributed to the effects of "Latin" backwardness. For anti-colonial thinkers such as Vasconcelos, who viewed Latin American racial, cultural, and political unity as necessary to counter US hegemony, articulating such a vision required directly refuting the tenets of racist science, particularly those of mestizo inferiority and Anglo-Saxon superiority. In the United States, meanwhile, miscegenation was one of the fulcrums of state policy on race in the United States during this era, and romances of white supremacy inspired by the ideas of racist science depicted interracial intimacy as monstrous and deviant. Du Bois and the National Association for the Advancement of Colored People (NAACP), founded in 1909, were directly involved in resisting the adoption of bans on interracial marriage in northern states between 1913 and 1929.[33] Beyond that, Du Bois and Vasconcelos formulated mestizo futurisms that refuted the dictates of scientific racism and provided alternative visions to racist white supremacist utopias.

On Method: Juxtaposition versus Comparison

One of the principal arguments advanced by this book is that we gain a better understanding of African American and Latin American ideas about race if we place them within a hemispheric frame, rather than reading the two traditions separately. The methodological approach pursued in this book is not conceived as an exercise in "comparison," however. As a number of scholars have noted, comparison is rarely neutral.[34] Some of the pitfalls of comparison that have plagued previous attempts at hemispheric analysis, including those undertaken by Douglass, Sarmiento, Du Bois, and Vasconcelos, include: (1) comparison constructs the racial, national, and cultural differences it purports to analyze; (2) comparison has been used to rank different units of analysis, which has obscured persistent forms of racial exclusion in both the United States and Latin America. As Micol Seigel observes regarding long-standing comparative exercises between the United States and Brazil, comparison helps produce the very national (or regional) characteristics that are its supposed object of study.[35] It assumes, or constructs, an illusion of coherence and distinctness of the units being compared. It thus tends to overlook moments of exchange or overlap, as in when ideas travel, or thinkers from different traditions engage with shared interlocutors.[36] Most centrally, however, there is also often an implied evaluative aspect of comparison, whereby it becomes an exercise in ranking. In the case of the thinkers analyzed in this book, for example, a common (and mistaken) assumption has been that its aim is to arrive at an assessment of which of the two traditions has formulated the better approach to race. Such evaluative stances have in fact suffused the way both US and Latin American thinkers have approached the task of hemispheric comparison. As a result they have been less concerned with finding out "the truth about the other America," than with setting it up as the antithesis to their America, and in turn as either object lesson or aspiration.[37] We have much to learn from a simultaneous reading of African American and Latin American thinkers's ideas about race, but not if we continue to conceive of hemispheric analysis as an exercise in ranking.

The anti-imperial strand of Latin American thought illustrates these pitfalls of comparison.[38] Comparison has been both a central thematic preoccupation and key methodological approach in Latin American political thought, particularly its anti-imperial strand. During the era of independence, Latin American colonial anxieties were directed at Europe, but they increasingly shifted to the United States in the post-independence era, as the United States emerged as the region's primary imperial threat. While the anti-imperial strand within Latin American political thought thus dates back to the nineteenth century, it reached its apex during the twentieth century, when Latin American thinkers of varied ideological and philosophical orientations—Marxists, nationalists, and liberals, as well as advocates of whitening, mestizaje, and *indigenismo*—all thematized the question of hemispheric power relations. Anti-imperial thinkers sought to both critique the United States and validate Latin America, and while there were a number of different axes on which the two regions were contrasted, race was a central feature of this exercise in hemispheric comparison, whose aim was to establish Latin America as the equal of its powerful northern neighbor. In the service of asserting the superiority of Latin American race relations, however, Latin American thinkers creatively misread certain aspects of US racial history, and they also downplayed or glossed over racial hierarchies and racism within their own countries. When comparison functions as a trope it thus involves creative misreading of the other refracted through one's own political concerns and philosophical dilemmas.[39] This kind of creative misreading is central to how many thinkers engage in "comparison," and, in fact, all of the thinkers examined here succumb to it at some point. A hemispheric genealogy of racial thought in the Americas thus reveals the paradoxes of comparison and exposes its methodological limitations in all contexts. The question, then, is how to still put thinkers and traditions in conversation while avoiding the various pitfalls of comparison.

I propose the concept of juxtaposition as a methodological alternative to comparison. By definition juxtaposition places two disparate objects side by side, and it is by being viewed simultaneously that the viewer's understanding of each object is transformed.[40] The metaphor of counterpoint in dance performance provides a useful illustration for how juxtaposition works as method. In dance, counterpoint is when two (or more) choreographic fragments with different uses of space, time, and/or body are executed simultaneously on the same stage.[41] The various elements on stage thus do not appear to be speaking directly to each other, but by being viewed side-by-side a relation between the pieces is revealed that would not be apparent if they were staged separately or sequentially. Juxtaposition thus allows us to ask: What happens when thinkers and traditions that are viewed as disparate are staged as proximate, what insights are revealed? "What can we see or understand differently by juxtaposing distinct and diverse . . . texts, contexts, and traditions?"[42] Most centrally, however, juxtaposition does not assume prior similarities or differences between thinkers and traditions. One of the problems with comparison is that it presumes the existence of stable and discrete traditions of thought that are available for comparison. But by assuming prior difference (or connection) between traditions, comparison does not interrogate the boundaries between traditions as contingent products of political power. In contrast, I view juxtaposition as a historical-interpretive approach that seeks to situate the resonances and/or discontinuities between traditions of thought within the specific historical, intellectual, cultural, and socioeconomic contexts in which they emerged.

In fact, juxtaposition as method reveals the importance of charting a hemispheric genealogy of how comparison itself is deployed as a trope by both African American and Latin American thinkers. The rhetorical and textual strategies of the thinkers analyzed here illustrate the difference between comparison and juxtaposition. Douglass, Sarmiento, Du Bois, and Vasconcelos all deployed hemispheric comparison as a trope, with its characteristic creative misreading of the other America. Du Bois's use of textual juxtaposition in *Darkwater* is closer to the methodological approach advanced here, however. Two key features of the use of juxtaposition in *Darkwater* are relevant to the approach to hemispheric analysis I adopt in this book. According to Susan Gilman and Alys Weinbaum, Du Bois deployed a textual "politics of juxtaposition" that connected questions of gender and sexuality present in *Darkwater*'s fictional pieces with the problems of race and empire analyzed in the book's nonfiction essays, yet these themes were not fully interwoven. They thus argue that it is necessary to read the fictional and nonfictional elements of Du Bois's multi-genre works alongside each other in order to fully understand his political ideas.[43] Lawrie Balfour meanwhile, focuses on the juxtaposition between romantic and tragic sensibilities in *Darkwater*'s fictional and non-fictional elements. Du Bois, she argues, included the fictional elements because straightforward philosophical argument was not sufficient to his ends; the fictional elements juxtaposed with the nonfictional did work that each separately could not.[44] Du Bois's use of juxtaposition in *Darkwater* is emblematic of two aspects of how it can function as method. First, juxtaposition does not require coherence between the elements being read alongside each other (as in Du Bois's use of dissimilar genres and forms). Second, juxtaposition enables greater theoretical complexity. As Balfour observes, Du Bois's juxtaposition of romantic and tragic sensibilities "dramatizes democratic possibility and foreclosure" simultaneously, which in turn serves to trouble the unwarranted optimism that is an underlying assumption of much of democratic theory. In a similar vein, hemispheric juxtaposition enables us to view African American and Latin American thought as related yet distinct. It also allows us to resist the impulse to engage with the other America only as comparative foil.

Questions of selection, of both thinkers and texts, are also clearly central to any exercise in hemispheric juxtaposition. For example, the pairings in this book seem to imply that Latin America and the United States are comparable units of analysis. But it actually pairs one country with a whole region, and a marginal strand within one tradition to elite thinkers from another tradition. It also pairs thinkers who think about race primarily in terms of the black/white divide with thinkers who do so primarily in terms of a white/indigenous white/mestizo/indigenous divide, as the two Latin Americans come from countries with relatively small and often socially invisible black populations. Mexico and Argentina are also situated at different ends of the spectrum of Latin American racial formation: one country has a high degree of mixture, while the other has one of the whitest populations in the region and a history of discouraging mixture.

Yet juxtaposition precisely entails placing disparate objects side by side. Rather than a problem of faulty selection then, the differences between the traditions and thinkers juxtaposed here are a feature of the methodological approach. Juxtaposition enables reading thinkers and traditions that are viewed as disparate alongside each other. Reading Douglass and Sarmiento and Du Bois and Vasconcelos simultaneously reveals that very different thinkers across the Americas were wrestling with the racial science of their time and engaging with some of the same interlocutors. Douglass and Sarmiento and Du Bois and Vasconcelos may not have read or commented on each other's works, but reading them alongside each other reveals them all as hemispheric thinkers in ways that have so far been underappreciated. It also reveals how what are viewed as the very distinct ideas about race formulated in the United States and Latin America, respectively, were in fact formed in relation to and in contrast to the other America.

There are other ways of undertaking the task of hemispheric juxtaposition than by examining a set of thinkers, however, so why choose to juxtapose Douglass, Sarmiento, Du Bois, and Vasconcelos specifically? Neither Latin American nor African American political thought is monolithic; each tradition is composed of different strands, some with very different approaches to racial identity and racial justice.[45] Sarmiento, for example, could be classified as an example of the de-racialized liberalism espoused by many Latin American thinkers, and as an advocate of whitening who rejected mixture. Vasconcelos, meanwhile, was one of the region's pre-eminent advocates of mestizaje who nevertheless coincided with Sarmiento in advocating indigenous assimilation. African American political thought is equally diverse; one of the major fault lines in the tradition is between integration or assimilation and black nationalism or separatism. Douglass is usually viewed as an assimilationist, while Du Bois advocated both at different moments in his career.[46] In a certain sense, then, because no two thinkers can be taken as representative of an entire philosophical tradition, a different lineup of thinkers would no doubt yield additional insights.[47]

Nevertheless, the choice of Douglass, Sarmiento, Du Bois, and Vasconcelos was not arbitrary. All four are recognized as key figures within the canon of African American and Latin American political thought. They all centrally engaged with race, and they were all politically influential. They all shaped racial discourses in their respective regions and remain points of reference for thinkers who followed them. Yet these are unlikely pairings. Despite the fact that they were contemporaries working during the same historical eras, and therefore can be said to have operated (up to a certain point) with similar lexicons of "race," Douglass and Sarmiento and Du Bois and Vasconcelos are seen as having formulated very different racial theories. At first glance, for instance, Douglass, the fugitive slave and US abolitionist has nothing in common with Sarmiento, the Latin American advocate of whitening. Similarly, there appears to be little over-lap between Du Bois, who supposedly reified US binary thinking about race, and Vasconcelos's celebration of Latin American mixture.[48] Each thinker is thus identified with a particular position on race that is seen as emblematic in some way of either US or Latin American ideas about race, but that is not adequate to their work and thought. In each case, hemi-spheric juxtaposition reveals the inadequacy of the orthodox interpretation of their ideas about race. It also demonstrates that a fuller appreciation of their political thought depends on a broader reading of their work, one that highlights their preoccupation with the other America. Even the most astute readers of Douglass, for example, have overlooked how his intel-lectual and political engagement with the Caribbean and Central America shaped his ideas at key moments. Sarmiento, likewise, is almost always depicted as a proponent of the Europeanization of Latin America, but is instead shown here to have quickly turned to the United States instead as the political model for Latin America. By decentering Europe and fore-grounding both Americas, hemispheric juxtaposition thus transforms our understanding of each of these thinkers and traditions, and brings to the foreground aspects of their thought that otherwise remain obscured.

Finally, textual juxtaposition—between texts written in different genres during different time periods—is a central feature of the kind of expan-sive reading this book advocates. Questions of textual selection are fun-damental because of the tendency to reduce a thinker's political ideas to static moments captured within iconic texts. All the thinkers analyzed here had long and productive careers, and their ideas shifted over time. Instead of focusing only on the early Du Bois of *Souls*, for instance, my reading of him centers later texts, such as *Dark Princess*, in which he spe-cifically focuses on questions of mixture. A similar problem is evident in readings of Sarmiento that focus only on *Facundo*, and as a result overem-phasize his arguments in favor of Europeanization without sufficiently considering his subsequent disenchantment with Europe. The project of hemispheric juxtaposition also requires drawing widely on a variety of less well-known texts—including Douglass's journalism, Du Bois's fiction,

Sarmiento's writings on the United States, and Vasconcelos's writings on racial discrimination against Latinos—because these are the sites where their hemispheric engagements were most clearly articulated.[49] Douglass, for example, emerges as a more radical thinker in his journalism via his hemispheric engagements. Similarly, Sarmiento's writings about the United States in the 1860s reveal traces of an anti-colonial preoccupation with the potential dangers of US hegemony in the hemisphere that are absent from his earlier work. The kind of intellectual genealogy of racial thought in the Americas that this book enacts thus raises important questions for political theory beyond the hemispheric context, such as what kinds of texts are legible as political theory. Implicitly this book argues for moving beyond a narrow understanding of what counts as a philosophical text. As political theorists seek to map a thinker's ideas, we need to think more broadly about the sites where those ideas have been formulated, rather than continually reifying a few canonical texts as the center of gravity of a particular thinker's oeuvre.

But if hemispheric intellectual genealogy requires reading a broad range of texts, it also requires reading texts in context. This is not to suggest that the ideas of Douglass, Sarmiento, Du Bois, and Vasconcelos were determined by the historical eras in which they lived, or that their arguments are only relevant to the contemporaneous debates from which they emerged. It is rather to note that by placing their political theorizing about race in its proper historical context we can better understand the philosophical and political moves each thinker was making. Situating their writings within the particular historical and intellectual contexts in which they each operated is thus key to understanding how their ideas evolved and shifted over time, and also why they did so depending on the racial politics of the moment. There is an enormous difference, for instance, between domestic racial politics in the United States during the height of Reconstruction and the racial terror and official adherence to white supremacy of "the nadir" era. Similarly, Latin American attitudes about the United States shifted significantly from the post-independence era of the late nineteenth century to the beginning of the twentieth century, which was the height of US imperial intervention in the region. Hemispheric juxtaposition thus requires more than just close textual reading, it also requires mapping the intellectual and political terrain in which these thinkers's ideas were formulated. It requires reading a broader set of texts, and all texts in intellectual, historical, and political context.

Chapter Outline

This book features multiple, nested juxtapositions: between two traditions, between the thinkers in each pairing, and between texts. This enables an analysis of common interlocutors and thematic concerns among paired thinkers, without our understanding of each thinker being overdetermined by the differences or commonalities with others within the same tradition or with the thinker to whom he or she is being juxtaposed. This allows for thinkers and traditions to be read on their own terms, but also alongside each other. The book's organization reflects this, as it features individual chapters on Douglass, Sarmiento, Du Bois, and Vasconcelos that function as part of two hemispheric pairings between thinkers from each tradition. Each chapter can thus be read on its own, but the book's insights only fully emerge when each is read alongside its counterpart.

The book is organized into two parts, each featuring individual chapters on one Latin American and one African American thinker, two from the nineteenth-century and two from the early to mid-twentieth century. Part I: Ambas Américas, juxtaposes two thinkers, Frederick Douglass (c. 1818–1895) and Domingo Faustino Sarmiento (1811–1888), in order to demonstrate the importance of Latin America for Douglass's political ideas, and the US's influence on Sarmiento's political thought and ideas about race in particular. Part II: Mestizo Futurisms, analyzes the conceptions of racial identity and racial mixture developed by W. E. B. Du Bois (1868–1963) and José Vasconcelos (1882–1959) in order to formulate anti-colonial political projects that ultimately fell short in different ways. I propose that their mestizo futurisms should be read as mixed-race utopias that sought to envision post-racist futures in the first half of the twentieth century in the Americas.

Sarmiento and Douglass and Du Bois and Vasconcelos did not read each other's works, nor were they directly in contact with each other. Thus, I am staging a "dialogue" that did not actually take place. There are some thematic threads that span all four thinkers, however, such as the fact that they all wrestled with the racial science of their day, albeit in different ways. Both Vasconcelos and Du Bois explicitly positioned themselves as Sarmiento and Douglass's intellectual heirs, and there are important continuities between Sarmiento and Vasconcelos and Douglass and Du Bois as hemispheric thinkers.[50] Du Bois, like Douglass, grappled with the question of what form black politics in the United States should take, while Vasconcelos, like Sarmiento, was preoccupied with the danger US imperialism posed for Latin America. In both cases, however, Du Bois and Vasconcelos significantly departed from their intellectual forefathers. Du Bois developed an analysis of the "global color line" that exceeded the hemispheric, and Vasconcelos, in contrast to Sarmiento's racial pessimism, would exalt Latin American mixture as the vanguard of historical progress. Most centrally, however, the hemispheric frame adopted here highlights underappreciated elements of the political thought of each of these thinkers, such as Douglass's search for sites of black freedom and multiracial democracy in the Caribbean and Central America, the importance of racial mixture to Du Bois's political thought, Sarmiento's preoccupation with establishing horizontal relations between the two Americas, and Vasconcelos's analysis of Latinos's position in the US racial order during "the nadir" era.

Chapter 1, "'A Black Sister to Massachusetts': Latin America and the Fugitive Democratic Ethos of Frederick Douglass," explores the hemispheric dimensions of Douglass's political thought, especially in relation to multiracial democracy. It traces the connections between Douglass's interventions into debates about US expansionism in the Caribbean and his arguments about immigration and racial politics in the United States. The chapter demonstrates that Douglass not only found exemplars of black self-government and multiracial democracy in the Caribbean and Central America, he also sought to incorporate black and mixed-race Latin Americans into the US polity in order to reshape its contours and challenge white supremacy. Viewed though a hemispheric lens Douglass is revealed as a more radical thinker whose ideas can be utilized to sketch a fugitive democratic ethos that contains important resources for contemporary democratic theory. Specifically, I explore how Douglass's political ideas allow for the articulation of a conception of democracy informed by a tradition of black fugitive thought that takes as its starting point the search for freedom of the enslaved.

Chapter 2, "'Mi Patria de Pensamiento': Sarmiento, the United States, and the Pitfalls of Comparison," traces Sarmiento's turn away from Europe to the United States as a political model for Latin America. In particular, I focus on Sarmiento's three-year stay in the United States during Reconstruction, which would shape his political thought in important ways. Sarmiento deployed a highly selective reading of US history that significantly misread the Civil War in the service of trying to grapple with Argentinean political problems and intervene in Latin American policy debates. He emerges as a hemispheric thinker preoccupied with Latin America's relationship, not to Europe, but with the United States. In fact,

Sarmiento's concern with establishing an egalitarian relationship between the two Americas situates him as an unlikely precursor to later Latin American critics of US imperialism, such as José Martí and Vasconcelos, locating him closer to a tradition that he is usually viewed as at odds with.

In contrast to most studies of Douglass and Sarmiento, which portray them as thinkers principally preoccupied with national problems in the United States and Argentina, respectively, Part I shows how their political ideas were shaped in key ways by hemispheric concerns, particularly debates about race and democracy and US expansionism to Latin America. In order to grapple with these questions, both Douglass and Sarmiento had to contend with debates about race and human capacity spurred by the transnational circulation of the tenets of the scientific racism of their time, particularly those of the American school of ethnology. Shifting hemispheric locations also played a key role in Douglass and Sarmiento's thinking about race. Douglass's most radical black fugitive moments occurred when he was able to conceive of an expanded geography that included other black populations in the Americas. Likewise, as has been noted by many commentators, geography was central to the binaries around which Sarmiento's key arguments were constructed: between the city and the countryside and Europe and Latin America in *Facundo*, and between the North and the South and the United States and Latin America in the texts he wrote during the 1860s. The hemispheric dimensions of Douglass and Sarmiento's ideas revealed by tracing the connections between theorizing about race across the Americas in Part I thus point to the value of resisting political theory's reflexive tendency to turn its gaze toward Europe. Reframing Douglass and Sarmiento as hemispheric political thinkers illustrates the pitfall of comparison as a trope, whereby a selective reading of "the other" serves as either mirror or foil. Both Douglass and Sarmiento romanticized the way race operated in the other America in the service of their own racial projects and politico-theoretical attachments. Part I thus speaks directly to debates about comparison as method.

Chapter 3, " 'To See, Foresee, and Prophesy': Du Bois's Mulatto Fictions and Afro-Futurism," analyzes the work of the later Du Bois, where racial mixture emerges as a key lens through which he moves beyond African American politics and extends his analysis to the global color line created by white supremacy, global capitalism, and colonialism. Du Bois has been read as a paradigmatic example of the binary US (black/white) approach to race, who downplayed racial mixing due to his investment in a narrow, and at times essentialist, conception of black identity in the service of a project of African American racial uplift. This chapter argues that if we move past the iconic texts of the early Du Bois, such as the essay on "The Conservation of Races" and *Souls of Black Folk*, which is perhaps his most widely read text, we see that mixture was in fact an important theme in Du Bois's writings. Specifically, I analyze Du Bois's varying portrayals of interracial intimacy in his "mulatto fictions" through the lens of Afrofuturism.[51] Doing so allows us to probe how and why narratives of racial mixture, such as *Dark Princess*, allowed Du Bois to imagine a yet-to-be Global South in which people of color forged transnational political alliances against white supremacy during the first half of the twentieth century. These narratives of mixture, I argue, became politically imaginable sites of racially just futures, as gendered and sexualized debates about interracial intimacy were at the core of racial politics during this era, even as they proved to be problematic post-racist utopias.

Chapter 4, " 'A Doctrine that Nourished the Hopes of the Nonwhite Races': Vasconcelos, Mestizaje's Travels, and US Latino Politics," traces the development of Vasconcelos's enormously influential conception of Latin American mestizaje as an anti-colonial ideology in response to US imperialism. It shows how Vasconcelos's ideas about race were developed in direct conversation with US racial politics. The chapter traces the differences in Vasconcelos's engagement with US racial politics in his most well-known text, *The Cosmic Race*, and subsequent works. In *The Cosmic Race*, the United States is selectively read in order to serve as a foil for Latin America's superior approach to race. In contrast, in *Indología* and *Bolivarismo y Monroísmo*, Vasconcelos urged Latin Americans to embrace a nonwhite racial identity that would challenge global white supremacy, based in large part on an analysis of racism against Latinos in the United States during the nadir era. The chapter moves full circle with an analysis of mestizaje's travels, specifically late twentieth-century invocations of *The Cosmic Race* by US Chicano/Latino thinkers, such as Gloria Anzaldúa. Anzaldúa's selective borrowing from Vasconcelos is especially surprising given that in contrast to his relative silence on gender and sexuality, she "queers" mestizaje by centering a feminist, female, queer, mestiza, border subject.

Part II's engagement with Du Bois and Vasconcelos as thinkers concerned with futurity and race mixture, on the one hand, and with challenging global white supremacy and probing the consequences of US empire, on the other hand, challenges dominant readings of both thinkers.

Foregrounding Du Bois's complex writings about mixture frees us to see him as more than just a thinker whose ideas about race remained strictly bound by a binary US racial logic that reifies essentialist conceptions of race. Similarly, engaging with Vasconcelos's writings about Latinos and US racial politics in the 1930s reveals him to have been less of a naïve believer in mestizaje as a form of post-racial utopia, and (surprisingly) more of a trenchant critic of the tendency of Latin American elites to identify with whiteness. The juxtaposition of Du Bois and Vasconcelos thus brings together two strands of oppositional thinking to eugenics and the scientific racism of the early decades of the twentieth century. At certain moments, for both Du Bois and Vasconcelos, anti-colonial mestizo futurisms were central to envisioning a post-racist world that was yet-to-be. In different ways the chapters in Part II thus interrogate the inescapable difficulties faced by attempts to forge black internationalisms and Latin American Pan-Americanisms that could challenge global white supremacy.

As participants in a philosophical tradition that is simultaneously Western and marginal, Latin American thinkers have been consistently concerned about questions of authenticity and charges of derivativeness. Because they (sometimes) draw on European ideas to speak to American realities, subaltern traditions such as African American and Latin American political thought are too often seen merely as poor copies of "the imported book" in Martí's evocative phrase.[52] This book resists that framing. Instead, it analyzes hemispheric American intellectuals on their own terms, tracing the discontinuities and resonances between thinkers from *"ambas Américas"* (both Americas) who were all in their own way (in Du Bois's felicitous coinage): "radicals trying to bring new things into the world."[53]

PART I

Ambas Américas

I do not despair of this country . . . the doom of slavery is certain. I therefore leave off where I began with *hope* . . . drawing encouragement from the Declaration of Independence, the great principles it contains, and the genius of American Institutions.

—FREDERICK DOUGLASS, *What to the Slave Is the Fourth of July?* (1852)

The principal element of order and morality on which the Argentine Republic relies today is the immigration of Europeans. . . . If there were a government capable of directing their movement, *this alone would be enough to cure* in ten years, at most, *all the homeland's wounds* made by the bandits, from Facundo to Rosas, who have dominated it.

—DOMINGO F. SARMIENTO, *Facundo* (1845)

FIGURE 1.1 Frederick Douglass, Prints & Photographs Division, Library of Congress

FIGURE 1.2 Domingo F. Sarmiento, Prints & Photographs Division, Library of Congress

1

"A Black Sister to Massachusetts"

LATIN AMERICA AND THE FUGITIVE DEMOCRATIC
ETHOS OF FREDERICK DOUGLASS

THE TRANSNATIONAL DIMENSIONS of Frederick Douglass's political thought have been neglected in prevailing interpretations of him as a thinker thoroughly focused on the United States, a perception further buttressed by his categorization as part of the assimilationist strand within African American philosophy or as an exponent of American liberalism.[1] In contrast, this chapter enlarges the conceptual terrain of Douglass scholarship by locating a more geographically capacious Douglass whose engagement with Latin America reveals an important hemispheric dimension to his political thought. It joins recent analyses by historians and literary critics that highlight the centrality of Douglass's engagement with the rest of the Americas to his political ideas, but shifts the locus of attention to read Douglass more expansively as a theorist of democracy.[2] Viewed through a hemispheric lens Douglass is revealed as a radical democratic thinker whose ideas can be utilized to sketch a black fugitive democratic ethos that contains important resources for contemporary democratic theory. Engaging with the hemispheric coordinates of Douglass's political reflections and investments and his support for a composite US nationality via immigration during the nineteenth century can illuminate early twenty-first-century debates about racial politics, shifting demographics, and the character of US democracy.

This chapter traces the connections between Douglass's positions on black emigration and US expansionism to the Caribbean and Central America and his conception of democracy.[3] I argue that the thread that unites Douglass's seemingly contradictory Caribbean interventions and his view of US racial politics was his commitment to multiracial democracy. For Douglass, Latin America and the Caribbean functioned as both models of racial egalitarianism and potential collaborators in the project of reshaping the US polity. Douglass and most of his African American contemporaries undoubtedly overestimated Latin America's racial egalitarianism. Even though racial hierarchy was maintained by different means in Latin America than the United States, the region was not the racial paradise depicted by many African American commentators.[4] For the present argument, however, what matters is Douglass's belief that "the other America" represented a preferable alternative to US racial politics.

Grappling with Douglass's writings on Latin America reveals a heretofore underappreciated element of his political thought: the articulation of a conception of democracy informed by black fugitivity that could enable the practice of egalitarian politics in multiracial polities. Douglass's conception of multiracial democracy envisioned the political coexistence on egalitarian terms of individuals of "all races and creeds" as fellow citizens. Unlike the myths of racial democracy formulated in Latin America during the twentieth century, however, which conflated racial harmony and political equality with mestizaje (racial and cultural mixing), Douglass envisioned a "composite nationality" anchored in the idea of a universal human right to migration and the Americas's political legacy as a multiracial space. Reading Douglass as a democratic theorist thus reveals how his arguments about US and Latin American racial politics intersect to formulate a black fugitive democratic ethos.

Douglass's arguments in favor of multiracial democracy were shaped in fundamental ways by his engagement with the racial science of his day. The question of the intellectual, moral, and civic capacities of nonwhites and the kinds of political relations that could be established between whites and nonwhites in the multiracial republics of the Americas were far from settled during the second half of the nineteenth century. The emergence and consolidation of scientific theories of race as heredity and fixed notions of biological racial inferiority—particularly the "new climatic racial determinism" propounded in part by the American school of ethnology that gained ascendance in the United States in the 1840s and 1850s, as well as racially deterministic theories of history that established the superiority of Anglo-Saxon civilizations—were the backdrop against which Douglass formulated his notion of multiracial democracy.[5]

Douglass for the most part staunchly rejected, but at times did echo, some of the tenets of the scientific racism of his time. In the 1840s and 1850s, the members of the American school of ethnology were among the most influential figures in US debates about race and slavery. Prior to emancipation their arguments that blacks belonged to a separate and inferior species were marshaled by defenders of slavery to buttress the case against abolition. Douglass was forced to rebut these arguments. He directly addressed the impact of the new racial science in an 1854 speech, "The Claims of the Negro Ethnologically Considered," in which he argued that science could not remain neutral on the moral problem of slavery. Taking on statements by Louis Agassiz and Samuel Morton that their claims about black inferiority were simply scientifically objective conclusions unrelated to political debates about slavery, Douglass contended to the contrary that on the question of slavery: "There is no neutral ground. He that is not for us is against us."[6] Douglass also disputed the objectivity of the new racial science:

> When men oppress their fellow men, the oppressor ever finds, in the character of the oppressed, a full justification for his oppression ... the inability to rise from degradation to civilization and respectability, are the most usual allegations against the oppressed. The evils most fostered by slavery ... are precisely those which slaveholders would transfer from their system to the inherent character of their victims. Thus the very crimes of slavery become slavery's best defense.[7]

It was thus not only empirically impossible to make definitive claims about black capacity on the basis of their condition under enslavement, Douglass argued, the claims of the American ethnologists in favor of polygenesis were also inextricable from the social and political context in which they were being formulated and received. "The debates in Congress ... show how slaveholders have availed themselves of this doctrine in support of slaveholding," he observed. "There is no doubt that Messrs. Nott, Glidden, Morton, Smith and Agassiz were duly consulted by our slavery propagating statesmen."[8] Prior to emancipation, Douglass also rejected the claim that there were separate climate zones destined for habitation by different racial groups. During the height of Reconstruction in the 1870s, however, he echoed some of the claims of "the historical school" of nineteenth-century scientific racism regarding the inevitable triumph of Anglo-Saxon over Latin civilizations to buttress his vision of a US polity reshaped by nonwhite immigration, including the incorporation of willing Latin American nations.[9] The tenets of various strands of nineteenth-century scientific racism were thus integral to key political questions with which Douglass was centrally concerned, such as what kind of multiracial polity the United States would become and the type of hemispheric relations it would establish with its Latin American neighbors.[10]

One of the reasons that many political theorists have missed the hemispheric dimensions of Douglass's political thought is that they tend to base their analyses primarily on his autobiographies or speeches concerned with US questions. Yet, as is widely acknowledged, the genre of the slave narrative in which Douglass's first autobiography was written placed certain constraints on the authorial voices of former slaves.[11] Extending this insight to his oeuvre as a whole, it may be that Douglass was able to express a more radical political imagination in his non-autobiographical writings, particularly his journalism. Indeed, most of the texts where Douglass's ideas about Latin America are to be found are in his newspapers and speeches on non-US topics.[12] In order to trace Douglass as a hemispheric thinker, I thus draw on a wide variety of texts, both his own writings and instances where he functioned as a curator in his role as newspaper editor and chose to publish work by others on Latin American topics. In particular, I focus on texts in which Douglass juxtaposed analyses of US and Latin American racial politics.

The chapter analyzes three key moments when Douglass engaged with Latin America most closely: his flirtation with African American emigration and search for alternative political spaces of black self-government in Haiti, Nicaragua, and the Mosquito Kingdom in 1852 prior to the US Civil War; his endorsement of the annexation of Santo Domingo in 1870–1871 following the abolition of slavery in the United States in accordance with his vision of a multiracial polity transformed in part by nonwhite immigration; and his defense of Haitian political capacity toward the end of his life, in particular at the 1893 World's Columbian Exposition in Chicago. In each of these moments, different aspects of a black fugitive democratic ethos are on display, but Douglass's commitment to multiracial democracy remains constant throughout. Overall, the chapter traces Douglass's enduring aspiration to reshape US democracy, for which he found inspiration by enlarging his reflections and investments into a hemispheric mode that encompassed all the Americas.

"We Owe Something to the Slaves": Rethinking Democratic Fugitivity

This chapter contends that Douglass forged a radical black fugitive democratic ethos that impacted his vision of a future US multiracial polity, and that there are two traditions of democratic thinking that are helpful for interpreting this theoretical move: Sheldon Wolin's notion of "fugitive democracy" and black fugitive thought. In so doing, I extend and sharpen Wolin's concept, by putting it in conversation with the experience of actual fugitive ex-slaves and the philosophical insights that have been culled from those experiences. Wolin understands democracy as "a project concerned with the political potentialities of ordinary citizens, that is with their possibilities of becoming political beings through the self-discovery of common concerns and the modes of action for realizing them."[13] He suggests that rather than thinking about democracy as a form of government, it would be more useful to reconceive it as a political moment that is rare and episodic: "a mode of being which is ... doomed to succeed only temporarily, but is a recurrent possibility."[14] Because the enlargement of the circle of those who can participate in politics generally requires the wholesale transformation of existing forms, democracy and revolution are related rather than opposed, and constitutionalism rather than institutionalizing democracy attenuates and limits it, because democratic founding moments are revolutionary moments "that activate the demos and destroy boundaries that bar access to political experience ... revolutionary transgression is the means by which the demos makes itself political."[15] Democracy thus requires moments of "democratic renewal" when ordinary individuals can create "new cultural patterns of commonality."[16] Wolin's notion of democratic fugitivity envisions democracy as a nonteleological, multifaceted practice that is never fully achieved.

Rethinking Wolin's theorization of democracy's evanescence in light of the experience of fugitive ex-slaves sharpens and amends his concept in significant ways. Douglass's understanding of citizenship and exclusion in his famous "What to the Slave Is the Fourth of July" speech of 1852, for example, proleptically articulates Wolin's qualms about the ossification of democracy. Fugitive ex-slaves also complicate notions of who the democratic citizen is and can be, however. Were they liminal citizens, as Douglass suggests at certain points in the speech?[17] If so, they could be seen as having developed enhanced democratic subjectivities because their experience of the democratic more closely maps onto its episodic and insurgent character. Such an understanding of fugitive slaves as liminal citizens would be in contrast with an understanding of fugitivity as flight, and specifically flight from slave law, however. From the perspective of black fugitivity, fugitive slaves are not citizens-to-be (as implied in the notion of liminal citizens), as their project is to evade the law. Instead, they have a constitutive outsider status as they repudiate both the law and the state that enacts it. Perhaps, however, it is not possible to remain a permanent fugitive, and there is movement from fugitivity to liminality (and vice versa?). Douglass rhetorically performs this civic in-between-ness of slaves, fugitive ex-slaves, and free African Americans in the speech by continually aligning and dis-aligning himself with the United States. He simultaneously addresses his white audience as "fellow citizens," yet reminds them that "this Fourth [of] July is *yours*, not *mine*. *You* may rejoice, *I* must mourn."[18] Douglass's rhetorical oscillations suggest that it is liminal citizens, in particular, who are called upon to mobilize in what Wolin identifies as revolutionary moments with the potential to engender democratic renewal and enlarge the scope of the demos.

There are thus at least two key ways in which engagement with the experience of fugitive ex-slaves reframes Wolin's notion of fugitive democracy: one has to do with the necessarily different and fraught relationship of the enslaved to the rule of law (and to the law in general), while the other is related to the temporality of fugitivity, and the way in which it might permanently shape political subjectivity. Douglass articulated both of these processes. While in general being committed to working within the parameters of the US polity, Douglass consistently articulated the idea that the enslaved had a different relationship to the law. In his autobiographies, for example, he suggested that slavery distorted the connection between the law and morality, between the right and the legal.[19] As a result, slaves learned to distrust and disobey the law; otherwise, it would not have been possible for them to engage in any kind of resistance or flight. In his third autobiography, for example, he argued: "The morality of free society could have no application to slave society. Slaveholders made it almost impossible for the slave to commit any crime, known either to the laws of God or the laws of man. If he stole, he but took his own; if he killed his master, he only imitated the heroes of the [US American] revolution."[20]

In order to challenge the idea that it was permissible to own a human being as property, which was enshrined in US law, Douglass and other enslaved persons had to sever the presumed link between the law, political right, and morality. As Douglass explained, enslaved persons learned to distinguish between the *force* of the law and political and moral right:

> The right [of the master] to take my earnings was the right of the robber. He had the *power* to compel me to give him the fruits of my labor, and this *power* was his only right in this case. . . . To make a contented slave you must make a thoughtless one. . . . He must be able to detect no inconsistencies in slavery. The man who takes his earnings must be able to convince him that he has a perfect right to do so. It must not depend upon mere force—the slave must know no higher law than his master's will.[21]

The fact that slavery produced a subjective morality (for the masters) that distorted the relationship between the right and the legal in turn meant that for the enslaved to assert their humanity they had to engage in activities that were proscribed in this context but that would have been hailed as exemplary political actions in others. Discussing a clandestine meeting with other slaves to plan an escape, for example, Douglass suggested that: "These meetings must have resembled, on a smaller scale, the meetings of the revolutionary conspirators [for US independence]. . . . We were plotting against our (so-called) lawful rulers, with this difference. . . . We did not seek to overthrow them but to escape from them."[22] Connecting the political practices of the enslaved engaged in flight and resistance to the United States's founding served to highlight the disjuncture between the law and political right during political founding moments or struggles for democratic renewal.

Douglass made this connection even more explicit in "What to the Slave Is the Fourth of July," when he interpreted the United States's founding as an anti-colonial, revolutionary event in which the rule of law was flouted in the name of higher moral and political principles. This, in turn, implied that in the pre–Civil War Era it was the enslaved and fugitive ex-slaves, who were not citizens, as well as (black and white) abolitionists, who were displaying exemplary civic virtue. The United States's founding fathers, Douglass argued: "preferred revolution to peaceful submission to bondage. . . . They believed in order; but not in the order of tyranny. With them, nothing was '*settled*' that was not right. . . . They seized upon eternal principles and set a glorious example in their defence [sic]."[23] By connecting the law-breaking of fugitive slaves to the United States's founding, Douglass can be read as suggesting that revolutionary acts of resistance are constitutive to the praxis of democratic citizenship.[24] Engaging with Douglass thus extends what it means to be a fugitive democratic thinker in Wolin's sense because Douglass moves beyond recognizing the revolutionary and unsettled character of democratic politics to demonstrating the permanently uneven reach of democracy and the rule of law, as struggles to enlarge the demos are likely to be resisted and viewed as anything but "lawful" protest. Today's fugitives are thus the DREAMers or Black Lives Matter protesters who enact exemplary democratic practices even as their status as citizens is precarious, and as their political activism renders them vulnerable to increased state reprisal.

Drawing on Douglass's discussion of slave fugitivity also alters the temporality of Wolin's concept beyond the evanescence of democracy, as it points to the ways the political practices of fugitives were permanently altered by the experience of flight and outlawry. As the most visible African American fugitive of his time, Douglass repeatedly analyzed what it meant to be a fugitive in plain sight. In the chapters of his autobiographies concerning his life in the antebellum North after his escape from slavery, for example, Douglass emphasized the precarious character of black freedom. In his first autobiography, *Narrative of the Life of Frederick Douglass, an American Slave* published in 1845, Douglass includes an extended (and chilling) account of fugitivity:

> Let him be a fugitive in a strange land—a land given up to be the hunting-ground for slave-holders—whose inhabitants are legalized kidnappers—where he is every moment subjected to the terrible liability of being seized upon by his fellow-men. . . . I say, let him place himself in my situation . . . among fellow-men, yet feeling in the midst of wild beasts. . . . I say let him be placed in this most trying situation,—the situation in which I was placed,—then, and not till then, will he fully appreciate the hardships of, and know how to sympathize with, the toil-worn and whip-scarred fugitive slave.[25]

For Douglass, flight from slavery thus did not immediately translate into freedom. The fugitive, like the slave, had a precarious legal status. Psychologically, the fugitive was in a state of constant fear, as bonds of human solidarity could not be relied upon. The fugitive was surrounded not by "fellow-men" but by "wild beasts," not by fellow citizens-to-be but by "legalized kidnappers." Douglass thus did not present fugitivity and enslavement as diametrically opposed conditions. He explained: "No colored man was really free while residing in a slave state. He was ever more or less subject to the condition of his slave brother. In his color was his badge of bondage."[26] Moreover, the insecurity experienced by the fugitive was not simply a result of the Fugitive Slave Act of 1850 that rendered "free" blacks constantly subject to re-enslavement; it resulted from the fact that the North "was not entirely free from race and color prejudice."[27] If in the Fourth of July speech Douglass was speaking for the slave, here he speaks for the fugitive.

Because racial barriers to black freedom transcended enslavement, the freedom of the fugitive was a precarious kind of freedom, and fugitivity bred practices of concealment and secrecy that Douglass found difficult to discard even after he became a public figure. Prior to his freedom being legally purchased in 1846, for example, he wrote: "I was constantly in danger of being spirited away at a moment when my friends could render me no assistance ... though I had reached a free state, and had attained a position of public usefulness, I was still under the liability of losing all I had gained."[28] Indeed, Douglass's understanding of fugitivity as a political practice with certain ethical commitments is clear in his reticence to reveal the details of his own escape in his first two autobiographies. In *My Bondage and My Freedom* (his second autobiography, published in 1855), Douglass included a stinging critique of abolitionists who publicized slave escape routes.

> The practice of publishing every new invention by which a slave is known to have escaped from slavery, has neither wisdom nor necessity to sustain it. ... I have never approved of the very public manner, in which some of our western friends have conducted what *they* call the '*Under-ground Railroad*'. ... Its stations are far better known to the slaveholders than to the slaves. ... In publishing such accounts the anti-slavery man addresses the slaveholder, *not the slave*. ... We owe something to the slaves.[29]

But it was not just a duty to enable continued fugitivity that compelled Douglass to abide by a commitment to secrecy and concealment, it was also a sense that the slaveholder should also be forced to experience some version, however attenuated, of the fear and radical uncertainty visited upon the fugitive and the enslaved. The slaveholder, he argued: "should be left to imagine himself surrounded by myriads of invisible tormentors, ever ready to snatch, from his infernal grasp, his trembling prey. In pursuing his victim ... let him be made to feel, that, at every step he takes ... he is running the frightful risk of having his hot brains dashed out by an invisible hand."[30] Douglass's analysis here suggests that rather than thinking about democracy's temporality in terms of periodic moments of renewal, fugitives develop enhanced democratic subjectivities because they are routinely exposed to experiences of risk and loss that are the hallmarks of democracy.[31]

In order to fully sketch the black fugitive democratic ethos that can be culled from his work, which both enlarges and challenges elements of Wolin's articulation of democratic fugitivity, it is thus also necessary to situate Douglass within the tradition of black fugitive thought. As Angela Davis has observed, fugitivity is a recurring theme in black political thought.[32] Fugitivity was a strategy that escaped slaves enacted both individually and collectively, and it has shaped the way black thinkers have understood some of the key concepts in Western political thought, such as freedom, justice, democracy, etc. Some of the key features of black fugitive thought include: (1) taking seriously as political activities the survival strategies of fugitives, such as secrecy, concealment, flight, outlawry, etc.; (2) highlighting the continuities between slavery and post-emancipation societies, thus approaching fugitivity as an enduring condition or orientation; (3) a concern with the creation of autonomous, and at times clandestine, spaces where black political agency could be collectively enacted, often coupled with a rejection of the strategy of seeking inclusion into existing racial states due to pessimism about their ability to be reorganized on bases other than white supremacy; and (4) embracing the intellectual orientations arising from fugitivity, such as imagining alternate racial orders, futures, and forms of subjectivity.[33] Ironically (given his status as an actual fugitive ex-slave), Douglass's placement within this tradition might be questioned by those who view him solely as an assimilationist thinker committed to integration into the US polity.[34] I argue that Douglass belongs squarely within the tradition of black fugitive thought, however, because enslavement and fugitivity shaped his political thought in ineluctable ways. In Douglass's own words at the end of his life summing up his political thought: "My part has been to tell the story of the slave. The story of the master has never wanted for narrators."[35] We can thus sketch an account of the fugitive Douglass by analyzing his positions vis-à-vis three key preoccupations of black fugitive thought: the question of slave agency, the afterlife of slavery, and the limits of fugitivity as an individual or collective practice.[36]

Black fugitive thought runs the risk of focusing on the dehumanization wrought by slavery and racism at the expense of the agency of the enslaved, and Douglass has sometimes been read as an example of a thinker who succumbed to this danger. Despite the prominent place afforded to the battle with the slave-breaker Covey in many analyses of Douglass's ideas, for example, Stephen Marshall has argued that he is a thinker primarily concerned with the way slavery distorted the ethical and political capacities of both masters and slaves. In his view, Douglass brilliantly exposed the dehumanization and moral corruption of slavery, but had comparatively less to say about slave agency and slave resistance.[37] Such readings of Douglass rely on texts in which he highlighted black subjection and decried slave subservience, particularly the *Narrative*.

It is equally plausible to read Douglass as a theorist of slave agency and fugitivity, however. Neil Roberts, for instance, has argued that Douglass provides an account of slave agency that allows us to move beyond the stalemate between static, polarized conceptions of negative and positive liberty that dominate debates about freedom in Western political thought. In Roberts's view, "Douglass develops a tradition of political theory centering attention on the psychological and physical acts of struggle and assertion that are integral to slave agency."[38] When Douglass claimed that he became a free man in fact even though he remained a slave in form after his victory in the climactic battle with Covey, he illustrated the possibility of slave agency and conceived fugitivity as a praxis and disposition of the enslaved.[39] Moreover, as Roberts and Anthony Bogues observe, the notion of comparative freedom Douglass articulates in his description of this moment in *My Bondage and My Freedom* allows us to conceive freedom, not as a static condition that one either does or does not possess, but as a critical human practice that is not reducible to the political.[40] This fugitive emphasis on process likewise informs black fugitive thought's approach to democracy, as a focus on politics as experienced by those that Bogues calls "living corpses," such as the enslaved, reveals democracy as a never fully achieved condition that has been fundamentally shaped by racial modernity. In other words, democracy is always incomplete because the denial of political rights to some, rather than being a contradiction of its core principles, has instead underwritten the ability of others to claim such rights. This black fugitive understanding of how democracy is shaped by white supremacy is especially evident in Douglass's political thought before and after Reconstruction, but is even discernible in his commitment to decentering whiteness within the US polity during the 1870s.

It is also important to consider how gender informed Douglass's account of slave agency. Douglass's gender politics were complicated. He supported women's suffrage and praised the political activism of female abolitionists at a time when women were not supposed to participate in the public sphere. Yet some black feminists have argued that Douglass espoused a masculinist understanding of freedom (i.e., one that reified male experience as normative) that overshadowed enslaved women's "gendered strategies of freedom."[41] Centering fugitivity as the preeminent example of slave agency would certainly privilege male experience, as enslaved men had more geographic mobility than enslaved women, and therefore greater opportunities for escape. Moreover, the conceptions of freedom that emerge from female slave narratives, such as Harriet Jacobs's *Incidents in the Life of A Slave Girl*, foreground issues that are less prominent in Douglass's *Narrative*, such as the collective liberation of a family unit, sexual agency as a core feature of individual autonomy, and a critique of marriage as a site of subordination for women.[42] As black feminists have noted, the harms of slavery were not confined to traditional civic forms of injustice such as the denial of legal personhood and political standing or economic exploitation, they also critically extended to more intimate spheres and encompassed the denial of bodily autonomy and the inability to preserve stable familial and romantic bonds.[43] This suggests that fugitivity may not have been the primary means through which enslaved women exercised agency, as rather than outright flight or escape they may have sought less drastic means of evading gendered forms of subjection (such as Jacobs's escaping sexual assault by being hidden in plain sight).

Douglass did acknowledge sexual violence against enslaved women, and he also identified the denial or distortion of familial bonds as one of the principal harms of slavery. Yet his depiction of enslaved women, particularly in the *Narrative*, has been critiqued for presenting black women's pained bodies as spectacle. Critics have argued that representations of enslaved women as objects of violence fail to envision them as agents struggling for their own freedom.[44] Moreover, as historians of gender and slavery have noted, emphasizing spectacular moments of defiance can lead to more everyday forms of resistance to slavery being overlooked.[45] Nevertheless, as Robert Gooding-Williams has argued, in *My Bondage and*

My Freedom Douglass emphasized the importance of slave community to black liberation.[46] In *Bondage*, Douglass highlighted everyday acts of resistance by women, including his mother, grandmother, and the slave-woman Caroline.[47] He also stressed the denial of family ties as one of the principal harms of slavery. Whereas in *The Narrative* Douglass described himself as having no meaningful attachments prior to being sent to Baltimore as a child, his relationships with his mother and grandmother emerge as central formative influences in the later autobiographies. In these texts, the moment of separation from his grandmother looms large. He writes of his sadness at his forced removal from her home, observing that "My grandmother was all the world to me." His grandmother likewise "looked sad. .... She was soon to lose another object of affection, as she had lost many before."[48] Douglass inserted detailed descriptions of his mother and grandmother in the later autobiographies, showing them both to have been strong women with a certain degree of independence but also as deeply burdened by the many and repeated familial losses imposed by slavery.

The centrality of intimate losses grounded in the denial of family bonds to Douglass's account of the harms of slavery in the later autobiographies is clear in his description of both his separation from his grandmother and his lack of connection with his siblings in *Bondage* as "my first introduction to the realities of the slave system."[49] In *Bondage* and *Life and Times*, Douglass took pains to describe his mother's sacrifices in order to see him (walking twenty-four miles at night without permission, for example, which was a punishable offense), and her actions become emblematic of enslaved women's refusal to accept slavery's distortion of family ties: "The pains she took and the toils she endured, to see me, tells me that a true mother's heart was hers, and that slavery had difficulty in paralyzing it with unmotherly indifference."[50] Indeed, there is another scene, the moment when his mother saves him from Aunt Katy's wrath, that can be read as the counterpart to the battle with Covey. In this scene, which does not appear in *The Narrative*, Douglass becomes, not an individual man, but a member of a family, via an everyday act of resistance by his mother. In *Life and Times*, Douglass wrote: "The scene which followed is beyond my power to describe. The friendless and hungry boy, in his extremest need, found himself in the strong, protecting arms of his mother. .... That night I learned as I had never learned before, that I was not only a child, but somebody's child."[51] Arguably, it was his mother's protective act, which showed him he was "somebody's child," which enabled Douglass to engage in his later assertion of freedom, and his insertion of the scene in *Bondage* suggests that this is how he understood the relationship between the two events. He described it as "a circumstance which is deeply impressed on my memory." Douglass's account of the harms of slavery in the later autobiographies is thus much closer to Jacobs's, and his understanding of slave resistance is also broader and more oriented toward the preservation of family ties and slave community rather than individual acts of fugitivity.

Finally, black fugitive thought has also been centrally concerned with what Saidiya Hartman has described as the entanglements of slavery and freedom. In other words, if we think of slavery as a form of racial governance, then certain practices and forms of subjection developed during it continue to shape post-emancipation polities.[52] Not only were there continuities between the forms of self-regulation and discipline imposed on enslaved and "free" black populations after emancipation, slaves who did not gain their freedom by flight generally became free by being exemplary slaves, by performing the epitome of subjection. Douglass was especially concerned with the problem of "slavishness." But he also believed that race was not constitutive to US democracy, such that it could be remade on more egalitarian grounds (this was particularly true during Reconstruction), which suggests that he was not especially attuned to slavery's afterlife.[53] Douglass was also quite clear about the fact that the legal abolition of slavery did not result in black freedom, however. He observed: "Though slavery was abolished, the wrongs of my people were not ended. Though they were not slaves, they were not quite free." Following emancipation, he argued, blacks "were called citizens, but left subjects; they were called free, but left almost slaves."[54] Douglass was also more attuned to the permanence of racism in his later writings. In the 1890s, for example, he connected the heightened racial terror that accompanied the end of Reconstruction to a residual "spirit of slavery" that continued to shape US democracy and black citizenship, in particular.

Perhaps the issue on which Douglass is most at odds with black fugitive thought is on the question of the creation of autonomous spaces for collective liberation.[55] Black fugitive thought has generally been concerned with the creation of autonomous sites of black freedom, such as maroon communities that existed at the margins of colonial states and their successors. Douglass, for the most part, was committed to working toward the re-foundation of the US polity on more egalitarian terms; he envisioned its radical transformation based on an expansive notion of multiracial democracy that would decenter whiteness to an extent that has not been achieved to this day. Yet at key junctures Douglass's concern with black freedom led him to look for models of political agency and black self-government in other parts of the Americas, such as Haiti, which he recognized as a state founded by fugitive slaves (in others words, a maroon state). Douglass also embraced US expansion into the Caribbean during the 1870s, however, which threatened the sovereignty of the Dominican Republic and Haiti, which he viewed as black republics. Douglass thus did not always fully embrace all the implications of black fugitivity, particularly the idea of creating autonomous spaces for black freedom. The black fugitive democratic ethos that can be extracted from his political thought was nevertheless shaped by black fugitive preoccupations that both extend Wolin's notion of democratic fugitivity and are in tension with it at times.

Douglass's political thought thus displays elements of both democratic fugitivity and black fugitivity. Yet democratic fugitivity and black fugitivity are in tension. They point in different political and philosophical directions, especially where the relationship to the state is concerned. Democratic engagement requires exposure to the state, for instance, but it is precisely the rule of law that is revealed as insufficient and dangerous by the black fugitive. Likewise, fugitive democratic politics would seek to reshape the moral dispositions of the dominant racial order, but black fugitivity is oriented instead to the creation of sites of black freedom that refuse or challenge the logics of coloniality and exceed or bypass the nation-state. I therefore trace the tensions between democratic fugitivity and black fugitivity in Douglass's political thought. Sediments of both are present throughout, but black fugitive commitments are most evident during those moments when Douglass despairs about the United States, while a fugitive democratic orientation is most apparent during Reconstruction, when he believed a revolutionary moment of democratic renewal was underway.

"A [Black] City Set on a Hill": Haiti, Nicaragua, and the Mosquito Kingdom

Douglass's trenchant critique of US democracy in 1852 in his "What to the Slave Is the Fourth of July" speech coincided with the emergence of an enlarged hemispheric sensibility that looked outward to the rest of the Americas for examples of black self-government. In 1852 *Frederick Douglass's Paper* was the discursive site of African

American reflections about Central America that directly contested US racism in light of political models of multiracial democracy drawn from Nicaragua and the Mosquito Kingdom. Douglass's curatorial practices as a newspaper editor in the 1850s—which highlighted African Americans's search for sites of black freedom outside the United States—can thus be read as a fugitive practice of concealing oneself in the service of sustaining an outlawed exercise of agency. By featuring other African Americans writing openly about voluntary emigration, Douglass was able to champion multiracial democracy without alienating white abolitionists opposed to black equality. Yet African American attempts to enact black fugitivity transnationally also ran the risk of establishing proto-imperial relationships vis-à-vis local populations in Latin America, including black and indigenous peoples pursuing their own quests for political autonomy.

Debates about African American emigration during the 1850s were shaped by the tenets of racial science, particularly the "new climatic racial determinism," which claimed that different racial groups were destined to inhabit separate climate zones. White colonizationist schemes to remove African Americans to Central America were premised on the claim that black and white coexistence on equal terms was impossible in the United States, and that blacks were meant to live in tropical regions.[56] Douglass generally opposed African American emigration. He also rejected the idea of separate climatic zones suitable to being inhabited only by certain races: the temperate zone for whites, the tropics for blacks. Bolstered by the new racial science, white colonizationists (including some abolitionists) envisioned a kind of Jim Crow American continent that disavowed the possibility of political coexistence between whites and nonwhites in the same polity. Douglass, in contrast, refused to concede that democracy was only possible in the context of racial homogeneity. Douglass's opposition to African American emigration was thus partly driven by his commitment to multiracial democracy, as well as his rejection of scientific racism, particularly climatic racial determinism. In opposition to Douglass, African American advocates of voluntary emigration viewed it as a means of fulfilling black desires for freedom and self-government. This was especially true of Douglass's onetime co-editor of *The North Star* and later rival Martin Delany, who was the most famous African American proponent of emigration in the nineteenth century.

Douglass and Delany are generally portrayed as representative of two diametrically opposed poles within African American political thought: integrationism and Black Nationalism. Unlike Douglass, Delany had given up hope for black equality in the United States; he highlighted African Americans's connection to Africa, whereas Douglass emphasized their status as Americans. It is thus Delany rather than Douglass that one would expect to have formulated a hemispheric vision connecting African Americans to black populations in Latin America. But Douglass and Delany had a complicated intellectual relationship. As Daniel Levine has observed, such simplistic binary oppositions overlook the fact that there was also significant overlap between their political ideas: "If Douglass can be viewed as a U.S. nationalist whose racial thinking surfaced at times of stress or dissonance, Delany can be viewed as a racial thinker whose U.S. nationalism expressed itself at moments of hopefulness."[57] This contention is borne out by Douglass's endorsement of African American emigration for a brief period prior to the Civil War, when the *Dred Scott* decision and other developments made the possibility of national inclusion in the United States appear distant.

In the 1850s, as his newspapers promoted emigration to Haiti and Central America, Douglass himself planned to visit Haiti in order to report on conditions there for African Americans interested in emigration. In "A Trip to Haiti" in *Douglass's Monthly* in May 1861, he explained that among his motives for going were "special ones growing out of things at present existing in this country. During the last few years the minds of free colored people in all the States have been deeply exercised in relation to what may be their future in the United States. To many it has seemed that the portents of the moral sky were all against us."[58] As a maroon state built by rebellious slaves, Haiti beckoned disillusioned African Americans "looking out into the world for a place of retreat, an asylum from the apprehended storm."[59] Haiti featured prominently in US debates about race and slavery during the nineteenth century. Haiti also played an important role in Douglass's thinking about black freedom. He believed that the success of Haiti's experiment in black self-government had implications for the cause of black equality everywhere, including the United States. Douglass explicitly extolled Haiti as an exemplary maroon community where black self-government was a reality:

> Born a slave as we were, in this boasted land of liberty . . . accustomed from childhood to hear the colored race disparaged and denounced, their mental and moral qualities held in contempt, treated as an inferior race, incapable of self-government, and of maintaining, when left to themselves, a state of civilization . . . we,

naturally enough, desire to see, as we doubtless shall see, in the free, orderly and Independent Republic of Haiti, a refutation of the slanders and disparagements of our race. We want to experience the feeling of being under a Government which has been administered by a race denounced as mentally and morally incapable of self-government.[60]

Douglass noted that because of the central place it occupied in US debates about race, civilization, and slavery, "both the press and the platform of the United States have long made Haiti the bugbear and scare-crow of the cause of freedom." One purpose of his trip was thus to reveal the truth about Haiti, "to do justice to Haiti, to paint her as she is," since "though a city set on a hill, she has been hid."[61] In this moment Douglass's journalism was thus serving black fugitive goals, revealing Haiti as an alternative political ideal to US blacks still living under slave law. Haiti was the living enactment of heroic black liberation in which blacks had been the principal actors. For US blacks, in Douglass's words, it was "the theatre of many stirring events and heroic achievements, the work of a people, bone of our bone, and flesh of our flesh."[62]

This was an era in which Douglass was especially attuned to black fugitivity. In his speech on the anniversary of West India emancipation in 1857, for example, he emphasized the importance of violent resistance by the enslaved, in contrast to his praise in 1880 for the peaceful process by which emancipation was achieved in the British Caribbean in another speech commemorating the same event. In 1857 he proclaimed: "This then is the truth concerning the inauguration of freedom in the British West Indies. Abolition was the act of the British Government. . . . Nevertheless, a share of the credit of the result falls justly to the slaves themselves. 'Though slaves, they were rebellious slaves.' . . . They did not hug their chains." What British abolitionists were trying to accomplish through persuasion, Douglass argued, "the Slaves themselves were endeavoring to gain by outbreaks and violence."[63] This is a moment when Douglass "extols the value of black revolutionary violence as modeled in the Southern Americas."[64] Indeed, Douglass's critique of the passivity of US blacks in the speech is consistent with black fugitivity because he was suggesting that even "free" blacks in the North were not truly free, that their moral capacities and political aspirations continued to be distorted by slavery. He explicitly stated that one of the aims of the speech was to exhort US blacks to display the same kind of civic virtue as non-US blacks. His hope was that the example of "rebellious slaves" in the Caribbean would inspire free and enslaved blacks in the United States to "the execution of great deeds of heroism ... I am free to say that nothing is more humiliating than the insignificant part we, the colored people, are taking in the great contest now going with the powers of oppression in this land." Indeed, Douglass confessed to being especially dismayed by "the stolid contentment, the listless indifference, the moral death which reigns over many of our people."[65] At this moment Douglass was clearly concerned with the question of slave agency. In this speech, the tension in his work between emphasizing the degradation produced by slavery, on the one hand, and the vital necessity of resistance, on the other hand, is mapped onto the comparison between rebellious non-US slaves and passive US blacks. Moving from a general observation about how it was imperative that the oppressed actively resist their subjection to a discussion of the implications of this maxim for US blacks, Douglass (as he had in *My Bondage and My Freedom*) argued: "Power concedes nothing without a demand. It never did and never will.... The limits of tyrants are prescribed by the endurance of those whom they oppress. In the light of these ideas, Negroes will be hunted at the North, and held and flogged at the South so long as they submit ... and make no resistance, either moral or physical."[66] In the 1850s Douglass thus emphasized a black fugitive hatred of mastery that rejected a quietistic politics of submission to the strictly legal.

Douglass did find examples of violent African American resistance to slavery to exalt in the 1857 West India emancipation speech. Those US examples of slave resistance raise other questions about whether his understanding of slave agency privileged particular kinds of heroic action, however. Douglass's list of "rebellious" African American slaves willing to sacrifice their lives and the lives of others in the pursuit of freedom begins with the rather bloodthirsty suggestion that "every mother who, like Margaret Garner, plunges a knife into the bosom of her infant to save it from the hell of our Christian Slavery, should be held and honored as a benefactress." He then proceeded to cite various instances of enslaved men and fugitive male slaves who violently resisted recapture, such as Joseph Cinque and Madison Washington, "who struck down his oppressor on the deck of the Creole."[67] Douglass's invocation of Garner is notable because she is the only woman in his pantheon of heroic slaves. Garner's presence among this list of fugitive slaves belies the absence of an active female protagonist in Douglass's 1853 novel *The Heroic Slave*, in which the only enslaved woman in the text, Madison Washington's wife (whom he risks recapture in order to be reunited with after having successfully fled to Canada), never speaks. She also becomes a fugitive, but is a silent presence in the text. In contrast, his inclusion of Garner in the 1857 speech shows that Douglass did not believe heroic forms of agency were restricted to men. Douglass's implied claim that she should serve as a role model raises other questions about what it means to interpret Garner's act as heroic in the first place, however.[68] In extolling violent resistance to slavery, Douglass was prizing flight and direct confrontation above forms of everyday resistance and the preservation of intimate bonds. In fact, with the exception of Cinque and Washington, the instances of African American resistance he extols were all individual acts of inward-directed violence, such as infanticide and suicide, rather than collective uprisings against slavery. Ultimately, then, Douglass's list of heroic slaves echoes his frustration with African American efforts to resist slavery and his search for sites of black freedom outside the United States.

In 1852, five years prior to Douglass's invocation of Caribbean models of slave agency in the West India Emancipation speech, Central America was prominently featured as a site of black freedom in Frederick Douglass's Paper. In April 1852, Delany published The Condition, Elevation, Emigration, and Destiny of the Colored People of the United States, in which he identified Central America, and Nicaragua specifically, as one of the most favorable destinations for black emigration.[69] It is not entirely clear whether Delany was already aware that he had been elected (in absentia) mayor of the port of San Juan del Norte when he wrote Condition, and Douglass never reviewed the book.[70] Delany's election was covered in Frederick Douglass's Paper in 1852, however, as was African American emigration to San Juan; that same year Douglass also published a review of Ephraim G. Squier's Nicaragua, Its People, Scenery, Monuments, and the Proposed Interoceanic Canal. While Douglass did not write any of the articles lauding the Mosquito Kingdom and Nicaragua as examples of black self-government, as publisher of the paper he made the editorial decision to include them. Douglass's curatorial choices as a journalist in 1852 could thus be read as a fugitive practice, whereby the measure of concealment offered by publishing pro-emigrationist texts written by other African Americans allowed him to challenge prevailing racial hierarchies in the United States.

In his two-part review of Squier's book, which appeared in Frederick Douglass's Paper in January 1852, James McCune Smith identified both the Mosquito Kingdom and Nicaragua as free states governed by blacks.

Writing under the pseudonym "Communipaw," McCune Smith explained to his African American readers: "The British Government claims protection over the mouth of the San Juan, for its ally the colored King of the Musquitos. The American Government claims protection over the rest of the route, for their allies the colored republic of Nicaragua. For Nicaragua is a *colored republic!*"[71] Mapping the one-drop rule onto Squier's description of Nicaragua's racial composition, McCune Smith observed that taking the "North American view" of the question, "Colored or Negroes" were the majority of the country's population. Reducing those originally counted as white (whose whiteness Squier himself had also questioned), and adding together those in the mixed-race and black categories, McCune Smith concluded that Nicaragua was a mostly black country, with a significant indigenous population, and few whites.[72] Nicaragua's *criollo* elite, which tended to downplay the country's black and indigenous ancestry, would have no doubt vigorously disputed his characterization of it as a black republic, but it was consistent with African American perceptions of Latin America as more racially egalitarian than the United States.[73]

In 1852, when slavery was still legal in the United States, African Americans found in Nicaragua an inspiring example of a "colored republic" in which blacks/mixed-race people of African descent were exercising political power. Yet African Americans migrating to San Juan were doing so only ten years after slavery had been officially abolished in the Mosquito Kingdom, and thirty years after Nicaragua outlawed slavery in 1821 (at independence). African Americans such as McCune Smith were thus undoubtedly romanticizing race relations in the Mosquito Kingdom and Nicaragua. But they were also using claims about Central America's more egalitarian racial politics to intervene in debates about multiracial political coexistence and black capacity in the United States. McCune Smith, for example, approvingly cited Squier's statement that in Nicaragua "notwithstanding the diversity of races, distinctions of caste are hardly recognized," and commented on its significance for US debates about the possibility of multiracial democracy: "All classes may aspire to the highest position in Church and State. Hear that, American Colonizationism! . . . and stand convicted of ignorance or falsehood when you say it is 'neither *natural* nor desirable that whites and blacks shall live together in the same community.'"[74] African Americans found in Central America evidence that both multiracial democracy and black self-government were possible. McCune Smith pointedly observed that Nicaragua's Foreign Relations minister at the time, Sebastian Salinas, was a mulatto: "Although

Mr. Squiers [sic] carefully conceals it, the truth is that *Senior Salinas is a black man!* . . . Here in Nicaragua, the . . . freest . . . region on the face of God's earth, where black and white interchange all the civil and social relations on the same platform . . . we find a black diplomatist of the first water."[75] Similarly, Douglass would later point to Latin America in a scathing rebuttal of Lincoln's flirtation with colonizationism in the midst of the Civil War in an editorial in *Douglass's Monthly* in September 1862: "Mr. Lincoln knows that in Mexico, Central America and South America, many distinct races live peaceably together in the enjoyment of equal rights."[76] We see here some of the earliest examples of a pattern whereby African Americans would deploy a romanticized depiction of Latin American racial politics to buttress their arguments for racial equality in the United States.

African Americans seeking sites of black freedom in Central America encountered complicated local racial politics upon their arrival, however, as illustrated by another article about San Juan del Norte that appeared in *Frederick Douglass's Paper* in May 1852 (a month after the publication of Delany's *Condition*). James Starkey, an African American immigrant, wrote a letter about attempts to export US-style racial segregation to San Juan. Having departed the United States on a vessel captained by a Virginian who enforced segregation aboard the ship, Starkey expected to be able to meet whites "on equal ground" in San Juan, but was disappointed to find that in "a town containing five hundred inhabitants, of which one hundred are white Americans . . . the other four hundred, which are composed of Indians and colored persons from the American States, suffer themselves to be ruled at the will and pleasure of the few pale faces."[77] Even more disturbing was the fact that it was sometimes transplanted African Americans who sought to enforce racial segregation in deference to the sensibilities of their white customers from the United States. Starkey described an incident involving an African American returning from California with white companions who was refused service by the "colored" landlord of a hotel, which resulted in a sound rebuke by the entire party which then moved to another "hotel kept by a *white man* . . . [where they] were entertained alike without distinction."[78] Starkey sought a space of black freedom in the Mosquito Kingdom, not just from slavery but also from US-style racial hierarchies:

> It is very strange that our people will suffer themselves to be carried away by this 'American character' even here, in a country like this, whose king is a colored man, and the police officers, colored

men. . . . And with this colored government, colored persons from the States, seek to enforce what they call the 'American character,' but more justly the slaveholding character, on their own color who come among them. . . . Is it not time that we had begun to appreciate freedom, and real liberty, particularly, in a country like this?[79]

Slavery might not have existed in San Juan, but due to the presence of white US Americans and transplanted African American subservience, blacks were still not free.

Starkey's concern that white immigration to black/mixed-race spaces in Central America could infuse them with the "slaveholding character" that US blacks were trying to escape was not unfounded, as the circumstances of Delany's election as mayor of San Juan reveal. Delany's election, which was reported in *Frederick Douglass's Paper* in May 1852, was orchestrated by a transnational, multiracial political alliance between African American migrants and San Juan's local black, indigenous, mixed-race inhabitants, against an effort by white US citizens to exclude nonwhites from political participation. As Jake Mattox has noted, "In the San Juan election purportedly won by Delany, white and black US Americans, Jamaicans, Miskito Indians, and Nicaraguans participated, pitting a white Cotton American ticket supported by southern US American residents against a 'native and colored' party."[80] Delany's election was subsequently annulled, yet this fugitive enactment of multiracial democracy epitomized the contradictions that plagued African Americans's search for sites of black freedom in Central America. For Carolina, a correspondent to *Frederick Douglass's Paper*, the event represented an actualization of fugitive democracy, when "the native and colored citizens of San Juan" were impelled to organize politically to counter the exertions of "a portion of the inhabitants of this town . . . to deprive us of our rights as citizens, to strip us of the rights of having a voice in choosing our own rulers, to subject us if possible to a system of slavery, equaled only by that of the Southern States of the United States of North America."[81] Read in light of black fugitivity, the precariousness of African American freedom (and citizenship) in San Juan is clear, as alluded to in Carolina's not-entirely metaphorical conflation of the denial of political rights with plantation slavery as practiced in the US South. Simultaneously, however, Delany's selection as a candidate, when he did not reside in, and had never even visited San Juan, points to the unequal power hierarchies within this transnational alliance of people of color. Black emigrationism thus involved a trade-off in which spaces of black freedom for African Americans might be achieved at the expense of the disempowerment of the Mosquito Kingdom's actual black and indigenous citizens, who were already involved in a struggle to preserve their political autonomy from Nicaragua, the United States, and Great Britain. Douglass's hemispheric vision was plagued by similar tensions, as we shall see.

In the 1850s Douglass (and Delany) found sites of black freedom, models of a black "city on a hill" in the Caribbean and Central America that demonstrated that black self-government and multiracial democracy were possible. Douglass's black fugitive sensibilities during this period can be discerned in his decision to allow his newspapers to function as a discursive space where collective black political agency could be envisioned. The tensions inherent in African American hemispheric visions would become even more apparent following emancipation in the United States, however, when Douglass (who rejected expansionism while slavery persisted) endorsed the incorporation of willing Caribbean nations as a means of remaking the United States in their more multiracial and (ostensibly) racially egalitarian image.

"A Black Sister to Massachusetts": Decentering Whiteness in US Democracy

In the 1870s, rather than looking for sites of black freedom elsewhere in the Americas, Douglass sought to refashion the US polity into his vision of a multiracial democracy, partly via nonwhite immigration and expansion to Latin America. Douglass's support for the annexation of Santo Domingo (the Dominican Republic) in 1870–1871 is generally viewed as an expression of his US nationalism. Without excusing his support for annexation, I suggest that Douglass's commitment to multiracial democracy informed his position in ways that have not been sufficiently appreciated. At this time Douglass had a much more negative assessment of the political capacities of the black republics of the Caribbean than in the 1850s, while he also viewed the Reconstruction–era United States as the vanguard of racial egalitarianism in the hemisphere. During this period, the fugitive democratic overtones of Douglass's political thought eclipse his commitment to black fugitivity. Paradoxically, Douglass at times echoed claims about Anglo-Saxon superiority in his arguments in favor of annexation, even as he disputed these same claims in his defense of an expansive immigration policy.[82] Debates about annexation and immigration during this era were closely tied to racial science and the way it shaped the kinds of hemispheric relations that were being envisioned by white elites in the United States, Caribbean thinkers, and US blacks. Douglass's support for annexation was driven by the belief that the willing incorporation of black, mixed-race Latin American states on terms of full equality would transform US racial politics by contributing to, as Millery Polyné has argued, "a diverse U.S. American identity that decentered whiteness."[83] The other prong of Douglass's project to transform US democracy during this era was expanded nonwhite immigration grounded in the notion of a universal human right to migration. Douglass's commitment to refounding US democracy on more racially egalitarian grounds led him to underestimate the threat US expansion posed to black freedom and sovereignty in the Caribbean, however.

Douglass's formulation of an expansive vision of US multiracial democracy in the 1870s fueled in part by the idea of a human right to migration is especially interesting in light of contemporary debates about immigration and cosmopolitanism in political theory. As Farah Godrej has noted, while work on cosmopolitanism has flourished in recent years, most of it continues to draw almost exclusively on Western sources and ideas.[84] Meanwhile, arguments for open borders have generally been grounded in liberal frameworks that give primacy to individual rights.[85] In contrast, I want to suggest that Douglass's project of decentering whiteness in US democracy in part via an embrace of immigration during Reconstruction offers an alternative genealogy for cosmopolitan arguments that might instead be traced back to the ethical commitments fostered by fugitivity. Douglass's thinking about a human right of migration cemented an analysis of how racial hierarchy had rendered the United States an uneven democracy, which could be remedied via a commitment to accepting nonwhite immigrants from all corners of the globe and including them as equal citizens. While Douglass's invocation of the idea of human rights could be taken as evidence of his adherence to liberal individualism, his analysis of racial hierarchy in the United States suggests that it might more properly be ascribed to the fugitive ex-slave's recognition that national borders alone did not determine the condition of citizen or non-citizen. Moreover, his foregrounding of the Americas as a geographic space characterized by multiraciality and immigration, and shaped politically by republicanism, marks this as a subaltern hemispheric approach to cosmopolitanism.[86]

During the nineteenth century, US views about expansion to Latin America were shaped by attitudes toward slavery and racial hierarchy, which were in turn influenced by the racial science of the day. Prior to the Civil War, white southerners promoted US expansion as a way to increase the number of slave states, while abolitionists opposed it for precisely the same reason. During Reconstruction, however, a reversal occurred, and many white southerners—driven by similar motives as in the past: antagonism to racial equality and a desire to enforce racial separation and white supremacy—opposed US expansion to Latin America because it entailed the incorporation of nonwhite citizens. Douglass's position also shifted at this time. Consistent with his opposition to racial segregation on a hemispheric level between the "white" US and black/brown Latin America, he rejected racist arguments against annexation.[87] Douglass supported voluntary annexation because he believed it could be beneficial to both Santo Domingo and the United States: it would help the former overcome the legacy of slavery and the deficient political culture inherited from Spain, and it would enhance the latter's emerging "composite nationality." He also believed that the annexation of Santo Domingo would help end slavery in Cuba and Puerto Rico.[88] Douglass's support was contingent on certain parameters for annexation, however: it could not occur by force, a majority of Dominicans had to support it, and the Dominican government should freely agree to it. "While we would gladly see San Domingo, Hayti, Cuba, and all the islands of the Caribbean Sea made a part of the United States, we would not accept any of them, or all of them, at the price of a single act of bad faith, or a single drop of blood. If we cannot have them without dishonor, rapine, and bloodshed let them stay out forever."[89]

Racial science played a key role in debates about the annexation of Santo Domingo. Much of the opposition to annexation was rooted in racist anxieties about the deleterious effects of incorporating black, mixed-race Caribbean bodies into the United States. Since African Americans had obtained the right to vote in 1870, Southern Democrats worried that annexation would add more black voters who would vote Republican, and contribute to the creation of a nonwhite majority that would entrench "black supremacy." Opponents of annexation drew on the new climatic racial determinism, which had also shaped debates about African American emigration, to argue against the proposal. Based on the notion that different races were suited to live in different geographical regions, "anti-imperialist racists . . . were concerned about a plan that would add 'tropical' blacks to the U.S. nation."[90] For example, Senator Carl Schurz of Missouri (himself an immigrant from Germany), imagined the following nightmare scenario: "fancy the Senators and Representatives of ten or twelve millions of tropical people, people of the Latin race mixed with Indian and African blood ... fancy them sitting in the Halls of Congress, throwing the weight of their intelligence, their morality, their political notions and habits, their prejudices and passions, into the scale of the destinies of this Republic."[91] Claims about the existence of natural geographic zones where only certain races could flourish also found their way into the arguments of Senator Charles Sumner, Douglass's political ally and champion of African American rights. Sumner framed his opposition to annexation as a defense of the right to self-government of nonwhite peoples in general, and Haiti in particular. But he also argued: "By a higher statute is that island [Hispaniola] set apart to the colored race. It is theirs by right of possession ... by tropical position ... and by *unalterable laws of climate.* Such is the ordinance of nature, which I am not the first to recognize."[92] The tenets of scientific racism were thus deployed at times to argue against US expansion.

Consonant with his earlier critique of how the tenets of racial science, particularly notions of permanent black inferiority, were used to support slavery in the United States, Douglass rejected the idea of a link between race and climate. As had been the case with his opposition to white colonizationist schemes in the 1850s based on the notion that black and white political coexistence was impossible after emancipation, in the 1870s Douglass rejected the anti-imperialist racist vision of a Jim Crow American continent composed of racially homogeneous nation-states. Against opponents of annexation, he argued: "We fail to see any serious objection to the measure on the grounds that the tropics, especially belong to the colored race ... *we are opposed to this parceling out the earth to different varieties of men*—locating one here and another there, and deeming this one and that out of its place, here or there ... reason, aptitude, and ability, rather than color ... must determine where ... a race of men must live."[93] Ironically, Douglass's critique of climatic racial determinism was thus deployed in support of US expansion to Latin America.

During Reconstruction, Douglass also formulated a cosmopolitan notion of multiracial democracy grounded in the idea of a universal human right to migration and the Americas as a multiracial space. In an 1869 lecture on the United States's emerging "Composite Nationality," for example, he linked the fact that "until recently, neither the Indian nor the negro has been treated as a part of the body politic" to opposition to

Chinese immigration.[94] He observed that those who objected to nonwhite immigration to the United States often wondered: "Should not a superior race protect itself from contact with inferior ones? Are not the white people the owners of this continent? Have they not the right to say what kind of people shall be allowed to come here and settle?" To these critics, Douglass forcefully replied: "There are such things in the world as human rights. They rest upon no conventional foundation, but are eternal, universal and indestructible. Among these is the ... right of migration ... which belongs to no particular race, but belongs alike to all and to all alike." Observing that it was only by virtue of said right that European settlers and their descendants could justify their presence in the Americas, he affirmed:

> I reject the arrogant and scornful theory by which they [whites] would limit migratory rights, or any other essential human rights, to themselves, and which would make them the owners of this great continent to the exclusion of all other races of men. I want a home here not only for the negro, the mulatto and the Latin races, but I want the Asiatic to find a home here in the United States, and feel at home here, both for his sake and ours.[95]

We can thus detect a residue of the black fugitive's refusal to be bound by the nation-state in Douglass's idea of a universal right to migration.

Douglass's support for annexation coincided with his view that the United States should embrace nonwhite immigration as a means to de-center whiteness, but he also believed that annexation would be advantageous to Santo Domingo, by helping to transform the deficient political institutions inherited from Spain and the distorted cultural habits that were the legacy of slavery. Annexation, he argued, should be viewed not in terms of "what Santo Domingo can do for us, but ... [rather] what we can ... and ought to do for Santo Domingo."[96] In contrast to his rejection of climatic racial determinism, in some of his pro-annexation arguments Douglass echoed the claims of "the historical school" of scientific racism that Anglo-Saxons were superior to Latins. He described Hispaniola as an island ruled by two governments, "both republican in form, yet both military and despotic in fact."[97] Contrary to his earlier positive assessment of Haiti in 1861, he now attributed the island's political dysfunction partly to the legacy of Spanish colonization: "In Santo Domingo were first planted the virtues and the vices, the beauties and deformities of European civilization ...

Spain, to whom it belonged ... was as remarkable for her piety as she was for her cruelty."[98]

Douglass's characterization of the negative effects of Spanish colonization in Santo Domingo echoes that of Latin American intellectuals such as Domingo F. Sarmiento. Indeed, a critique of the deleterious effects of the Spanish legacy on Latin America was a consistent element in Sarmiento's political thought. In *Facundo* (published in 1845), for example, Sarmiento famously ascribed Argentina's political disorder partly to the stultifying effects of Spanish colonization, even as he embraced other European influences.[99] Later in 1865, a few years before Douglass's arguments about annexation, Sarmiento deplored the "many evils of bad Spanish colonization," and even claimed that "the ignorance of the Spaniards of the fifteenth century, perpetuated in a savage land, the abject condition of the rude Indian incorporated into colonial society, fanaticism and the loosening of every moral bond, have produced in South America greater depravity than slavery in the [US] South."[100] Douglass, in passages that could have been written by Sarmiento, attributed Santo Domingo's sluggish and unimaginative national character to Spain's intolerance of religious diversity. He claimed that "dark and sanguinary as may have been the barbarism of the island, prior to its discovery and settlement by the Spaniards, the state of things which then existed seems to have been far more friendly to human life and happiness than after it ... [came into] the hands of the Christian Spaniards."[101] It is doubtful that Sarmiento (who was as scathing in his assessment of Argentina's indigenous inhabitants as he was about its Spanish colonizers), would have agreed with this assessment, but the similarities between their indictments of Spain point to the pervasiveness of the notion of Anglo-Saxon superiority at the time.

Douglass also attributed Santo Domingo's political disorder and economic underdevelopment to the legacy of slavery. Rather than emphasizing slave agency in the Caribbean as he had in the 1857 West India Emancipation speech, in the 1870s Douglass focused on slavery's deforming effects on the enslaved:

> When we think of the slavery, both of the natives, and the Africans in that Island; when we think of the ten thousand evils that slavery entailed upon that country ... the indolence and repugnance to labor which slavery left behind it, and the misrule, and bad government which have followed to this day ... the wonder is not that civilization is feeble, but that there is civilization at all.[102]

Slavery, he argued, contributed to political instability by fostering a political culture prone to violence and disorder: "While a large portion of the people of Santo Domingo are peaceable and orderly . . . owing to the ignorance and barbarism left them by slavery, they are the sports of designing chiefs, of educated and ambitious leaders who manage to keep the country in a chronic state of revolution."[103] Douglass's reference to the "barbarism left by slavery" is noteworthy given pre–Civil War anti-abolitionist arguments that slavery had a "civilizing" effect on blacks.[104]

During Reconstruction, Douglass's commitment to the United States was at its apex; he believed the US polity was in a process of radical refounding and retreated from political ideas consonant with black fugitivity. Hence, the paternalistic overtones of his arguments about the beneficial effects of transplanting US political institutions to Caribbean nations. For example, in a strange moment indeed for the author of "Claims," he argued that there would be no greater achievement for "the Anglo-Saxon race" than "the redemption of the tropics from Latin mis-rule, ignorance and superstition."[105] While his aim was to decenter whiteness within the US polity, here Douglass unreservedly echoes the historical school of scientific racism's arguments about Anglo-Saxon superiority. Douglass viewed the United States as the vanguard of racial egalitarianism in the Americas at this time. Explaining his switch from opponent to supporter of US expansion, he wrote: "That was a time when extension meant more slavery, more ignorance and barbarism, but that time is now gone by. Extension now means freedom . . . this Republic is now the hope of freedom throughout the world."[106]

Writing at the height of Reconstruction, when racial equality seemed like a distinct possibility in the United States, Douglass linked his support for expansion to progress toward multiracial democracy:

> All signs indicate that . . . the continent is ultimately to belong to us. Latin civilization, the only present obstacle to our southern dominion, is rapidly getting itself into the grave. . . . The sentiments of our people are shaping themselves for this multiform composite nationality. Prejudice against color once thought to be natural and invincible alike to time and reason, can no longer be relied upon. The idea that this is exclusively the whitemans [sic] country—and the whitemans [sic] government—has already become a superstition. The irrepressible negro . . . is now a member of Congress, and elegeable [sic] to any office of honor or profit in the land.[107]

Douglass deployed the language of Anglo-Saxon superiority, but bent it to his own purposes in order to argue for multiracial democracy. It was precisely by contributing to the democratic ideal of making it no longer "exclusively the white man's country" that the annexation of Santo Domingo was beneficial to the United States. Douglass believed that the voluntary incorporation of Latin American states would help transform the United States into a more racially egalitarian and multiracial polity.[108] Annexation "would make her [Santo Domingo] the black sister to Massachusetts, and transplant within her tropical borders the glorious institutions which have lifted that grand old Commonwealth to her present commanding elevation. ... Since the downfall of slavery and the enfranchisement of the colored race, we have recognized the *composite* character of the nation, and considered it a blessing rather than a misfortune."[109] Douglass in the 1870s thus borrowed selectively from racial science in order to advance a cosmopolitan, multiracial vision of the US polity.

Douglass envisioned a multiracial US democracy in which whiteness was decentered in multiple ways: through political and social equality for African Americans and Native Americans, Asian immigration, and the addition of black, mixed-race Latin Americans, all of whom would be integral elements of a new "composite nationality."[110] By composite Douglass did not mean a blending together of different racial groups into a homogeneous mestizo national type, however. Rather, as some of the definitions of "composite" in the *Oxford English Dictionary* suggest, he was referring to a polity: "Made up of various parts or elements. ... Consisting of an organic aggregation of individuals, or of distinct parts ... made from two or more physically different constituents each of which largely retains its original structure and identity."[111] Douglass's concept of "composite nationality" thus envisions an egalitarian democracy in which multiple racial groups could coexist, and in which whiteness was not dominant. We can see the fugitive democratic elements of his political thought at work here because he envisions a political community of ordinary persons with the common goals of racial redress, material survival, and dismantling racial oligarchy.

Douglass welcomed the idea of a nonwhite majority in the United States that would transform white supremacy, such that "the old question as to what shall be done with the negro will have to give place to the greater question 'what shall be done with the Mongolian,' and perhaps we shall see raised one still greater, namely, 'what shall the Mongolian do with both the negro and the white?' "[112] He believed that the United States was uniquely suited to become the site of such a composite nationality because of its anti-colonial, revolutionary foundation: "our greatness ... will be found in the faithful application of the principle of perfect civil equality to the people of all races and creeds. We are not only bound to this position by our organic structure and by our revolutionary anteced- ents but by the genius of our people. Gathered here from all quarters of the globe, by a common aspiration for national liberty as against caste, di- vine right and privileged classes."[113] Grounded in a cosmopolitan notion of the virtue of migration, Douglass argued that the United States "should welcome ... all nations ... tongues and peoples, and as fast as they can learn our language and comprehend the duties of citizenship, we should incorporate them into the American body politic."[114] He thus took the nightmare scenario of the racist anti-annexationists and reshaped it into a fugitive democratic vista in which US democracy would be enhanced by having a "black sister to Massachusetts" of Caribbean origin and non- white immigrants from around the globe.[115]

Douglass was undoubtedly overly optimistic in his hopes that racial inclusion during Reconstruction constituted a permanent democratic recomposition of the US polity, but his ringing endorsement of immigra- tion a century-and-a-half ago is striking in light of some of the contempo- rary xenophobic responses to Latino and Muslim immigration. Efforts to enact multiracial democracy during Douglass's lifetime evoked many of the same fears and racial resentments elicited today by the United States's changing demographics and the election of its only African American president. Ironically, given that it perhaps should have led him to doubt the lasting effects of Reconstruction–era experiments in racial equal- ity, Douglass was prescient about the possibility of such a backlash. He observed that for some of his contemporaries African American enfran- chisement had conjured a "new danger ... the phantom of black suprem- acy." He reassured his white audience that "black supremacy need not much disturb you" as it was an as yet distant prospect.[116] Douglass may have mocked fears of a "black emperor," but he certainly envisioned the transformation of the US polity via an expanding multiracial citizenry that would challenge white supremacy. In contrast to his search for sites of black freedom and racial egalitarianism in Latin America in the 1850s, during Reconstruction Douglass endorsed expansionism (and nonwhite immigration) in order to transform the United States into his vision of a city on a hill: a multiracial democracy with a composite nationality in which individuals of "all races and creeds" could be equal co-citizens. The failure of Reconstruction would render Douglass much more skeptical about the prospects of multiracial democracy in the United States. As a result, traces of black fugitivity resurfaced in his thinking in the 1890s, and he once again highlighted Haiti as an exemplary site of black freedom linked to African Americans by transnational forms of racial solidarity.

"We Must Rise or Fall with the Race": Black Fugitivity and Racial Solidarity

The final sentence of the 1892 edition of Douglass's third autobiography, *The Life and Times of Frederick Douglass*, published three years prior to his death, reads: "I have been the recipient of many honors, among which my unsought appointment ... to represent the United States to the capital of Haiti, and my equally unsought appointment ... to represent Haiti ... at the World's Columbian Exposition, are crowning honors to my long career and a fitting and happy end to my whole public life."[117] That Douglass would cite this as a fitting coda to his extraordinary life might come as a surprise to both Caribbean critics of his support for US expansionism and those who view him as only concerned with US political problems. Douglass's decision to discursively align himself with Haiti is consistent with his defense of Haitian sovereignty and political capacity in the 1890s, however. This was a moment when Douglass's earlier black fugitive commitments resurfaced as he extolled the heroic collective struggle for liberation of Haitian slaves as an exemplary political act. Yet Douglass's attempt to enact a transnational form of black solidarity in the 1890s could not escape the tensions that plagued African American quests for black freedom in Central America in the 1850s. Throughout his career Douglass oscillated between the two polarities of democratic and fugitive hope. Democratic hope recognizes democracy's impermanent, contingent, and imperiled character but nevertheless remains committed to the struggle to perfect the polity, whereas black fugitive hope seeks to enable black freedom while maintaining distance from the inheritances of slavery and white supremacy because the polity is not easily reconstituted on more racially egalitarian grounds. We find traces of both in Douglass's engagement with Haiti in the 1890s.

Douglass served as US Minister Resident and Consul General to the Republic of Haiti from 1889 to 1891, a tenure marked by controversy over the Môle St. Nicolas. The failure to secure a lease of the Haitian port of Môle St. Nicolas as a US naval fueling station would lead to Douglass's resignation in 1891 and to a public dispute over who was responsible for the failure of the negotiations. Rather than accept that Haiti, as an independent republic, had rejected an arrangement that Haitians perceived as a breach of national sovereignty, the US press blamed Douglass (who was not the lead negotiator) and suggested that his racial sympathies had compromised his ability to defend US interests. Douglass's criminalization in the press (through implicit accusations of treason) figuratively returned him to the status of a fugitive whose national belonging was in doubt. Disgusted with US efforts to strong-arm Haiti into submitting to the lease, and distressed by his portrayal in the press, Douglass published two articles shortly after his resignation that exposed the racist logic behind the criticisms.[118]

Douglass claimed not to have opposed the idea of the lease per se, as "the concession asked for was in the line of good neighborhood and advanced civilization, and in every way consistent with the autonomy of Haiti," but rather to have objected to the manner in which the United States sought to gain Haitian agreement to it.[119] He then exposed the hypocrisy of claims that a white diplomat would have been able to establish better relations with Haiti:

> One of the duties of a minister in a foreign land is to cultivate good social as well as civil relations with the people and government to which he is sent. Would an American white man, imbued with our national sentiments, be more likely than an American colored man to cultivate such relations? Would his American contempt for the colored race at home fit him to win the respect and good-will of colored people abroad? Or would he play the hypocrite and pretend to love negroes in Haiti when he is known to hate negroes in the United States? . . . Haiti is no stranger to Americans or American prejudice. Our white fellow-countrymen have taken little pains to conceal their sentiments.[120]

As Douglass observed, the only putative advantage to appointing a white diplomat in his stead was the expectation that it would lead to more deference by Haiti, a racist assumption that betrayed ignorance of the country's history. Douglass also cited his prior support for the annexation of Santo Domingo as evidence that he was not uniformly opposed to US expansion to Latin America, but rather wanted the United States to treat Latin American nations as equals, and to have such incorporation be voluntary and mutually beneficial. The United States, he argued, "should ask nothing of Haiti on grounds less just and reasonable than those upon which they would ask anything of France or England. . . . Are we to wring from it by dread of our own power what we cannot obtain by appeals to its justice and reason? If this be the policy of this great nation, I own that my assailants were right when they said that I was not the man to represent the United States in Haiti."[121] Douglass's futile attempt to enact horizontal hemispheric relations in the 1890s was incompatible with US racism and imperialism.

If the negative reaction in the United States to Douglass's egalitarian approach to hemispheric relations reflects a process by which he was "blackened" (i.e., where he was seen as too sympathetic to Haiti because of racial solidarity), Caribbean intellectuals critical of his role engaged in an inverse "whitening" of Douglass, where they viewed him solely as an agent of US empire. The Cuban nationalist José Martí, for example, writing in exile from New York in 1889 in the Argentinean newspaper *La Nación*, described Douglass in rather disparaging terms:

> About Haiti there has been a scandal in these days because the minister sent by the United States is the gray-haired mulatto Douglass, married to a white woman; and he goes there to tell them that they should love the United States and especially the Republicans that are currently in power, because they have been like a father to the black man, and the blacks of the Americas should place themselves in their [capable] hands and follow them if they wish to be saved.

Martí did not mince words about what he viewed as Douglass's complicity in US imperial ventures in the Caribbean, and even accused him of being animated by greed: "[for] Douglass, who has rented out his old age . . . those [Caribbean] waters are not unknown, because he voyaged in them years ago, as a commissioner for Grant, when there was a plan for the annexation of Santo Domingo."[122] As Jossianna Arroyo has observed, Martí's critique of Douglass on behalf of Haitian sovereignty is ironic, given that most Spanish Caribbean "intellectuals turned their backs on Haiti because the country clearly mirrored their own sociopolitical fears for their nations . . . becoming a black nation governed by blacks."[123] In contrast to the widespread disavowal of the Haitian Revolution by Latin American and Caribbean intellectuals, in the 1890s Douglass would again cite Haiti as an inspiring black collective freedom project that was even more exemplary for having been enacted by rebellious slaves.[124]

The tensions between black fugitivity and democratic fugitivity in Douglass's political activities during this era are perhaps most evident in his curation of the Haitian exhibit at the 1893 World's Columbian Exposition in Chicago. In keeping with the heightened exclusion and racial domination that characterized the post–Reconstruction period, African Americans were not represented in any of the US exhibits. Indeed, the Exposition's spatial design followed a white supremacist logic whereby "the sequence of exhibits was supposed to demonstrate the advance of civilization from so-called primitive cultures, such as those in Africa, to the supposedly higher stages represented by Europe and North America."[125] African American inclusion in the US exhibit would have disrupted the racist evolutionary premises underlying its design. Nevertheless, because Douglass was asked by Haiti's government to organize their country's exhibit, he was able to ensure African American presence in the Exposition. The Haitian pavilion became a site for the celebration of African American achievements since emancipation, displaying the writings of notable African American intellectuals such as Paul Laurence Dunbar and Ida B. Wells. Yet Douglass's curatorial efforts at the Exposition can be read in multiple ways. For instance, he could be viewed as having coopted the Haitian Exhibit by using it to feature African Americans, such that this was a moment when the power hierarchies that plagued earlier attempts to link black struggles across the Americas resurfaced, when the quest for citizenship of African Americans once again displaced, if not erased, the autochthonous political concerns of local black populations, in this instance Haitians. Whatever the truth of this assessment, it appears that most Haitians held Douglass in high esteem and viewed him as an advocate and ally of Haiti in the United States.[126]

Read in light of democratic fugitivity, however, Douglass's efforts to ensure African American representation at the Exposition (and thereby symbolic inclusion in the US polity), coupled with his vehement denunciation of lynching and post–Reconstruction Era violence, could be seen as an attempt to facilitate a fleeting mobilization of the demos against white supremacy. Douglass's writings in the 1890s are suffused with vivid demonstrations of attenuated black citizenship, as in the pamphlet he and Wells published in 1892, "Why the Colored American Is not at the World's Columbian Exposition," that simultaneously documented African American progress since emancipation and the escalating forms of racial terror they faced in the period after Reconstruction. Douglass wrote an introduction to the volume that preceded an essay by Wells on lynching, in which his denunciation of the failings of US democracy evince a reemergent black fugitive orientation. Douglass attributed escalating racial terror in the post–Reconstruction United States to the persistence of a residual "spirit of slavery." African Americans, he proclaimed:

> would like . . . to tell our visitors that . . . barbarism and race hate [have been banished] from the United States; that the old things of slavery have entirely passed away . . . that American law is now the shield alike of black and white . . . that here Negroes are not tortured, shot, hanged, or burned to death merely on suspicion of crime . . . that the American Government is in reality a Government of the people, by the people and for the people, for all the people . . . that to the colored people of America, morally speaking, the World's Fair now in progress, is not a whited sepulcher. . . . But unhappily, none of this can be said . . . without flagrant disregard of the truth.[127]

While Douglass ends the essay on a somewhat positive note—exhorting African Americans to struggle for their rights, since "manful contention" was "itself ennobling" even when it did not necessarily result in victory—this spirit of rebellious prophetic critique is also present in his other writings on lynching and racial terror in the 1890s.[128]

In "The Lessons of the Hour," published in 1894, for example, Douglass described the US body politic as "disfigured" by the "ghastly horrors" of lynching. In his telling, US democracy was being rendered monstrous by the accumulating bodies of black dead produced by unchecked racial violence. He wrote: "there is nothing in the history of savages to surpass the blood-chilling horrors and fiendish excesses perpetrated against the coloured people of this country, by the so-called enlightened and Christian people of the South . . . [who] gloat over and prey upon dead bodies."[129] Douglass connected the systematic assaults on black life and citizenship of the post–Reconstruction Era to the persistent inheritances of slavery, arguing that "the sentiment left by slavery is still with us, and the moral vision of the American people is still darkened by its presence."[130] If US democracy as a whole was haunted by the specter of slavery, the North was not exempt from critique, as Douglass observed that its acquiescence to lynching and less violent forms of inclusion made it equally complicit in black oppression. "You [the South] kill their bodies, we [the North] kill their souls."[131] Douglass even went so far as to confess to his faith in US democracy being shaken as a result: "events have made me doubtful . . . [they have] shaken my faith in the nobility of the nation . . . the immediate future looks dark and troubled. I cannot shut my eyes to the ugly facts before me."[132] In this text, in contrast to the concluding exhortation to African Americans in the Columbian Exposition pamphlet two years earlier, Douglass argued that because racism was a white, not a "negro problem," it required changes on the part of whites, not black striving. In words that acquire a particularly poignant resonance in light of the shooting of nine unarmed African Americans at the AME Emanuel Church in Charleston, South Carolina, by a millennial white nationalist in 2015, Douglass concluded that the only peaceful solution to white supremacy was to: "Let the white people of the North and South conquer their prejudices. . . . Let them give up the idea that they can be free while making the Negro a slave. Let them give up the idea that to degrade the colored man is to elevate the white man. . . . They are not required to do much. They are only required to undo the evil they have done, in order to solve this problem."[133] Douglass's fugitive democratic commitments are clearly in evidence at this moment. He still believed that it might be possible for the white majority to disavow racial terror, even as the insights derived from black fugitivity suggested the futility of the strategy of continuing to petition the racial state for inclusion. For the fugitive democrat, this risk might be preferable to giving in to the temptation of democratic despair, whereas black fugitivity would point toward the search for alternative sites of liberation.

The powerful lecture on Haiti Douglass delivered at the Exposition, in which he rearticulated the notion of Haiti as a black city on a hill and celebrated the political activities of revolutionary Haitian slaves, provides even stronger evidence of his reorientation toward black fugitivity at this time.[134] The official purpose of the Exposition was to commemorate the 400th anniversary of Columbus's arrival in the Americas. In his January 2, 1893, lecture inaugurating the Haitian pavilion, however, Douglass reframed the event and turned it into a celebration of the 90th anniversary of Haitian independence in 1804, of the establishment of "the only self-made black republic in the world." Rather than a celebration of the advent of European colonialism, it became a celebration of the revolutionary activities of rebellious slaves. The Haitian Revolution, Douglass argued was "one of the most remarkable . . . events . . . in the history of mankind." Comparing it to the US struggle for independence, he observed that the

founding fathers benefited from "long years of personal and political freedom. They belonged to the ruling race of this world and the sympathy of
the world was with them." In contrast, the Haitian revolutionaries "were
slaves. . . . Their education was obedience to the will of others. . . . Yet
from these men of the negro race came brave men, men who loved their
liberty more than life [Applause]; wise men, statesmen, warriors and
heroes . . . men who have gained their independence against odds as for-
midable as ever confronted a righteous cause or its advocates."[135] It was the
courage, resilience, and sagacity of the enslaved who fought for freedom
that accounted for Haiti's enduring power as a political example: "It will
ever be a matter of wonder and astonishment to thoughtful men, that a
people in abject slavery, subject to the lash, and kept in ignorance of letters, as these slaves were, should have known enough, or have had left in
them enough manhood, to combine, to organize, and to select for themselves trusted leaders and with loyal hearts to follow them into the jaws
of death to obtain liberty."[136] Douglass also reiterated a frequent trope in
his work that struggling for freedom from enslavement was the source of
valuable political lessons that could not be taught: "The freedom of Haiti
was not given as a boon, but conquered as a right!"[137]

In the 1893 lecture on Haiti, Douglass envisioned an alternative political lineage for the Americas that equally foregrounded the contributions
of its black ancestors. He argued that Haiti was an exemplary American
space because:

> She was the first of all the cis-Atlantic world, upon which the firm
> foot of the . . . white man was permanently set. . . . She was also the
> first to witness the bitter agonies of the negro bending under the
> blood-stained lash of Christian slave-holders. Happily too, for her,
> she was the first of the New World in which the black man asserted
> his right to be free and was brave enough to fight for his freedom
> and fortunate enough to gain it.[138]

Douglass's inclusion of the Haitian Revolution as part of the political
legacy of the Americas points to the notion of diasporic currents of circulation of ideas and practices, not only of slavery, but also of freedom.[139] In
contrast to his emphasis on Santo Domingo's deficient political culture
during Reconstruction, in the 1890s Douglass praised the achievements
of ordinary Haitians and challenged attempts to attribute Haiti's political instability to "the character of the race." Haiti's political conflicts, he

argued, were the result of self-interested Haitian and US elites: "The common people of Haiti . . . have no taste for revolutions. The fault is not with the ignorant many, but with the educated and ambitious few. Too proud to work . . . they make politics a business of their country. . . . I wish I could say that these are the only conspirators against the peace of Haiti, but I cannot. They have allies in the United States."[140] Douglass's assessment of Haiti in 1893 was thus much closer to his pre–Civil War views.

Douglass's articulation of a notion of transnational black solidarity in his 1893 lecture on Haiti, based in part on shared subjection to anti-black racism and the linkages forged by rebellious slaves, further supports the view that this was a moment when he once again looked beyond the United States to the rest of the Americas for political inspiration. He displays a black fugitive sensibility at this time, envisioning a non-nation-state-based solidarity that could engender freedom and cultivate distance from white supremacy. At the outset of the lecture, for example, he argued that Haiti was intimately linked to black struggles everywhere, including those of African Americans:

> The people of Haiti, by reason of ancestral identity, are more interesting to the colored people of the United States than to all others, for the Negro . . . can never part with his identity and race. . . . No matter where prosperity or misfortune may chance to drive the negro, he is identified with and shares the fortune of his race. We are told to go to Haiti; to go to Africa. Neither Haiti nor Africa can save us from common doom. Whether we are here or there, we must rise or fall with the race.[141]

In addition to bonds of racial solidarity, Douglass also invoked links forged on the basis of exemplary political actions, such as the Haitian Revolution, that exemplified universal civic virtues:

> Haiti is the black man's country, now forever. . . . She has grandly served the cause of universal human liberty. We should not forget that the freedom you and I enjoy to-day; that the freedom that eight hundred thousand colored people enjoy in the British West Indies; the freedom that has come to the colored race the world over, is largely due to the brave stand taken by the black sons of Haiti ninety years ago. When they struck for freedom, they builded [sic] better than they knew. . . . They were linked and interlinked with their

race, and striking for their freedom, they struck for the freedom of every black man in the world.[142]

In the 1890s Douglass again found in Haiti a model of black political agency that served as the basis for a form of black fugitive hope. Having recognized the fragile character of the United States's commitment to racial egalitarianism following Reconstruction, Douglass chose to highlight Haiti as the source of an alternative founding genealogy for all of the Americas, one committed to racial justice and enacted by heroic ex-slaves.

This chapter has sought to highlight a different dimension of Frederick Douglass as a democratic theorist, and to show that Latin America played an often-overlooked yet important role in shaping his political thought, particularly his arguments about multiracial democracy. A key element of Douglass's vision of democracy, which was informed by the experience of black fugitivity, was an enlarged account of political founding moments that foregrounded black contributions and the development of a broad and inclusive notion of an American (in the hemispheric sense) political inheritance. Recovering this element of Douglass's political thought has important methodological implications for political theory, and comparative political theory in particular. The dominant impulse in the field to turn to Europe for models and sources is replicated in comparative political theory by the default comparison between Western and non-Western thinkers and ideas. This reflexive turn to Europe diverts attention from alternative philosophical, political, and intellectual contexts, such as the hemispheric connections and genealogies traced in this book, which provide other sources for rethinking democracy, migration, and cosmopolitanism. This analysis of Douglass's political thought, which enables us to rethink democracy in light of black fugitivity, demonstrates that we have much to learn from a hemispheric conceptual frame that rigorously interrogates the intellectual connections and political genealogies of the Americas.

The black fugitive democratic ethos sketched here, which emerges from a hemispheric reading of Douglass's political thought, is particularly relevant today because it can serve as a resource in ongoing debates about racial justice, immigration, and US democracy. There is a striking parallel between the nineteenth-century fears of black supremacy elicited by attempts to enfranchise African Americans and twenty-first century accusations of executive overreach and Caesarism leveled against President Barack Obama. Similarly, fears that the United States is being overrun by hordes of Latino immigrants, resulting in the displacement of its Anglo-Saxon political culture, mirror earlier objections to Chinese immigration. There is a stark contrast between twenty-first-century anti-immigrant hysteria and Douglass's embrace of a right to migration in the nineteenth century. His embrace of a composite US nationality fueled by nonwhite immigration in order to transform white supremacy and build an egalitarian multiracial democracy where solidarities could be forged across racial and cultural boundaries thus serves as an important counter-point to arguments that such developments threaten both the cohesion of the United States and African American interests. Highlighting African American political thought's hemispheric engagements also upends the claim that only Latin America has produced positive conceptions of multiracial democracy. It also serves as a counter to recent attempts to read Douglass as an unabashed believer in the redemptive power of a de-racialized American liberalism, by highlighting his at times quite radical black fugitive commitments to racial justice. When Douglass proclaimed of Haitian slaves, "when they struck for freedom they builded better than they knew," he should also be read as staking a claim for the revolutionary potential and relevance of black fugitivity as a resource for rethinking the spatial logic, temporal contours, and hemispheric intellectual lineage of democratic theory.

"Mi Patria de Pensamiento"

SARMIENTO, THE UNITED STATES, AND THE
PITFALLS OF COMPARISON

AMONG THE LEAST discussed texts by the prolific Argentinean statesman
and *pensador* Faustino Domingo Sarmiento is *Vida de Abran Lincoln*, which
was published shortly after Sarmiento's arrival in the United States to take
up his appointment as Argentinean ambassador a month after Lincoln's
assassination in 1865. The most interesting section of *Vida* is not the bio-
graphical sketch of Lincoln's life, but rather Sarmiento's introduction,
which lays bare both the vicissitudes of comparison as a method and the
complicated place of the United States in Sarmiento's political thought.
Sarmiento tells his Latin American readers that "in Lincoln's life existential affinities are to be found between both Americas; and from the facts
related to it, useful lessons and warnings for our own government are
necessarily inferred. ... South America's school in politics is the United
States."[1] If *Vida* is symptomatic of Sarmiento's practice of reading US history in light of Latin American realities, it also reveals another underappreciated element of his political thought: his presence in the country at
the height of Reconstruction, and the impact of the United States on his
ideas about race. While Sarmiento's admiration for the United States is
well known, he is nevertheless generally characterized as emblematic of a
strand of Latin American political thought that valorized European models and political ideas at the expense of indigenous American sources and
practices.[2] This account of Sarmiento's political thought is the result of the
overwhelming focus on his first and most famous text, *Facundo: civilización
y barbarie*, published in 1845. In *Facundo*, Sarmiento framed Argentina's
post-independence political dysfunction in terms of the binary opposition

between civilization and barbarism. This formulation succinctly encapsulates Latin American political thought's recurrent preoccupation with questions of authenticity and originality. On the one hand, American political practices appeared to encompass only conflict-prone societies and "primitive" indigenous peoples. On the other hand, the pursuit of "progress" led to the artificial imitation of ill-fitting European models and ideas. As Katherine Gordy has argued, however, a careful reading of *Facundo* reveals that even Sarmiento, the supposedly preeminent advocate of the Europeanization of Latin America, undermines his own attempt to celebrate European ideas.[3] Moving beyond *Facundo*, I argue that Sarmiento's approach to the question of Latin America's subaltern philosophical position (as both Western and marginal simultaneously) is best understood by grappling with his engagement with the United States, which shaped his political thought, and particularly his ideas about race, in important ways. This chapter thus departs from and challenges dominant assessments of Sarmiento's political thought by focusing on his post-*Facundo* writings, particularly those about the United States.

On the basis of *Facundo*, Sarmiento is rightly characterized as preeminently attentive to Argentinean national problems; in subsequent texts, however, he undoubtedly emerges as a broader hemispheric thinker focused on comparison between the United States and Latin America.[4] Beginning with his account of his first visit to the United States (and Europe) in 1847, and continuing in the various texts published during his three-year residence in the United States in the 1860s, there was an emphasis on democracy and republicanism in Sarmiento's work that is in contrast to the civilization/barbarism dichotomy that dominates *Facundo*. Similarly, while geography remains a central theme in his later writings, the topography shifts from the intra-Argentine split between the city and the countryside to a broader hemispheric juxtaposition between the United States and Latin America. Particularly in the 1860s and 1880s Sarmiento was concerned with the question of hemispheric power relations, of how Latin America could establish an egalitarian relationship with the United States.[5] As with the romanticized vision of Latin American race relations that Douglass and other African Americans used to critique US racism during the nineteenth century, Sarmiento read US history selectively, in a way that significantly misunderstood its political conflicts, especially the Civil War, in the service of intervening in and shaping Latin American debates about democracy, education, and the design of political institutions (especially federalism and executive power). In his writings about the

United States, Sarmiento thus exemplified one of the pitfalls of comparison, namely the way in which "the other" is selectively read or flattened in order to function as a mirror that reflects back a thinker's particular political and philosophical preoccupations. Sarmiento's selective reading of US history refracted through a Latin American lens is thus emblematic of the way comparison can serve to obscure rather than illuminate the realities it purports to represent.

While comparison remained a key conceptual and methodological tool throughout Sarmiento's oeuvre, after 1847 he was far more concerned with how to avoid power imbalances between *"ambas Américas"* (both Americas), that is, Latin America and the United States. Locating Sarmiento within a hemispheric intellectual genealogy dislodges the focus on Europeanization in dominant interpretations of his political thought, and in turn situates him as an unlikely precursor invoked by later and much more radical Latin American critics of US imperialism, such as Cuban nationalist José Martí, Peruvian Marxist José Carlos Mariátegui, and Mexican philosopher José Vasconcelos. Martí, Mariátegui, and Vasconcelos all invoked Sarmiento as an important intellectual precursor. This is surprising given the differences between their ideas and his, and also because Martí, Mariátegui, and Vasconcelos all belonged to different currents within Latin American political thought.[6] Yet, at the same time, it makes sense that they would reference Sarmiento, as he exemplifies Latin American thinkers's complicated relationship with European political thought since the era of independence. On the one hand, Latin American thinkers have drawn on Western ideas and categories but, on the other hand, they have had to fundamentally transform them to fit the region's realities. Since Simón Bolívar (the region's preeminent founding father) Latin American thinkers have been preoccupied with the question of what it means to forge a subaltern philosophical tradition that draws on European ideas and models while wrestling with problems and issues that have not been central to Western political thought, such as multiracial democracy, postcolonial statehood, cultural syncretism, and so on. Latin American thinkers have worried that because their political ideas were derived from Europe this has resulted in derivative, inauthentic, imported, and alienated forms of political association and philosophical production.

Sarmiento was a key voice in this debate. For example, as numerous literary critics have noted, while on the surface *Facundo* promotes the Europeanization of Latin America, Sarmiento's arguments in the text are contradictory and complex. He attributed the origins of political instability to Argentine geography, but the sections of *Facundo* devoted to describing the country and its people in the style of the literary genre of the travel narrative in fact read like a celebration of Argentina. Sarmiento was also a fierce critic of the effect of the Spanish colonial legacy on Argentina and of the negative consequences of blind imitation of Europe. In fact, he attributed Argentina's post-independence turmoil in part to the whole-sale application of European ideas without taking into account Argentine realities. He observed that Europeans were in no position to "reproach South America its mistakes and bloody conflicts. They blame her for their own doing, asking her to repair in thirty years *the errors they bequeathed during three centuries of colonization.*"[7] After 1847, however, Sarmiento's theoretical gaze shifted decisively to the Americas, as he drew on the United States to formulate ideas suited to hemispheric political realities. Rather than simply replacing one political model with another, however, this switch reflected an altered intellectual trajectory that became preemi-nently hemispheric, after which European thought remained present, but in the background.[8]

Despite his undisputed prominence within the canon of Latin American political thought, Sarmiento is now a controversial figure because of his undisputed racism.[9] Yet traces of Sarmiento's ideas about race endure. In Chile, for example, in contrast to the adoption of multicultural rights for indigenous peoples in other Latin American countries, current state policy and public reactions toward Mapuche mobilization demonstrate that Sarmiento's vision of indigenous people as savage and in need of civilization have not been entirely disavowed.[10] Moreover, as chapter 4 on Vasconcelos demonstrates, the notion that Latin America developed a superior approach to race emerged as a central argument of twentieth-century anti-imperial thinkers seeking to critique the United States and validate "their America." Latin American racial thought is varied, but claims about its advantages vis-à-vis other traditions need to be historicized and understood in light of their origins in moments of anti-imperial anxiety about hemispheric power relations. It would thus be a mistake to view Sarmiento as unrepresentative of Latin American thinking about race. Argentina, with its small black pop-ulation and rejection of mestizaje, may be at one end of the Latin American spectrum of racial politics, but Sarmiento was not only part of a broader regional conversation about race, his racist attitudes did not make him an outlier among his contemporaries.

Like other Latin American thinkers of his era, Sarmiento drew on and at times echoed the claims of US and European scientific racism.[11]

Sarmiento articulated unambiguously racist views throughout his career, but his last major work, *Conflicto y armonías de las razas en América* (1883), was especially marred by virulent anti-indigenous racism and his endorsement of the American school of ethnology's anti-miscegenationist strictures. The evolution of Sarmiento's political thought from *Facundo* to *Conflicto* is thus generally interpreted as a calcification of his ideas about race. This narrative of linear evolution overlooks the middle period in the 1860s, however, in which Sarmiento engaged most directly with the United States. The 1860s, I argue, was a moment when there was an important shift in emphasis in Sarmiento's political thought from the geographical proto-determinism of *Facundo* to a (mostly) de-racialized liberalism grounded in the twin pillars of education and democracy. Because there is no linear progression in his ideas about race, it is therefore important to avoid retrospective interpretations of his earlier texts in light of *Conflicto*. Without excusing or obscuring Sarmiento's racism, this chapter analyzes the shifts in his views about race over time.

The premise of my analysis is that a more useful way of approaching the question of Sarmiento's racism is to explore how the United States influenced his ideas about race. In the 1880s Sarmiento adopted some of the tenets of racial science to condemn mixture and buttress his critique of indigenous peoples. But at other moments in his career he also challenged certain tenets of scientific racism. In the 1840s, for example, Sarmiento refused to attribute United States progress to Anglo-Saxon racial superiority. Throughout his career he also consistently inverted the dominant racial hierarchy of the era that ranked Indians above blacks (although it is important to note that this inversion was based on paternalistic premises). And the texts he wrote during his stay in the United States at the height of Reconstruction in the 1860s, "are among the least tainted by racism that Sarmiento produced about blacks during his long career as a writer."[12] The point is thus not to suggest that Sarmiento was ever a champion of racial egalitarianism, nor that his ideas about race simply replicated US racial science, but rather to show that his exposure to US racial politics exacerbated trends that were already present in *Facundo*, in both negative and positive directions.

I focus on three important moments in Sarmiento's political thought in order to trace these shifts. The first is the 1840s, when Sarmiento turns away from Europe as the political model for Argentina to the United States, a shift that is evident in the contrast between the solutions to *caudillismo* presented in *Facundo* and *Viajes en Europa*,

Africa y América. The second moment, which is underemphasized in dominant readings of Sarmiento, is his tenure as Argentina's Ambassador to the United States (1865–1868), during which he wrote and published a number of important texts about hemispheric relations. In some of these texts Sarmiento functioned as a curator, as in the short-lived journal he founded during his stay in the United States and which circulated in Latin America called *Ambas Américas*. In *Ambas Américas* and *Las escuelas* (a "report" on public education in the United States) Sarmiento selected texts by US authors for the benefit of his Latin American readers. Additionally, the extensive correspondence between Sarmiento and Mary Mann is key to tracing Sarmiento's intellectual influences during his stay in the United States.[13] Sarmiento's writings about the United States are among the least discussed in his vast oeuvre, yet they are crucial to a full understanding of his political thought, as they reveal a shift in emphasis from geographic determinism as a justification for centralized state authority in *Facundo*, to calls for Latin America to follow the US model of popular democracy and universal public education. These texts also demonstrate Sarmiento's consistent tendency to read US history in light of Argentina's political problems, and his growing concern with the threat of US hegemony in the Americas. Finally, I turn to the 1880s, after Sarmiento's term as president of Argentina (1868–1874), to briefly consider his rereading of Latin America's relationship to the United States in *Conflicto*, at a time when social Darwinist views that whites were destined to worldwide dominance had gained widespread purchase.[14]

Focusing on the impact of the United States on Sarmiento's ideas avoids the tendency of centering *Facundo*, and reveals the extent to which it was the Americas rather than Europe that shaped his political thought. If Douglass looked south to Latin America and the Caribbean for political models and inspiration, Sarmiento looked north to the United States for the same. Their understanding of the other America was also similarly distorted by the particular political problems driving their search in the first place. Sarmiento's ideas thus cannot be understood apart from the scientific racism of the mid- to late-nineteenth century and his investment in Latin American progress to match the achievements of the United States. His appeal to successors such as Martí and Vasconcelos, as well as his failings, reflect the centrality of debates about race and postcolonial identity to subaltern intellectual traditions such as Latin American political thought.

"El Sabio Agassiz": Sarmiento and US Scientific Racism

The intellectual background against which Sarmiento's critique of Latin American political institutions and admiration for the United States emerged were the linked debates about race that were taking place in the United States and Latin America during the second half of the nineteenth century, which were in turn shaped by scientific racism. Sarmiento was not an outlier either in his earlier reliance on proto-racist environmental explanations of human difference in *Facundo*, or his later engagement with scientific racism in *Conflicto*. In the mid-nineteenth century, "the environmentalism characteristic of Enlightenment thinking about human differences" according to which "differences in pigmentation were a comparatively short-range result of climate and geography" was supplanted by full-fledged scientific ideologies of permanent, biological racial hierarchy.[15] By the end of the nineteenth century, scientific racism had solidified, and the effects of these intellectual trends reverberated in Latin America. As Thomas Skidmore has observed, at the same time as slavery was abolished, US and European "thinkers were articulating systematic theories of innate racial differences," and Latin Americans were "vulnerable . . . to racist doctrines from abroad. It could hardly have been otherwise, since these doctrines were a vital part of the North Atlantic civilization so fervently and uncritically admired by most Latin American intellectuals before 1914."[16] Many of the region's most influential thinkers attributed post-independence political turmoil to Latin American racial deficiencies, an explanation that conveniently justified the continued political dominance of the descendants of the *criollo* elite.[17] Simultaneously, comparisons between Latin America and the United States identified race as a key factor in the latter's post-independence success. Many Latin American intellectuals accepted that "the United States had developed because it was a nation of Anglo-Saxon immigrants in which the Indians had been pushed aside and the blacks segregated."[18]

The claims of the US school of ethnology, which also bedeviled Douglass (as shown in the previous chapter), became influential in Latin America via the work of Louis Agassiz, the Swiss biologist who became a professor at Harvard University in 1848. Agassiz was one of the racial theorists most cited by Latin American intellectuals.[19] He was influenced by the work of the craniologist Samuel Morton, whom he met when he first visited the United States in 1846. In his studies on human crania Morton ranked the human races on the basis of skull size, and concluded that different racial groups had always exhibited physical differences, thereby discrediting monogenesis. Eventually Morton went on to claim that blacks had been separately created to inhabit tropical regions, an argument that resonated with Agassiz because it was consistent with his own theory that plant and animal species had been created separately in accordance with the varying environmental conditions of different regions of the earth. As a corollary of the argument that racial groups had been created as separate species rather than as different varieties of a single human species, the US school of ethnology argued that hybrids or mixed-race stocks were sterile and would eventually die out.[20] The "ethnological-biological school," thus offered a scientific rationale for white supremacy, the subjugation of non-whites (even after the legal abolition of slavery), and racial segregation.[21]

Agassiz described himself as a disinterested scientist whose arguments about black inferiority were not meant to influence public policy. He disclaimed "all connection with any question involving political matters. It is simply with reference to the possibility of appreciating the differences existing between different men, and of eventually determining whether they have originated all over the world and under what circumstances, that we have tried to trace some facts representing the human race."[22] Agassiz was a staunch opponent of slavery, so he may not have intended his arguments to be used to oppose abolition, but he certainly believed in racial segregation. In a letter to his mother in 1846, for example, he recounted a visceral reaction to his first in-person encounter with blacks (the waiters at his Philadelphia hotel):

As much as I try to feel pity at the sight of this degraded and degenerate race, as much as their fate fills me with compassion in thinking of them as really men, it is impossible for me to repress the feeling that they are not of the same blood as us. Seeing their black faces with their fat lips and their grimacing teeth, the wool on their heads, their bent knees, their elongated hands, their large curved fingernails, and above all the livid color of their palms, I could not turn my eyes from their face in order to tell them to keep their distance, and when they advanced that hideous hand toward my plate to serve me, I wished I could leave in order to eat a piece of bread apart rather than dine with such service. What unhappiness for the white race to have tied its existence so closely to that of the negroes in certain countries! God protect us from such contact!

Given how repulsed he was by black people, Agassiz was also a staunch opponent of miscegenation. The government, he argued, ought "to put every possible obstacle to the crossing of the races, and the increase of half-breeds. It is immoral and destructive of social equality."[23] Agassiz would find much to validate his opposition to racial mixture when he traveled to Brazil twenty years later in the 1860s, as we shall see.

The members of the US school of ethnology ascribed intellectual and moral traits and capacities onto aesthetic characteristics of physical bodies. Aesthetic judgments about black "ugliness" were an important aspect of scientific rationales for polygenesis, as the slave daguerreotypes commissioned by Agassiz illustrate. The daguerreotypes were taken for Agassiz in 1850 in Columbia, South Carolina. They consist of fifteen images showing front and side views of seven slaves, male and female, in which the subjects are largely nude. Agassiz specifically wanted to find "pure" examples of the African race in the United States, which is why he chose slave plantations in South Carolina. He personally selected the slaves to be photographed, and the African origin, names, and owner of each enslaved person were carefully recorded. The daguerreotypes are divided into two series. One series consists of front, side, and rear views of two standing, fully nude male subjects in order to record body shape, proportions, and posture. The second series focused on the shape and form of the skull, and shows front and side views of the heads and naked torsos of three men and two women.[24] The images are deeply unsettling. It is impossible to look at Delia, Jack, Alfred, Renty, Drana, Jem, and Fassena—the persons compelled to participate in Agassiz's attempt to prove the inferiority of their race through the reproduction and display of their naked bodies—without seeing their humanity. But this was clearly not what Agassiz and his collaborators saw. One of the premises underlying polygenesis was the idea of a direct link between physical beauty and level of civilization. "Ugly" images of blacks, such as Agassiz's daguerreotypes, were thus judged against idealized images of Western notions of beauty, and were adduced as proof of black inferiority. Moreover, the use of full frontal nudity, which was rare in early US photography, gave the images pornographic and sexualized overtones.[25] Agassiz never published the daguerreotypes, but they illustrate the importance of visual representations of blackness to nineteenth-century racial science, particularly claims that racial hierarchy was inherent and natural.[26]

Frederick Douglass, who became the most photographed US person of the nineteenth century, was especially attuned to the role played by a biased visual economy of comparison in the racial science of his day. He observed that it was common to: "exaggerate the differences between the negro and the European. If, for instance, a phrenologist, or naturalist undertakes to represent in portraits, the differences between the two races—the negro and the European—he will invariably present the *highest* type of the European, and the *lowest* type of the negro."[27] Douglass argued that visual depictions of racial difference for ostensibly scientific purposes both performed and constructed arguments about white superiority and black inferiority. In these representations:

> The European face is drawn in harmony with the highest ideas of beauty, dignity and intellect. ... The negro on the other hand, appears with features distorted, lips exaggerated, forehead depressed—and the whole expression of the countenance made to harmonize with the popular idea of negro imbecility and degradation. I have seen many pictures of negroes and Europeans, in phrenological and ethnological works; and all, or nearly all ... have been more or less open to this objection. I think I have never seen a single picture in an American work, designed to give an idea of the mental endowments of the negro, which did any thing like justice to the subject; nay that was not infamously distorted.[28]

Douglass (who as numerous scholars have noted was keenly aware of the importance of representation) sought to undermine this biased visual record of blackness, of which Agassiz's slave daguerreotypes are a particularly haunting example, in the very dignified poses he adopted in photographs.[29] Douglass's portraits visually contested Agassiz and the US school of ethnology's aesthetic exercises in comparison to buttress hierarchical rankings of different races.

Agassiz, who was regarded as a scientific luminary during his lifetime, was one of the distinguished "American wise men and literary figures" to whom Mary Mann introduced Sarmiento during his stay in the United States in the 1860s.[30] In two letters to Sarmiento written shortly after his arrival in 1865, Mrs. Mann described Agassiz as being "highly valued among us." She also suggested that Agassiz's visit to Brazil in 1865–1866 would foster interest about Latin America in the United States "because Mr. Agassiz is a great pet [?] here, and every thing he does & every point he visits will be interesting to our community."[31] After Agassiz returned from Brazil, she suggested that Sarmiento write to him directly to elicit his support in marshaling US public opinion on behalf of the Triple Alliance's side in the Paraguayan war and suggested that he read Agassiz's account of his scientific expedition to Brazil. Sarmiento did both, and reported that "I am reading Agassiz's book as if I were reading a novel."[32] Agassiz and Sarmiento established at least a brief correspondence. In his reply to Sarmiento's letter about the Paraguayan war Agassiz mentioned that "in a letter I wrote some time ago to the Emperor of Brazil I told him how energetically . . . you were working in the good cause of S. American civilization and progress."[33] In his correspondence with Mary Mann, Sarmiento also mentioned plans to translate and publish one of Agassiz's essays in the journal *Ambas Américas*, although he does not appear to have done so.[34] Agassiz's status as a prominent academic who had published important scientific works on the region, and who had also traveled to Brazil, probably contributed to the frequency with which Latin American intellectuals referenced his racial theories.

Sarmiento was aware of Agassiz's racial theories in the 1860s, as they are peppered throughout Agassiz's account of his trip to Brazil, in which he discussed miscegenation on multiple occasions. Sarmiento did not cite them directly at that time, however. In fact, Sarmiento's analysis of hemispheric relations in the 1860s was not fundamentally shaped by race as it would be later in the 1880s. His speech before the Rhode Island Historical Society in 1865, for example, contains only a brief reference to the theory that blacks were destined to inhabit tropical zones: "Perhaps the Amazon is destined to be the means of restoring the countries of the torrid zone to the negro race, to whom God has adjudicated it, raising up Punic nations along the course of the powerful river, by the freedom of Brazil and the United States."[35] This was a reference to the climatic racial determinism that had become dominant in the racial science of the time, but it was an exception in a speech that overall did not attribute US success to racial superiority. Sarmiento, like Douglass, was forced to grapple with the claim of the historical strand of scientific racism that Anglo-Saxons had developed superior civilizations to Latins. In the 1840s, however, Sarmiento refused to attribute US success to race. It was not until *Conflicto* in 1883 that he directly incorporated the American ethnologists's strictures against mixture. He then also echoed, without fully accepting, social Darwinist claims that Anglo-Saxon domination over Latin "races" was inevitable.

Agassiz is referenced multiple times in *Conflicto*. Sarmiento calls him "el sabio Agassiz" (the learned Agassiz), and his racial theories, specifically his negative observations about racial mixture in Brazil, are quoted directly in the text twice.[36] In one passage Sarmiento invoked Agassiz's strictures against miscegenation approvingly:

> Let us now hear the learned Agassiz on the moral character of these races. 'Any one who doubts the evil of this mixture of races, let them come to Brazil, where the deterioration consequent upon amalgamation, more widespread here than in any other country in the world, is effacing the best qualities of the white man, leaving a mongrel nondescript type, deficient in physical and mental energy.' (Agassiz, pág. 293).[37]

At the same time, however, Sarmiento also suggested that Agassiz was mistaken in believing that mestizos and mulattoes would eventually die out. Sarmiento also omitted a few key phrases from the passage he cited from Agassiz's *A Journey to Brazil*. Agassiz's book, which was published after the end of the US Civil War and emancipation, included admonitions against more than just miscegenation. It was addressed at anyone "inclined, from a mistaken philanthropy, to break down all barriers between [the races]." In one of the omitted phrases, Agassiz claimed that it was not only the best qualities of whites that were being wiped out by mixture but also those of "the negro and the Indian." The United States, Agassiz concluded, should view Brazil as a cautionary tale:

> At a time when the new social status of the negro is a subject of vital importance in our statesmanship, we should profit by the experience of a country where, though slavery exists, there is far more liberality toward the free negro than he has ever enjoyed in the United States. Let us learn the double lesson: open all the advantages of education to the negro, and give him every chance of success which culture gives to the man who knows how to use it; but respect the laws of nature, and let all our dealings with the black man tend to preserve, as far as possible, the distinctness of his national character, and the integrity of our own.[38]

This recommendation was consistent with Agassiz's simultaneous opposition to slavery and endorsement of racial segregation and strict opposition to miscegenation. Agassiz's anti-black racism was somewhat at odds with Sarmiento's racial ranking, however. Sarmiento tended to view blacks more positively (albeit for paternalistic reasons rooted in problematic racist stereotypes) than indigenous peoples, toward whom most of the racial animus in *Conflicto* is directed.

In sum, Sarmiento was clearly influenced by the US school of ethnology and Agassiz's ideas in particular, but even in the 1880s he did not adopt all its tenets wholesale. *Conflicto* undoubtedly echoed the racial science of its time, but in the book Sarmiento depicted his ideas about race as more consistent over time than they actually were. In a letter to Mary Mann, to whom *Conflicto* was dedicated, Sarmiento explained that "this book would like to be *Facundo* grown old. . . . It is or will be, if I manage to express my idea, a scientific *Civilization and Barbarism* . . . based on modern sociological and ethnological science."[39] Yet, contrary to his suggestion that there was a seamless progression between the two texts, *Facundo* and *Conflicto* do not exhibit the same level of racial pessimism. Despite Sarmiento's invitation to read *Facundo* retrospectively in light of *Conflicto*, the binary of civilization and savagery in *Facundo* is a much less rigid account of race and national character than the anti-miscegenationist strictures and notions of Anglo-Saxon racial superiority reproduced in *Conflicto*.

"Mi Patria de Pensamiento": From Europeanization to North-Americanization

Unlike the United States, where the fundamental political question in the mid-nineteenth century was slavery, in Argentina (as in much of Latin America), it was political instability and *caudillo* rule. This is an important point of contrast between Douglass and Sarmiento's political ideas. For Douglass, slavery, and the struggle against it, was central to the history of the Americas, not just in the United States but also in the Caribbean. It shaped his view of Haiti throughout his life and was an important part of his calculus about the advantages of annexation for the Dominican Republic in the 1870s. In Latin America, meanwhile, the desire for black participation in independence struggles against Spain led to gradual, if contested, emancipation. For Sarmiento slavery was thus marginal to Argentinean political development.[40] The legacy of slavery, which was so central to Douglass's understanding of US democracy, is almost entirely absent from Sarmiento's analysis of Latin American political problems in his pre-*Conflicto* writings. In *Facundo*, for example, Sarmiento located the roots of the violent, personalistic politics and lawlessness that characterized Argentina during the post–independence era in Argentinean geography, and advocated Europeanization as the solution. Yet, as Gordy observes, Sarmiento's ambivalence about the transplantation of European ideas to American soil is reflected in the text's lack of "sustained engagement with European ideas."[41] This struggle between European and American sources came to a head in 1847, when Sarmiento turned away from Europe as his political model and looked to the United States instead.

While Sarmiento's admiration for the United States is well known, the extent to which it shaped his political thought has been underappreciated. According to Emilio Carilla, "it is impossible to understand" Sarmiento "outside of this influence and admiration [which] . . . in large part, coincides with ideas and dreams of his own. The Argentine sees in the United States much of what he aspires to for his own nation."[42] In fact, Sarmiento referred to New England, which for him represented the best of the United States, as his "patria de pensamiento" or intellectual homeland.[43] After 1847, then, Sarmiento's particular understanding of US history, and the lessons he derived from it, are integral to understanding his political thought. Reading *Facundo* (1845) and *Viajes* (1847) alongside each other reveals that rather than viewing Sarmiento solely as a thinker who favored the Europeanization of Latin America, it is necessary to consider why he felt compelled to defend himself "from a charge often leveled against me" of citing US "authors, adopting its principles of government, and wishing to *North-Americanize* [Argentina]."[44]

The problem of *caudillismo* was one of the principal concerns of Sarmiento's political thought. In a letter to his grandson in 1874, for example, he identified the two great themes in his life and work as "the destruction of the caudillos . . . and promoting the education of the people."[45] After gaining independence from Spain in 1810, Argentina suffered from continuous political strife. The conflict between *unitarios* (who favored a strong centralized government under the leadership of elites from Buenos Aires), and *federales* (who believed that the provinces should maintain a good measure of autonomy within an equal federation, and who tended to be more populist) reflected a broader split between the cities and the countryside.[46] Sarmiento was born in the provinces, but he sided with the *unitarios* because he believed that a strong central government was the only way to address the danger of *caudillismo*, or rule by a charismatic individual leader at the expense of established institutions. *Caudillos* such as the Argentine dictator Juan Manuel de Rosas established personalist governments based on direct relationships with the masses, which tended to view them as more responsive to their concerns than liberal elites espousing abstract theories of republican government.[47] *Facundo*, which was written while Sarmiento was in exile in Chile working against the Rosas regime, is an extended meditation on the problem of *caudillo* political rule, which in turn had a profound effect on Sarmiento's views of democracy.

In *Facundo*, Sarmiento attributed Argentina's deficient political culture to the natural environment, specifically the plains or *pampas*. Reflecting environmentalist accounts of political development, Sarmiento argued that in order to understand the origins of *caudillismo* it was necessary "to look to national precedent, to the physiognomy of the land, to popular traditions and customs."[48] He argued that the *pampas* were the cause of the *gaucho*'s hostility to political authority and settled political life: "The disease from which the Argentine Republic suffers is its own expanse. ... This insecurity in life, which is customary and permanent in the countryside, imprints upon the Argentine character, to my mind, a certain stoic resignation to violent death."[49] Drawing on European ideas about how geography shaped national character, Sarmiento argued that the Argentine landscape shaped the civic capacities of its inhabitants: "Many philosophers, too have thought that the plains prepare the way for despotism, in the same way that the mountains have lent support to the forces of liberty."[50] He concluded that "in Argentine life, the predominance of brute force, the preponderance of the strongest, authority with no limits and no accountability for those in command, justice administered without formality and without debate, begin to be established because of these peculiar characteristics."[51] *Caudillismo* was thus the opposite of the rule of law.

The Argentine countryside was the site and source of barbarism in *Facundo*, and it shaped its indigenous and European inhabitants equally. Barbarism, Sarmiento argued, was the result of environmental and cultural conditions, not inherent racial characteristics. Despite the dichotomy between civilization and barbarism, Sarmiento left open the possibility that under the right conditions the inhabitants of the *pampas* could become "civilized." His description of the *gaucho*, for example, was not entirely negative: "although the conditions of pastoral life, as constituted by colonization and negligence, give rise to grave difficulties for any sort of political organization and many more for the triumph of European civilization ... it cannot be denied that this situation also has a poetic side, and aspects worthy of the novelist's pen."[52] As many literary scholars have observed, Sarmiento's evident admiration and respect for the *gaucho*'s physical courage and unfettered way of life undermines the civilization/barbarism binary. Sarmiento appears "more fascinated by barbarism than by civilization ... [his] loving descriptions of the Pampas and its gauchos are among the most enduring pages in *Facundo*."[53] At the same time, *Facundo* contains descriptions of the Argentine population that are extremely disparaging of both indigenous peoples and their Spanish colonizers.

> The fusion of these three families [Spaniards, Indians, and blacks] has resulted in a homogeneous whole, distinguished by its love for idleness and incapacity for industry. ... The incorporation of indigenous races caused by colonization has contributed much to produce this unfortunate result. The American races live in idleness, and demonstrate an incapacity, even when forced, to apply themselves to hard, uninterrupted work. This prompted the idea of bringing blacks to America, which has produced such fatal results. But the Spanish race has not shown itself to be any more given to action, when, in the American deserts, it has been left to its own instincts.[54]

Despite his statements to the contrary, then, Sarmiento's text itself deconstructed the argument that Europe was infallibly associated with civilization and America with barbarism.

Sarmiento's arguments about race in *Facundo* were in fact somewhat out of sync with the emerging scientific consensus in the United States around permanent, inherited black inferiority.[55] His statement that the forced importation of enslaved Africans had "fatal" consequences, for example, is decidedly ambiguous given its placement in the text, which follows a rather positive, if deeply paternalistic, assessment of the black presence in Argentina: "The black race, now almost extinct except in Buenos Aires, has left its *zambos* and mulattoes, inhabitants of the cities, as a link connecting civilized with rustic man; a race inclined to civilization, gifted with talent and with the finest instincts for progress."[56] Blacks ranked above indigenous peoples in Sarmiento's racial ranking, probably because they lived mostly in urban spaces, which would have placed them away from the barbarism of the countryside and in closer proximity to civilization in his schema. *Facundo* also contains various admiring references to the military service of black soldiers who participated in the struggles for independence, such as: "[Lorenzo] Barcala, the black colonel who had so gloriously distinguished himself in Brazil, the freed slave who devoted so many years to showing artisans the right road, and to making them love a revolution that considered neither color nor class when recognizing merit."[57] As Lea Geler has observed, "even though it is clear that Sarmiento considered both Indians and blacks as inferior races that had not yet fully developed ... he valued Africans and their descendants more positively."[58]

Sarmiento's scathing assessment of the Spanish colonial legacy in *Facundo* also undermined the idea that European civilization was uniformly superior. "Sarmiento's critique of Spain was constant: in this or that occasion he censured her for what he calls her fanaticism and absolutism."[59] Sarmiento rejected Spain's colonial legacy as backward and static, especially when compared to other European nations. For him, as for most other Latin American intellectuals of his era, the political model was France. Describing the competing political factions that emerged in post-independence Argentina, for example, he sketched another binary comparison between: "Córdoba, Spanish ... stable, and hostile to revolutionary innovations, and Buenos Aires, all novelty, all revolution and movement ... each nourished by ideas extracted from different sources: Córdoba, from Spain, the Councils, the Commentators, the Pandects; Buenos Aires, from Bentham, Rousseau, Montesquieu, and all of French literature."[60] Echoing Bolívar, Sarmiento believed that Spain had passed on her defective political culture to her colonies.[61] The United States, in contrast, had a different colonial legacy: it had inherited progressive political institutions from England (such as religious freedom and popular sovereignty), while Latin America's founding fathers had embraced liberal political principles in opposition to the autocratic ideas prevalent in Spain, creating an unbridgeable chasm. Spain could never serve as a political model for Latin America because the independence movements were fought precisely in order to reject its backward political ideas and cultural habits.[62]

Sarmiento's advocacy of European immigration in *Facundo* thus needs to be understood in light of his concern with the political problem of *caudillismo*, which in his view was closely related to the deficient citizens produced by Argentina's political culture and geography: on the one hand, violent and lacking respect for established institutions in the case of the *caudillos*, and, on the other hand, servile and too-easily-led in the case of their followers among the popular classes. *Caudillismo*, which he understood as a form of populism in which the support of the masses for an authoritarian leader restricted elite political influence, indelibly shaped Sarmiento's views on democracy. He simultaneously condemned the arbitrary, personalistic politics practiced by the *caudillos* and the blind political support that they received from the uneducated masses. It was in response to these concerns that Sarmiento proclaimed European immigration to be the solution to Argentina's political problems, as it would endow Argentina with "active, moral, and industrious inhabitants" who would become neither *caudillos* nor passive followers of charismatic leaders.[63] Sarmiento's advocacy of European immigration was thus also arguably rooted in his recognition that the insufficient commitment to democracy and the rule of law of "white" Argentineans was partly responsible for *caudillismo*. Below its surface endorsement of Europeanization, therefore, *Facundo* could also be read as an indictment of the political deficiencies of Argentina's poor whites, who despite their European ancestry, had failed to become active yet self-regulated citizens.

In 1847, a mere two years after *Facundo*'s publication, Sarmiento traveled to Europe and the United States for the first time, and turned decisively away from Europe and to the United States instead as the political model for Argentina. According to Sarmiento's biographer David Bunkley, "North America replaced France and Europe as his model for civilization. The United States became his idol . . . [it was] a living model."[64] Sarmiento only spent about seven weeks in the United States in 1847, but they were to have a decisive influence on his political ideas. The shift from Europe to the United States as the political model for Latin America was accompanied by a shift in emphasis in Sarmiento's political thought away from the civilization/barbarism binary toward democracy and public education.[65] Like other Latin American intellectuals of his time, prior to his trip Sarmiento derived many of his ideas about the United States from reading Alexis de Tocqueville's *Democracy in America* (1835), after which he modeled *Viajes en Europa, Africa y América*.[66] Sarmiento explained the source of his disillusionment with Europe and newfound enthusiasm for the United States. France, his previous political model, turned out to be a disappointment, while in Spain he found confirmation for his negative assessment of Spanish colonization. Comparison, which was a central feature of Sarmiento's intellectual method, continued to function as a key rhetorical and conceptual device in *Viajes*. Whereas in *Facundo* the key dichotomy was between the city and the countryside, however, in *Viajes* the fundamental contrast was between Europe and the United States, to the point that Sarmiento claimed that Europe and Latin America were equally backward in certain respects.

Throughout the second volume of *Viajes* dedicated to the US portion of his trip, Sarmiento repeatedly compared Europe and the United

States, almost invariably concluding that the United States had surpassed Europe. Much of Europe reminded him of Latin America, particularly the condition of the masses: their low level of education, poverty, and lack of participation in politics. Sarmiento explained that "a man does not achieve his full moral and intellectual development except through education.... I come from traveling through Europe, from admiring her monuments, and bowing before her science, in awe yet at the wonders of her art; but I have [also] seen millions of her peasants, workers, and artisans, vile, degraded, unworthy of being counted among men."[67] The situation in the United States was different, in his view. While Sarmiento was extremely impressed with the country's wealth and industrial progress, it was its relative political and economic egalitarianism compared to Europe that was the decisive factor in his admiration for the United States. The discovery that Europe remained deeply unequal despite the enlightened social and political theories it had produced led to his disillusionment with France in particular. In characteristically hyperbolic fashion, he wrote:

> I am convinced that the North Americans are the only cultivated nation that exists on the earth. ... The only country in the world where the ability to read is universal, where writing is practiced by all in their daily lives, where 2,000 newspapers satisfy public curiosity, and where education, like welfare, is everywhere available to all those who want it, is the United States. Is there any country in the world that can compare with it in any of these respects? In France there are 270,000 voters; that is, among 36 million individuals in the oldest civilized nation, only 270,000 are not considered beasts according to the law. ... In the United States every man has a natural right to participate in political affairs, and he exercises it. France, on the other hand, has a king ... and a people dying of hunger.[68]

In *Viajes*, we can thus observe a crystallization of Sarmiento's ideas about democracy, where "civilization" is understood to mean political equality, the material welfare of the common man, individual freedom, and public education. As an ardent educational reformer, much of Sarmiento's admiration for the United States in *Viajes* was due to the quality of and access to public education there; by this measure Europe was just as barbarous as Latin America. In the United States, in contrast: "They have no kings, no privileged classes, nor men born to rule, nor human machines born to obey."[69]

Sarmiento devoted much of *Viajes* to trying to understand the roots of US success, but he never attributed it to race. In *Viajes*, Sarmiento alluded to the claims of the emerging historical strand of racial science that Anglo-Saxons were superior to Latins, but quickly dismissed them. If in *Facundo* Sarmiento was trying to identify the source of Argentina's political problems, in *Viajes* he sought to isolate the cause of US success. He singled out an agricultural model based on small-landholding, a free press, and religious tolerance as important factors that had facilitated US development, but race did not figure among them. Instead, Sarmiento clearly stated that "at this time I will only establish one fact, and that is that the aptitude of the [Anglo] Saxon race is also no explanation of the cause of North America's enormous progress."[70] He would later argue precisely the opposite in *Conflicto*. But in 1847 Sarmiento attributed US success to a widespread spirit of republican liberty: "the mass of the population of the United States has acquired this feeling, this political consciousness. ... In England there is political and religious liberty for the lords and the merchants, in France for the writers and rulers; but the people, the poor, disinherited masses do not feel anything yet regarding their position as members of society. ... In North America the Yankee is fated to republicanism."[71] Sarmiento was so disillusioned with Europe in *Viajes* that, in contrast to his prescriptions for Argentine progress in *Facundo*, he argued that European immigration actually had a negative impact in the United States. "There, European immigration is an element of barbarism; who would have believed it! The Irish, German, French or Spanish European, with few exceptions, comes from the poorest classes in Europe, is usually ignorant, and is unaccustomed to republican practices."[72] Indeed, in contrast to twentieth-century eugenicists who objected to an influx of non-Aryan Southern European immigrants, for Sarmiento the problem was that the new arrivals were uneducated and unprepared to exercise republican virtues.

Reflecting how marginal it was to his political thought (in contrast to Douglass), the most glaring blind spot in Sarmiento's depiction of the United States in *Viajes* was slavery.[73] Strikingly for someone visiting the country during the heyday of abolitionist agitation in 1847, slavery is rarely mentioned in *Viajes*. Sarmiento did make it clear that the political virtues he admired in the United States were lacking in the South. He observed that civilization and progress were not uniformly distributed across the United States and argued that "if one region of the Union defends and maintains slavery, it is because in that part the moral sentiment toward the racial other, imprisoned, hunted, weak, ignorant, is as toward an *enemy* . . . but in all the other States . . . the *political* feeling that should be as inherent to man as reason and conscience, is fully developed."[74] Sarmiento viewed it as a paradox that the United States, which was otherwise the most egalitarian society of its time, should "be condemned" to fight the final battle against the ancient injustice of slavery. In fact, he characterized slavery as a European inheritance: "Slavery is a parasitical plant that English colonization has left attached to the leafy tree of American liberty. They did not dare uproot it when they pruned the tree, leaving it to time to kill it off, and now the parasite has grown and threatens to break off the entire tree." In addition to absolving the United States of responsibility for slavery by characterizing it as a legacy of English colonization, Sarmiento echoed one of Thomas Jefferson's conclusions in *Notes on the State of Virginia*. He suggested that peaceful coexistence between blacks and whites after emancipation would be difficult if not impossible:

> Today slavery in the United States is an insoluble issue: there are four million blacks. . . . If they are freed, what is to be done with this black race hated by the white race? . . . The separation into free and slave states . . . would lead to the disappearance of slavery. But where would four million freemen go? Here is a Gordian knot . . . that fills the clear and radiant future of the American Union with mournful shadows. They can neither advance nor turn back, and in the meantime the black race teems, develops, becomes civilized and grows. A race war within a century, a war of extermination, or a backward and abject black nation alongside a white one, the most powerful and advanced in the world![75]

Sarmiento's disregard for the horrors of slavery in *Viajes* is in stark contrast to Douglass's assertion that slavery made a mockery of vaunted US liberty.[76] Not only did Sarmiento display remarkably little concern for the plight of enslaved blacks in *Viajes*, the existence of slavery hardly detracted from his rosy depiction of US republican freedom.

Sarmiento's understanding of the United States in *Viajes* was thus undoubtedly highly selective and shaped by his own political and philosophical concerns. Its lasting impact on his thought is undeniable, however. In 1886, two years before his death, he wrote to Luis Montt, who was compiling the first edition of Sarmiento's collected works, asking him to "highlight the part devoted to the United States [in *Viajes*] . . . because . . .

I regard my revelations about that country as of paramount importance. ... My trip was as Marco Polo's. I discovered a world and I adhered to it."[77] While Sarmiento's belief in the United States as the political model for Latin America remained unwavering, he became increasingly concerned about the threat of US expansionism. By the 1860s the question of the relationship between the two Americas had thus acquired greater urgency. In contrast to the idea of the United States as the political model for Latin America articulated in *Viajes*, in the 1860s Sarmiento envisioned hemispheric relations as an intellectual exchange among equals, a project rendered increasingly uncertain by the threat of US expansion.

"Ambas Américas": North–South Dialogue in the Context of US Expansionism

During the three years he lived in the United States in the 1860s, Sarmiento developed a more nuanced view of it, and particularly of what its relationship to Latin America should be. His view at this time combined continued appreciation for US achievements in popular education with a critique of US expansionism to Latin America. Geographically, Sarmiento's concerns during this middle period thus expand from the national to the hemispheric. The overarching theme of his writings as Argentinean ambassador was to foster a mutually beneficial hemispheric intellectual exchange between the United States and Latin America. In contrast to *Facundo* and *Viajes*, Europe and Europeanization had thus thoroughly faded from view in the 1860s. Instead, Sarmiento's comparative method during this era was focused on what "ambas Américas" (both Americas) could learn from each other. He had an expansive notion of his mission as Argentine ambassador that went beyond merely representing the national interests of his country to the dissemination of useful information about education and democracy in the United States to Latin America, as well as correcting mistaken ideas about the region in the United States. He clearly stated, for example, that "the ostensible topic" of the speech he gave to the Rhode Island Historical Society was "the United States's influence on Latin America and its real purpose, to rehabilitate the name of those nations, viewed from here as a shapeless blob agitated by perverse passions."[78] Sarmiento's goal in the 1860s was thus to tell the United States the truth about the other America.[79]

Notably, during the 1860s Sarmiento's analysis of hemispheric relations was not fundamentally shaped by race as it would be later on in the 1880s, even as he alluded to the solidifying scientific consensus on racial hierarchy. By the 1860s the new climatic racial determinism (which claimed that different racial groups were destined to live in separate climate zones) and arguments about Anglo-Saxon racial superiority as justifications for US expansionism toward Latin America were in full swing.[80] Yet Sarmiento's publications during his US stay did not accept the notion of Latin American inferiority based on the tenets of racial science. Instead, he articulated a vision of the two Americas as each other's natural interlocutors. He argued that they were political equals who should establish a horizontal intellectual dialogue and mutually beneficial exchange of ideas and models. In the 1860s Sarmiento envisioned the relationship between the United States and Latin America as more of a two-way street than he had in *Viajes* in 1847. He moved beyond claiming that the United States was a model that Latin America should follow, to a vision of mutual learning between political and intellectual equals. In various texts, he made a point of not only showing Latin Americans what they could learn from the United States but also including instances of the reverse, where the United States had learned from Latin America. In *Las escuelas*, for example, he recounted the story of Edelmiro Mayer, an Argentinean who wrote an editorial advocating that black freedmen be allowed to fight on behalf of the union, and who later served as lieutenant colonel of the 45th US Colored Troops during the Civil War. According to Sarmiento, Mayer pointed to the example of blacks who fought in the Latin American wars of independence in exchange for their freedom as evidence for his argument.[81] This emphasis on what the two Americas could learn from each other is present not only in Sarmiento's writings directed at US audiences but also in texts intended for Latin American readers, such as *Las escuelas* and the journal *Ambas Américas* (of which four issues appeared between 1867 and 1868). Indeed, the journal's title is evidence of this aim.

Establishing an American (in the hemispheric sense) intellectual dialogue that bypassed Europe was a central theme of Sarmiento's writings during his stay in the United States in the 1860s. The stated aim of *Ambas Américas*, for example, was to disseminate viable ideas that had already been successfully implemented in the United States to its southern neighbors, and also to establish intellectual dialogue throughout Latin America, among Latin Americans. As Sarmiento explained in the introduction to the first volume, the title itself was meant to convey that this was meant to be a multidirectional learning process: "It is in both their interests for each of the two Americas to enter into intellectual dialogue and establish means of communication." The journal's aim was thus to take the first step toward "bridging the wide chasm that separates *Ambas Américas* [both Americas], and if a solicitous hand in Latin America" were to also take up the task on the other end, Sarmiento would have begun to build the robust link "that must unite intellectual activity in both continents."[82] The format he chose for *Ambas Américas* reflected this aim. A journal allowed him to reproduce work by others on a variety of topics (mainly education and agriculture), and to include a correspondence section, which Carilla suggests is evidence of his desire to "establish a real dialogue."[83]

While there is no doubt that Sarmiento continued to find much to admire in the United States in the 1860s, this was also a period in which the threat of US expansion to Latin America became an increasing concern. The various titles given to his speech to the Rhode Island Historical Society reflect the anxieties about US empire that troubled Sarmiento at the time, as well as subsequent Latin American readers. The original Spanish title of the speech was "North and South America," and the original English translation included the subtitle: "A Discourse delivered before the Rhode Island Historical Society." Sarmiento later included the speech in *Las escuelas* under the title "Ambas Américas." It was then assigned the title "La Doctrina Monroe" in the first edition of his *Obras* published in 1895–1900, which is how the text is known to Latin Americans. Sarmiento formulated a strong critique of US expansionism in both "Discourse" and *Vida de Lincoln*. In "Discourse," he also forcefully articulated the idea that the two Americas were equals whose fates were inextricably linked. For example, he suggested that once ancient archaeological finds in Latin America received proper scientific study, "the history of both Americas will begin upon the same page." He argued that North and South America started off on equal footing and later divided "into two great chapters" during the colonial and independence eras, only to later "evolve the common history of the great American family."[84] A key theme of "Discourse" is thus this idea of a shared "American" hemispheric trajectory, in which Europe plays little to no part.

According to Sarmiento the links between the two Americas were recognized in the United States during the era of independence, but this sense of kinship with their South American republican brethren had since been lost. He cited Daniel Webster's declaration in 1826 that his sympathy for the Latin American independence movements led him "to feel that I am an American," for example, in order to contrast that prior moment when "the two continents were united in sympathy and opinion," to the public opinion of his time that viewed Latin America as decidedly different from (and inferior to) the United States.[85] Against the latter view, Sarmiento portrayed the United States and Latin America as having shared anti-colonial roots: "The United States, from afar, hurried on the independence of South America ... [via] the proclamation of the right of colonies to emancipate themselves. ... South America felt itself evoked by this herald."[86] But he also argued that following the US example had not always served Latin America well. Echoing Bolívar, he attributed the adoption of federalism in the region to too great an adherence to foreign models, specifically the United States:

> Why this general persistency to adopt a form which had no precedent in their history? Because the only existing Republic, the United States of America, presented itself in this form.... Here then is another influence of the United States on South America ... the cause of many changes and revolutions. One half of the disturbances of Mexico, of Colombia, and of the Argentine Republic, which have lasted for half a century ... have been caused by the indirect but powerful influences of the United States.[87]

Sarmiento thus cleverly managed to both redeem Latin America from responsibility for its post-independence political instability and implicate the United States as a partial source of the region's turmoil.

Sarmiento's determination to place Latin America and the United States on equal footing is especially salient in his discussion of slavery in "Discourse," which was very different from his brief reference to it at the end of *Viajes*. In contrast to the claim that slavery was a European remnant in *Viajes*, in "Discourse" Sarmiento used it to establish similar levels of political virtue between the two Americas: "Four years of war, the loss of a million of men, and three thousand millions of debt, it has cost the United States to be *the last on earth* which has abolished slavery. Their own experience has taught them to be indulgent with those audacious and determined South American patriots, which, since 1810, undertook at the same time to be independent, [and] give liberty to their slaves as they wished it for themselves." If Latin Americans had suffered more post-independence turmoil, they had also faced greater obstacles than the United States. Moreover, Latin America deserved credit for consistency in the application of the principle of republican freedom, unlike the US founding fathers. Yet Sarmiento continued to evade or ignore the horrors of slavery. He went so far as to suggest that "the ignorance of the Spaniards ... the abject condition of the rude Indian incorporated into colonial society, [and] fanaticism ... have produced in South America greater depravity than slavery in the south, here."[88] Sarmiento's casual disregard for the brutality of slavery is troubling, as is the fact that the greater attention to slavery in "Discourse" appears to have resulted from a desire to point out US hypocrisy in condemning Latin American internal conflicts given its own civil war. "What we ask for South America is not indulgence, but justice. ... Let us compare South America with your country. The United States occupied ten years in the war of Independence, and four years in the war against slavery. We fought for both causes at the same time, and won them both in fifteen years. So far we are equals."[89] Sarmiento's hoped-for vision of egalitarian hemispheric relations would prove increasingly difficult to sustain given the specter of US expansionism, however.

In the 1860s Sarmiento simultaneously articulated an ideal of hemispheric intellectual dialogue with a strong critique of US imperial ambitions in Latin America, particularly as expressed in self-serving interpretations of the Monroe Doctrine. He argued that imperial expansion contradicted not only the United States's republican principles but also its distinctively "American" character. "The subsequent introduction of an old material, heretofore repudiated, which is the conquest and absorption of peoples and territories by arms, was to turn back to two thousand years ago, and utterly to renounce the initiation of the new reconstruction of human society. *It was rechanging Americans into Europeans.*"[90] The historical context for Sarmiento's statement was a combination of European attempts to recover lost colonies in the Americas, and (most crucially) the Mexican-American War that resulted in the annexation of Mexican territory to the United States.[91] Sarmiento concluded "Discourse" with the suggestion that "what South America needs and would accept" from the United States were teachers who could help spread high-quality public education in the region. "This is the only conquest really worthy of a free people; this is the 'Monroe Doctrine' in practice."[92] Presumably what Sarmiento meant is that the United States could best express its commitment to preserving republicanism in the

Americas by helping to spread to Latin America those characteristics, such as public education, that had helped it safeguard democracy and entrench the rule of law. Sarmiento's admiration for the United States thus did not extend to condoning the incorporation of Latin American nations, as Douglass would envision during the debate over the annexation of Santo Domingo a few years later.

Sarmiento's concerns about US expansionism are also evident in the introduction to *Vida de Lincoln,* which contains the clearest statement of Sarmiento's anti-imperialist critique of the United States during the 1860s. *Vida* was written for a Latin American audience. It was published in Spanish before the Rhode Island speech and was never translated into English. In *Vida* Sarmiento praised Lincoln because of his opposition to the annexation of Mexico. He argued that Lincoln's critique of "the South's expansionist policy, embodied in the conquest of Mexico," revealed his "sense of fairness toward other nations." Citing speeches by Lincoln and Horace Mann that articulated Northern opposition to the Mexican-American War because it was a means of trying to extend slavery, Sarmiento warned his fellow South Americans that it was an example "of the influence over the fate of a nation that can be exerted by the domestic factions of a powerful neighbor."[93] He cautioned that in its desire to extend slavery, the pro-slavery South had "opened the door to all future US [expansionist] attempts over South America."[94] If political instability could serve as a justification for annexation (as it had during the Mexican-American War), Sarmiento asked his Latin American readers: "What will then be visited upon those States that suffer from constant changes?" By seizing the richest of Mexico's provinces, he argued, "the United States has trampled upon ... the rights of nations" and retarded Latin America's democratic development.[95] Sarmiento also argued that expansionism was a Pandora's box for the United States because historically imperialism and republicanism had proven to be incompatible, but his main concern was preserving Latin American sovereignty. The Mexican-American War had revealed that rather than a safeguard against re-colonization by Europe, the Monroe Doctrine's famous dictum of "*America for the Americans* ... encompasses a double meaning, like the answers of the oracle at Delphos. The United States of [all] America would be sufficient to fulfill its meaning."[96] In the 1860s, the threat of US expansion over the hemisphere had thus replaced *caudillismo* as Latin America's gravest danger.

"A Vast Seminar of Moral and Intellectual Instruction": Civilization and Barbarism in the US South during Reconstruction

The three years he spent in the United States immediately after the end of the Civil War at the height of Reconstruction could arguably be characterized as a moment of relative racial optimism in Sarmiento's oeuvre. During this era, Sarmiento found inspiration for his vision of educational reform in Argentina in the efforts of US freedmen's organizations to educate ex-slaves and poor whites in the South. He wrote extensively about this aspect of attempts to implement a more racially egalitarian society during Reconstruction, and to a lesser extent about black suffrage, about which he was more skeptical. Sarmiento compared both recently freed blacks and poor whites in the South to Argentinean *gauchos* and found many other parallels between the US South and Latin America. In fact, Sarmiento's desire to provide his Latin American readers with a useful political model led him to misread US political history, and the Civil War in particular, in significant ways. Sarmiento's selective reading of the US Civil War and Reconstruction as analogous to the struggle between civilization and barbarism in Argentina is emblematic of the dangers of comparison as a trope. In this case Sarmiento saw echoes of "his" America everywhere in the US South in the 1860s; it was a mirror that constantly reflected back (his understanding of) Argentine realities.

Sarmiento's friendship with Mary Mann, a fervent abolitionist, likely also influenced his ideas about race during this era. Their correspondence contains numerous references to the education of the freed ex-slave population and black suffrage. In her case, it also reveals a degree of commitment to racial egalitarianism unusual for the era, even among white abolitionists. For example, Mrs. Mann, recommended that Sarmiento recruit Charles Babcock, a would-be black emigrationist, to move to Argentina:

> He is a very intelligent & pretty well-educated colored man, who wishes to emigrate to some warm country where color is not made so great a criterion of respectability as here, for notwithstanding the wonderful change in public sentiment in regard to the colored races, they still suffer sadly in a social point of view. I believe Mr. Babcock has not African blood in his veins—he is a descendant of the Narranganset[t] Indians of Massachusetts—now a mixed

race,—and several friends of his own & the other colored race think of emigrating with him, to some place where there is free suffrage to all. Is it so there?[97]

There is no record of Sarmiento's reply to this suggestion, as he failed to mention it in his July 28th reply to her letter, but given his more negative view of indigenous peoples than blacks, it is not clear that he would have been more welcoming of either type of nonwhite immigrant to Argentina.[98] Mary Mann kept Sarmiento apprised of developments related to black political incorporation in the United States even after his return to Argentina. For example, in a November 11, 1869, letter written to her during his presidency, he said: "I very much congratulate you on the appointment of two colored men to the Massachusetts legislature, you will recall that I have mentioned that here we always have one or two representatives. It is a very opportune step."[99] Sarmiento's reply implies support for black political participation, but in fact he and Mary Mann disagreed on the question of black suffrage in the United States, even as they agreed on the need for black education.

The education of freed blacks is a major theme of Sarmiento's US writings in the 1860s, partly because the paternalistic tenor of the discourse of self-help and moral uplift that characterized Northern efforts to assist the freedmen in the South resonated with his view of the need to "civilize" barbarous populations via education. *Las escuelas* (which was ostensibly a report on public education in the United States for Argentina's minister of education) and *Ambas Américas* both include information on the education of freed blacks and statistics on the freedmen's schools taken from *The American Freedman,* the organ of the American Freedmen's Union Commission (AFUC). Sarmiento's correspondence with Mary Mann also contains numerous references to black education and suffrage. Yet, as Barry Velleman observes, "Sarmiento's links to the Freedmen's organizations have been largely overlooked."[100] Sarmiento viewed the Freedmen's Aid Society as continuing the work of social equality begun by the admission of colored troops into the Union army championed by the Argentinean Meyer. He was particularly interested in their efforts to educate former slaves by founding schools and sending northern schoolteachers to rural areas of the South, which he viewed as the solution to the dilemmas created by partial black emancipation. Sarmiento cited a speech by the president of the Freedmen's Aid Society, who argued that "the special mission entrusted to this society is to prepare the freedmen for the new duties and responsibilities that already weigh on them ... its long-term aim is to enable them to provide for themselves and convert them into useful citizens."[101]

Thus, many of the northerners involved in Freedmen's organizations in the South in the post–Civil War Era described their efforts in civilizing terms that echoed Sarmiento's civilization/barbarism dichotomy. Indeed, Mary Mann, in a November 5, 1868, letter to Sarmiento, suggested that "in the southern people with their millions of uneducated freedmen we have almost as great a difficulty as you have with your gauchos."[102] The parallel between Sarmiento's views of the role of education and northerners's paternalistic understanding of their mission vis-à-vis freedmen in the South is consistent with Saidiya Hartman's claim that there was no categorical distinction between freedom and slavery for US blacks in the post-emancipation era because they continued to be subjected to discourses of responsibility, manhood, and fitness for citizenship aimed at fostering various forms of disciplined subjectivity.[103] As a result of Sarmiento's absorption of the educational lessons of Reconstruction, we see how technologies of subjection formulated to train "free" black populations in the United States migrated to shape the incorporation of "poor whites" in Argentina.

Sarmiento's interest in the question of the education of ex-slaves was largely driven by how it could serve as a model for his project of "reconstructing" public education in Argentina, which had a distinctly gendered dimension. According to Sarmiento the near-saintly efforts of female schoolteachers from the North in freedmen's schools had transformed the South into "a vast seminar of moral and intellectual instruction," and he wanted them to do the same for Argentina.[104] One of his goals during his stay in the United States was thus to recruit female schoolteachers from the North to travel to Argentina to assist in his efforts to "civilize" the country. With the assistance of Mary Mann, he succeeded in recruiting a number of young women to go teach in Argentina, some of whom had been teachers in freedmen's schools in the South.[105] Sarmiento's vision of educational reform in Argentina thus drew on a maternal vision of women as ideally suited to teaching. He explicitly argued that women were "natural" teachers. In a letter to Mary Mann, he congratulated her on their success in "bringing preferably female schoolteachers, instead of males, to spread the best methods and art of teaching, which they possess by right of conquest, by birthright, because in women it only entails directing and perfecting their instincts as ... mothers, teachers."[106] Sarmiento also supported women's suffrage, however, and their right to work outside the home. He particularly admired the level of education that northern women had achieved in the United States and viewed them as more prepared for the duties of citizenship than uneducated men. In a February 15, 1866, letter to Mary Mann, for example, he critiqued women's exclusion from suffrage in New England, arguing that "they are more capable of discernment than all the Europeans put together."[107] As a result of his belief in women's natural aptitude for education and admiration for Northern schoolteachers in particular, US women would play a role as co-civilizers in Sarmiento's project of Argentine reconstruction.

Sarmiento found many parallels between US Reconstruction and the prospect of Argentine refoundation following Rosas's ouster. In a speech to US school superintendents in Indianapolis on August 17, 1866, for example, he drew a parallel between the situation of whites and blacks in the South and that of *criollo* elites and *gauchos* in Latin America: "Only you sirs, who have taken the Southern states as the object of your studies ... can understand the situation of our America. ... Our *poor whites* have not overcome the moral decay in which they had long ago fallen; and the *rich whites* educated according to colonial traditions, are indifferent to those ills that appear not to affect them directly, even if they are the cause of the disturbances that destroy wealth and impede development."[108] In *Las escuelas*, Sarmiento discussed the situation in the South following emancipation for the benefit of his Latin American readers. He argued that Latin America should follow the US example in public education:

> I have arrived in the United States in a solemn moment. Slavery having being abolished, there is an attempt to admit into political association a race held in ignorance and inferiority for centuries. All are perplexed as to whether they who are so unprepared for high office will have the right to suffrage, i.e. to govern, and yet colored men in the United States are not more uneducated than the white inhabitants of our plains. But while this issue agitates the field of politics, citizens of all the United States have begun to work on addressing the gap, and in six months have done more to spread education among blacks in the South, than we have in three centuries for our compatriots and kin, as you will see in the pages that follow. They have shown us the means and the path, and those peoples that do not follow it will be guilty of suicide.[109]

In another article entitled "Education of Freed Blacks," he argued that these "hordes of peaceful barbarians" had wandered the South after emancipation out of a desire to experience freedom, "without being settled, possessing land, or power."[110] While Sarmiento did not further address the question of land, which was pivotal to the formerly enslaved, he undoubtedly viewed the education of blacks and poor white southerners as one of the major accomplishments of Reconstruction.

Sarmiento was especially concerned about the lack of education of poor whites in the South, whom he saw as analogous to the *gauchos* in Argentina. He cited a letter by General Howard, the head of the Freedmen's Bureau, in which he reported that "when I have traveled through Georgia and South Carolina I have hardly ever *encountered a white child who could read!*"[111] Sarmiento cited this statement to demonstrate "suspected similarities between the South of the two Americas."[112] While Latin America had fortunately rid itself of slavery at the time of independence, he argued, the US South suffered from a problem "worse than black servitude," the ignorance and lack of education of poor whites. Completing the geographical conflation of the US South and Latin America, Sarmiento claimed that "we now find ourselves, then, fully in South America."[113] In *Vida de Lincoln*, he stated the point even more forcefully: "In addition to slaves, the South contained white *plebs* or poor whites ... who occupy a similar position as the descendants of the Spaniards in South America, who are called gaucho."[114] During the 1860s Sarmiento was thus clearly reading US history in light of (his diagnosis of) Argentinean political problems. He approvingly cited the admonition of a southern politician prior to the Civil War that, rather than focusing solely on the plight of enslaved blacks, it was also necessary to consider "the millions of poor, ignorant, and degraded whites that live among us, and who in a land of plenty live comparatively naked and hungry."[115] Sarmiento thus found multiple echoes of the *gaucho* in the situation of poor whites in the US South during Reconstruction.

The analogy between the *gauchos* and poor whites and blacks in the South served to buttress Sarmiento's claim that Latin America should emulate the monumental efforts on behalf of public education in the United States after the Civil War. "In five months mere businessmen have created more schools [in the South] than ... more than each of the republics of South America in half-a-century of turbulent independence. Is it impossible to ever evoke a shift in public opinion among us, not in favor of a race reputed to be inferior, but in favor of our [poor] whites, black by ignorance and social inferiority?"[116] As an example of what such "public spirit"

could achieve Sarmiento included extensive statistics and qualitative information on the schools founded by the Freedmen's Aid Society taken from
the *Freedman*. He also reprinted a speech on civic education by Emory
Washburn that criticized the misguided notion of government held by
both poor whites and freed blacks in the South. According to Washburn,
they both looked to the government as either an owner or a provider, and
thus needed to be inculcated with the principles of republicanism and
self-help.[117] In Sarmiento's view Washburn had identified the key issues
facing the United States during Reconstruction: (1) how to prepare freed
blacks to exercise the functions of citizenship, and (2) how to inculcate
republican qualities among "the *poor* whites of the South, and the immigrants that by the tens of thousands were arriving annually from Europe
and who possess or easily acquire citizenship. The South American reader
will find in this text some descriptions so vivid and accurate of what occurs
among us, that it will seem as if this text speaks instead of what we should
ourselves undertake."[118] On matters pertaining to public education and
citizenship Sarmiento found in the United States during Reconstruction,
and especially the South, a mirror image of Latin America. Geography was
thus also a central theme in his writings on race in the United States in the
1860s, via a remapping of the US South as Latin American. This remapping led him to misread US racial politics in important ways, however.

Sarmiento's skepticism about black suffrage in the United States, for
example, derived from his understanding of how uneducated voters contributed to the problem of *caudillismo* in Latin America. He distrusted
uneducated voters, both white and black. Emancipation, he argued, had
raised the question of whether the United States should "submit its great
destiny to influences with a reputation for idiocy? . . . Would barbarism be
the first consequence of the triumph of freedom over the last remnants
of social oppression?"[119] Sarmiento and Mary Mann totally disagreed on
the answer to this question. In January 29, 1866, he wrote that he was
working on a speech for a convention of school superintendents "on the
admissibility of the colored people to citizenship, with the qualification
that whites and blacks must be able to write, as proof that at least through
reading they possess the means of uniting their existence, ideas and judgments to the human tradition, which in my estimation is the foundation of
liberty."[120] In a subsequent letter on February 15, 1866, Sarmiento reported
that he did not deliver the speech because "it was not entirely suitable
under the circumstances."[121] He later admitted that "truth be told, they
had not much desire to hear it. These are my ideas. In politics I am always

the schoolteacher."[122] Mary Mann vehemently objected to Sarmiento's view that there should be a literacy requirement for black suffrage. In a February 20, 1866, letter, for example, she argued that:

> I agree with you theoretically about the suffrage—but this seems to me a peculiar case. Our slaves were freed not by general consent & harmoniously as in your country, but against the will of those among whom they live, whose injustice and oppression can be staid [sic] in no other way than by giving them the suffrage. It is the only protection they can have that is adequate to the circumstances, & therefore I think they should have it. Afterwards ... let [there be] a new bill from Congress limiting the suffrage of both *whites & blacks* to those who can read, but the blacks are really better & more intelligent than the poor whites of the South, & better capable to vote. The hatred borne the blacks by these poor whites is so deadly, the rage of the slaveholders so intense, that the two classes together can *exterminate* the blacks if they are not protected ... the slaves [here] ... are in a better condition probably than your slaves were for freedom. .... If they were not to be taxed till they could be allowed the suffrage, it would be more just, but since they are taxed I see not what mortal has a right to say that they shall not have the suffrage. The right is *inalienable*. The educational qualification for all would be better, but the right cannot now be taken from whites without making more trouble than to give the negroes an equal chance.[123]

Mary Mann was not able to persuade Sarmiento to alter his opinion about black suffrage, but neither did she waver in hers. In March 6, 1867, for example, she rejoiced in the fact that black men had gained the right to vote: "I know you are afraid of the uneducated voter. ... However, I am not afraid of the voter who cannot read."[124] In her observation that suffrage was essential to protecting the gains blacks had made after emancipation given the intransigence of southern whites, Mary Mann showed herself to be a more astute reader of US racial politics than Sarmiento, who viewed them through the prism of Argentine conflicts.

As a result of reading US history as analogous to Argentinean post-independence conflicts Sarmiento developed a problematic understanding of US racial politics and, in particular, the Civil War. His vision of the struggle between North and South as one between civilization and barbarism echoed northern intellectuals's understanding of the Civil War. Sarmiento depicted the US Civil War as a struggle between civilization and barbarism. He argued that "The South with slavery was like a previous geological layer of the current soil: it was the intermediary between Europe and America: the natural descent of South America into ... North [America]."[125] The existence of slavery created a situation in which there was European-style aristocracy and social hierarchy in the US South, in contrast to American progress and equality in the north. Yet this reference to slavery is rare in a text in which Sarmiento emphasizes other causes of the US Civil War. Anticipating Southern historians's later rewriting of Civil War history, Sarmiento attributed the origin of the conflict to a dispute over federalism, not slavery. In a September 23, 1865, letter to Mary Mann, for example, he wrote: "I have nearly out a life of Lincoln with an Introduction written by me, which ... contains some general appreciations of the past slave policy of the United States and the labors of the abolitionist."[126] This is a misleading description of *Vida*, however, as Sarmiento devoted little attention to the abolitionist struggle, and instead focused on the useful lessons Latin America could derive from Lincoln's leadership during the Civil War.

According to Sarmiento in *Vida*, the main cause of the Civil War was centralized state power versus states's rights. "What was, at its core, the issue that three million soldiers have debated through arms and blood...? While slavery, as an institution, was the proximate cause of the war, and its abolition the obvious result of it, other more vital issues to the preservation of the Republic, were behind this great façade of the body politic; and it is important to know them in order to understand" it.[127] The "issue graver than slavery" faced by the United States, Sarmiento told his Latin American readers, was: "Can Republics founded on popular sovereignty be dissolved"?[128] This was a question Latin America had struggled with repeatedly since independence, hence the relevance of the US conflict and its resolution. In particular, Sarmiento praised Lincoln's use of executive power during the Civil War as a model for Latin American statesmen. Lincoln, he argued:

> defended the faculties and prerogatives of the Executive, so exposed to being attacked and undermined by the Legislature, by judges, by the people itself, who forget that the Executive is their instrument, and that civil war is a curse for all, for the winners and the losers. This principle established in the United States, this faculty used

honestly and only for the purposes established in the Constitution, will save the States of South America from many days of shame.[129]

Because he had not behaved as a *caudillo*, despite preserving the authority of the central government, Sarmiento argued that Lincoln's life was destined to be "a lesson for all peoples. Not the violence of the barbarian ... not the demagogue. ... He is the honest worker who studies the laws of his country, and reading the signs of the times, proposes to lead the people and achieves it ... above all it is an example of good republican governance."[130] Just as Sarmiento imagined the "poor whites" of the South as US *gauchos*, so too he recast the Civil War, not as a struggle over slavery, but as a lesson on how to avoid *caudillismo*.

Ironically, Sarmiento's selective reading of the US Civil War in terms of Argentinean political history actually appealed to his US audience because it confirmed their preferred interpretations of the war. This was reflected in the favorable reception to the publication of Mary Mann's English translation of *Facundo* in 1868 in the US press. Sarmiento's portrayal of Argentine history as a conflict between civilization and barbarism in *Facundo* coincided with northern views of the Civil War. One reviewer argued that a US reader could not read the book without "seeing in it again and again the broken image of his own country." The reviewer went on to opine that if the post–Civil War task facing the United States was "the preparation for the highest social freedom of the forces, black and white, set free by the victory of civilization ... at the Southern extremity of the continent, a society accepting the same instrument of government which we have had, has likewise had to pass through a conflict, more open, and lasting for a longer period than our own, but, alike with ours, the conflict of civilization and barbarism."[131] If Sarmiento saw in the South a reflection of Argentina's social inequality, US readers of *Facundo* also found in Argentina's post-independence conflicts a reflection of their own recent Civil War. US readers also found it flattering that Sarmiento viewed their country as a political model for Latin America. One reviewer of *Vida*, for example, suggested that the text might be of use to "our suffering neighbors the Mexicans ... for Sarmiento has dwelt with great minuteness upon all those features of our institutions which younger republics need to know in detail. It is, indeed, a manual of instruction for any young republic."[132] After a bloody civil war, it was no doubt reassuring to Sarmiento's US readers that their country could still be viewed as a model for Latin America.

Yet, in contrast to 1847, Sarmiento's admiration for the United States in the 1860s was tempered by concerns about hemispheric expansionism. He would therefore no doubt have disapproved of another reviewer's conclusion that US citizens were indebted to him for having shown that "if there is a manifest destiny in our Republic, it is to extend the idea of civil liberty, regardless of whether the area of the United States be extended with it."[133] This reviewer of *Facundo* might be excused for believing that Sarmiento, as an advocate of Europeanization, might have welcomed US imperial expansion to the rest of the Americas. It is ironic that he was read that way in the 1860s, however, as the anti-imperial aspects of Sarmiento's political thought are evident in his writings about the United States during this era. Sarmiento may have continued to argue that Latin America could learn from the United States in the 1860s, but his method cannot be described as a straightforward application of US ideas, especially when one considers his selective reading of the Civil War through the lens of Argentine history. Instead, there is a process of double refraction at work, whereby Sarmiento reads the United States in light of Argentina's ills, and on the basis of this selective reading endorses it as a useful model. Sarmiento's description of himself in a May 12, 1866, letter to Mary Mann captures the driving force behind his engagement with the United States in the 1860s: "I have taken a most active part in the *reconstruction* of my country. ... My goal even as a youth was to *constitute* a *Republic.*"[134] Sarmiento found both a model and a looming threat in the United States during Reconstruction, which led him to produce one of the first iterations of the comparative formulation of "the two Americas" that would become a central trope for anti-imperialist strands of Latin American political thought in the twentieth century.

"What is America? Who Are We?": Racial Pessimism and US Empire in the 1880s

Sarmiento's refusal in the 1840s and 1860s to attribute hemispheric power imbalances to inherent racial characteristics (as was commonplace in the racial science of the day), was replaced at the end of his life by a more rigid application of scientific racism. In *Conflicto*, his last major work, "the influence of land and geography is displaced by race as an explanatory master code."[135] By the time Sarmiento published *Conflicto* in 1883, new social Darwinist understandings of global differentiation were in full swing.[136] The question of US expansion to Latin America was thus debated in relation to the arguments of this strand of racial science. If white Europeans (and Anglo-Saxons in particular) were destined to rule over the rest of the world, Latin American thinkers were faced with the dilemma that racial science endorsed US expansion. Given its large non-white population and "Latin" European colonial legacy, Latin America was supposedly destined to backwardness. The relationship between "the two Americas" was thus an even more urgent question by the 1880s. *Conflicto* was ostensibly about Latin American race relations, but its dominant theme is actually Sarmiento's anxiety about US hegemony in the hemisphere. Sarmiento's fierce critique of the impact of indigenous survival and mestizaje on Latin American political development in *Conflicto* was driven by his anxieties about US expansion. Sarmiento's evolving view of the United States reflects a broader trend among Latin American intellectuals, who shifted from seeing it as a model in the nineteenth century to growing anti-imperialism in the twentieth. Sarmiento was no doubt one of Latin America's most ardent admirers of the United States, but his concern with the relationship between "Ambas Américas" also situates him as a bridge figure who anticipated some elements of the full-fledged critique of US imperialism developed by later figures such as Martí, Mariátegui, and Vasconcelos.

Sarmiento's preoccupation with Latin American vulnerability vis-à-vis the United States in *Conflicto* fairly oozes from the text. The very first sentences of the book pose the dilemma of Latin American identity. "What is America? Who are we? ... Are we Europeans? So many copper colored faces prove us wrong! Are we indigenous? The disdainful smiles of our blond ladies may give us our only answer. Mixed? No one wants to be that. ... Are we a nation? A nation without a blending of the accumulated materials, with neither adjustment nor foundation. Argentines? Until when and since when, it would be good to know."[137] In contrast to earlier texts, in *Conflicto* Sarmiento attributed US success to specific racial policies, particularly racial separation. During North American colonization, he argued: "the Anglo-Saxons did not admit the indigenous races, not as partners, nor as servants, into their social compact."[138] He claimed that the principal difference between the United States and Latin America was the absence of racial mixture and (white) political equality in the United States. "The North American, then, is the Anglo-Saxon, free from any mixing with races lacking in energy, with political traditions that have been preserved without being degraded by the racial ineptitude for government that is inherent to prehistoric man."[139] In the 1880s Sarmiento's prescription for how to counter US dominance was for Latin America to emulate it where race was concerned: "What can this America do to attain the free and prosperous destiny of the other? It must become its equal, as it has begun to do with the other European races, correcting indigenous blood with modern ideas. . . . It must become equal by reaching the same intellectual level and in the meantime only admitting into the electoral body those who are capable of carrying out its functions."[140] The driving force behind Sarmiento's endorsement of Agassiz's strictures against racial mixing in *Conflicto* was thus his growing concern that Latin America would be unable to match the success of the United States.

If the central geographic binary in *Facundo* was domestic (city versus countryside), in *Conflicto* the key comparative dichotomy is hemispheric (the United States versus Latin America). Indeed, Sarmiento's growing pessimism about the prospect of egalitarian hemispheric relations between the United States and Latin America explains why he would adopt some of the tenets of racial science regarding race's impact on political development in 1883, at a time of political stability and economic growth in Argentina. The country's main political problem was no longer *caudillismo*, but rather political cohesion and economic development as a bulwark against the danger of US expansion. Sarmiento made this clear in the letter to Mary Mann that served as the prologue to *Conflicto*. He explained that he had begun: "to suspect that there is something more than merely mistakes by the rulers or unchecked ambitions, but rather a general tendency of events to take a similar course in Spanish America. . . . Do you understand now the aim of my book about the conflict of the races in America? The conflict of the races in Mexico led it to lose California, Texas, New Mexico, Arizona, Nevada, Colorado, Idaho, which are now flourishing states within the United States."[141] Sarmiento's reliance on race as the main explanatory variable for US progress and Latin American lag in *Conflicto* had a perverse logic, however. It conveniently absolved Latin America's white-identified *criollo* elite of responsibility for the fate of "their America."

Yet, even in *Conflicto*, Sarmiento did not endorse all the precepts of the scientific racism of the era. He still held out hope that Latin America could become the equal of the United States. Racial science may have been pervasive in its intellectual impact, but this did not mean that individual thinkers had no agency in how they chose to understand and apply these ideas. Indeed, throughout *Conflicto* Sarmiento adopted those elements of scientific racism that buttressed his views, while ignoring less-congenial arguments. Notions of Anglo-Saxon racial superiority derived from the historical strand of racial science, for example, comported with his critique of the effects of the Spanish colonial legacy on Latin America. He argued that "Spanish colonization . . . was carried out by a monopoly of its own race that had not left the Middle Ages when it transplanted itself to America and absorbed there within its blood a prehistoric, servile race."[142] His assessment of indigenous peoples and blacks, meanwhile, continued to invert the dominant racial ranking of the time that placed Indians above blacks.

Conflicto is rife with virulent anti-indigenous racism. In it Sarmiento repeatedly describes indigenous peoples as examples of "prehistoric man . . . who is tame as a llama in the vast expanse of Peru; lazy, dirty, a thief, as he is in the pampas; and drunk and cruel in the whole world." He also claimed that indigenous peoples were savage, uncivilized, lazy, lacking the capacity for political rule, and generally deficient in moral character. He described them as "primitive, prehistoric . . . races destitute of any rudiment of civilization and government."[143] He even claimed that indigenous men were especially sexist, engaging in polygamy and exploiting indigenous women's labor in the fields and at home, to the point that he marveled at "how much Indian women have gained by their proximity and even servitude to the European race!"[144] Ironically, Sarmiento, the opponent of mixture, here prefigures a central element of twentieth-century discourses of mestizaje in Latin America: the beneficial effects of the paternalistic relations between European colonizers and black and indigenous women on slave plantations and colonial haciendas.[145]

Sarmiento's description of indigenous peoples as "prehistoric" in *Conflicto* was not accidental, it served to justify state policies to subdue and conquer indigenous territories in order to make way for European immigrants.[146] In fact, Sarmiento's indigenous policy reveals the limits of his anti-imperialism. Like many Latin American thinkers who criticized US hegemony in the hemisphere, Sarmiento did not apply the same scrutiny to his and other nineteenth-century nation-builders's efforts to dismantle indigenous communities and dispossess them of their lands, which was essentially a continuation of the unfinished Spanish colonial project.[147] As contemporary theorists of decolonization have noted, this is consistent with Latin American intellectual elites's continued adherence to Eurocentric colonial models and ideas, even as they launched anti-imperial critiques of the United States and Europe from their subaltern position within global political and intellectual hierarchies.[148]

If, as its title suggests, *Conflicto* was a book about the "harmony" as well as the conflict between the races in Latin America, Sarmiento located harmonious race relations in Argentina's (supposedly) dwindling black population. Sarmiento had much less to say about blacks than indigenous peoples in *Conflicto*, virtually all of it positive, albeit in a highly paternalistic vein. He described blacks as courageous, hardworking, and faithful servants who had established close bonds with whites, even during slavery. He recognized black participation and bravery during the wars of independence in Latin America and claimed: "The negro, even though a slave, was a friend to the young *criollo*, his owner, with whom he had in any case been raised in the family, and in whose games and inclinations he had participated. His race is faithful and enthusiastic and serving voluntarily as an assistant he would accompany his 'owner' to war."[149] In Sarmiento's racial imaginary blacks were more docile and adaptable to Western civilization, while indigenous peoples (for the most part) were savage, warlike, and stubbornly resistant to assimilation. As a result, blacks were "disappearing" in Argentina:

> There are a few youth of color left, who work in service as high-class coachmen, as porters in public buildings and other lucrative jobs, but as a race, as a social element, they are no longer more than a passing accident, having disappeared altogether in the provinces, and having been unable to establish themselves outside of the city.[150]

In keeping with this narrative of absorption and disappearance, Sarmiento claimed that the future of blacks was in Africa, not the Americas. He suggested that "the world is full of rumors of Africa, of the discoveries, greatness, and splendors of Africa, because all feel that its time has come for justice, dignity and reparation."[151] Sarmiento did not view blacks as an obstacle to Latin American development, either because they were in the process of being absorbed, or because their destiny lay outside the Americas.

Even in the 1880s, however, at the height of his concern about US hemispheric dominance, Sarmiento continued to believe in education as the solution to Latin America's racial dilemmas; he did not fully succumb to the racial pessimism about Latin American development prognosticated by scientific racism. In *Conflicto*'s unfinished conclusion he argued that "only the school can plant the seed that in adulthood will enable participation in social life; and to introducing this vaccine to extirpate the mortality inoculated into our veins by barbarism, has the present author dedicated his entire life, even when the political aim of his labors was not always understood."[152] Perhaps, then, even at a moment of despair about Latin America's ability to match US success and thereby withstand the threat of US expansion, Sarmiento had not completely abandoned the lessons imparted by the educational experiments of Reconstruction.

Sarmiento has presented a conundrum for scholars of Latin American political thought, partly because of his overt racism (especially in *Conflicto*), and partly due to his apparent advocacy of Europeanization and rejection of American sources. David Solodkow, for instance, has described Sarmiento as a prototypical example of postcolonial melancholia. He "is the intellectual that floats in the paradox and in the periphery of modernity, of that modernity that denies him systematically as a subject. A modernity to which he wants to belong, but from which he is excluded."[153] Yet, rather than viewing Sarmiento as a thinker who succumbed to the allure of European ideas and was forever trying to emulate them, he should instead more accurately be read as a thinker who was thoroughly preoccupied with American (in the hemispheric sense) political problems. By this I do not mean that the United States supplanted Europe in his political thought, since as this chapter has shown, Sarmiento's understanding of US history was itself shaped by Latin American realities. Rather, Sarmiento is an example of the way Latin American ideas about race were shaped in foundational ways by comparisons to the United States and concerns about hemispheric power relations. Shortly after writing *Facundo*, Sarmiento turned his gaze away from Europe to the United States, which functioned as both political model and threat. It was thus this supposedly most Europeanized of Latin American thinkers who sought to initiate a transnational dialogue between "ambas Américas" (both Americas) that predated the discourse of "nuestra América" (our America) that emerged as a central trope of twentieth-century anti-imperial Latin American political thought. Reflecting a later historical moment, when US imperial presence in the region was no longer a fear but a fait accompli, the discourse of "nuestra

América" eschewed North–South intellectual exchange in favor of Latin American cultural and political unity against a common foe. Sarmiento's more radical successors developed a thorough critique of US empire that advocated Latin American Pan-Americanism, contrasted US racism to Latin American racial harmony, and explicitly valorized the mestizaje he rejected. Yet, in ways that have thus far been insufficiently appreciated, after *Facundo* Sarmiento's gaze shifted decisively away from Europe to the Americas.

PART II

Mestizo Futurisms

We believe it is a duty of the [US] Americans of Negro descent, as a body, to maintain their race identity.

—W. E. B. DU BOIS, *The Conservation of Races (1897)*

We in [Latin] America shall arrive ... at the creation of a new race fashioned out of the treasures of all the previous ones: the final race, the cosmic race.

—JOSÉ VASCONCELOS, *The Cosmic Race (1925)*

FIGURE 11.1 W. E. B. Du Bois, Prints & Photographs Division, Library of Congress

FIGURE 11.2 José Vasconcelos, Prints & Photographs Division, Library of Congress

3

"To See, Foresee, and Prophesy"

DU BOIS'S MULATTO FICTIONS AND
AFRO-FUTURISM

RACIAL MIXTURE IS not generally viewed as a salient theme in W. E. B. Du Bois's political thought.[1] He has mostly been read as a thinker who downplayed mixture due to his investment in a narrow, and at times essentialist, conception of black identity in the service of a project of African American racial uplift. Du Bois is seen as a paradigmatic example of the static US approach to race encapsulated in a rigid, binary (black–white) racial order. By reaffirming a notion of blackness based on hypo-descent Du Bois is viewed as having restricted any recognition or affirmation of the United States's interracial history and having endorsed an unduly restrictive conception of black identity that assumed that all persons with any degree of African descent were black and would identify as such.[2] Such readings of Du Bois are partly a result of the preponderance of certain iconic early texts, particularly *The Souls of Black Folk* (1903). In his later works, however, Du Bois displayed an increasingly global vision that situated US African American politics in light of broader black internationalisms and Afro-Asian alliances. In texts from the 1920s such as *Darkwater* (1920) and *Dark Princess* (1928), for example, Du Bois envisioned political movements of people of color worldwide, and race mixture served an important political function in these attempts to imagine postcolonial futures.[3] As the later Du Bois sought to envision a post-racist world, he increasingly turned to the iconography of mixture to work out the potential grounds of, and challenges to, global anti-colonial politics and proto-socialist solidarities.

Du Bois's writings about mixture resulted from his effort to make a conceptual and temporal leap beyond the simultaneously rigid (but also in practice constantly trespassed) "color line." The politics of interracial intimacy in the early twentieth century were such that Du Bois's revolutionary arguments about mixture and black politics were subversive for the time, even as the terminology he utilized and the gendered implications of some of his arguments may strike us today as anachronistic and dated. Through them he sought to overcome the difficulties of attempts to forge black internationalisms. Reading Du Bois's portrayals of interracial intimacy through the lens of Afro-futurism thus allows us to probe how and why race mixture emerged as a way to envision a Global South in which people of color forged transnational political alliances during the first half of the twentieth century. As exemplified by Du Bois's novel *Dark Princess*, narratives of racial mixing became politically imaginable sites of racially just futures in early- to mid-twentieth-century African American (and Latin American) political thought that nevertheless proved to be problematic post-racist utopias.[4]

During the early twentieth century, racial politics in the United States was closely bound up with questions of interracial intimacy to a remarkable extent. Racial mixing, rather than an individual choice or question of personal freedom, was a matter of state policy until fairly late in the twentieth century in the United States. During the decades prior to World War II, during what is known as "the nadir" era in US race relations—which saw the consolidation of Jim Crow racial segregation in the South, widespread lynching, and other forms of racial terror—prohibitions against racial mixture were at the forefront of state policy on race.[5] Objections to racial egalitarianism or "social equality" during this era were directly linked in public discourse to fear of mixture.

US state policy on race in the early twentieth century codified the dominant scientific consensus on mixture. All strands of scientific racism, including the US school of ethnology, historical accounts of Aryan superiority, and social Darwinism, coincided that miscegenation led to degeneration and that crossing between so-called superior and inferior races should be avoided at all costs. The early decades of the twentieth century was also the high point of eugenics, whose dictates further entrenched negative views of mixture. Eugenics, which was based on supposedly more sophisticated understandings of the laws of human heredity, sought to improve human "stock" by encouraging those individuals and groups deemed most "fit" to reproduce and discouraging or preventing the "unfit" from doing so. In the United States, the dictates of eugenics translated into legislation mandating forced sterilization of "the feebleminded" as well as bans on interracial marriage.[6]

Scientific racism shaped multiple areas of official state policy in the United States in the decades prior to World War II. Eugenicists such as Madison Grant combined the racial determinism of the historical school with new notions of racial hygiene to argue in favor of racial purity, segregation, bans on nonwhite immigration, and restrictions on Southern European immigration. In *The Passing of the Great Race or The Racial Basis of European History* (which was first published in 1916 followed by multiple reprints), Grant argued that the superior "Nordic" race needed to be defended against the threat of mixture with inferior races. Embracing the dictates of eugenics, he urged the separation and eventual removal (via sterilization) of undesirables, defectives, and inferior race types. Grant's ideas helped shape immigration policy. They paved the way for restrictions on immigration to the United States from Southern and Eastern Europe and total bans on Asian immigration, as reflected in the national origin quotas of the Immigration Act of 1924. Grant was also a proponent of racial classification and anti-miscegenation laws that helped codify the "one-drop rule" and Jim Crow racial segregation in Virginia in the 1920s. Demonstrating the influence of eugenic ideas on public policy at the time, the Virginia Racial Integrity Act of 1924, which became a model for other racial segregation statutes in the US South, was passed at the same time as a forced sterilization act for the "feebleminded." The resurgence and expansion (to include all nonwhites, not just blacks) of anti-miscegenation law in the first decades of the twentieth century in the United States directly reflected the dictates of the racial science of the day, especially eugenics.

Interracial intimacy was also gendered and sexualized in particular ways in public policy debates about anti-miscegenation law in the United States. It had different political valences depending on who was involved. Interracial intimacy between white men and black women was both ignored and assumed to be consensual, with black women cast as hypersexual and incapable of suffering sexual violation. Meanwhile, state prohibitions on miscegenation were overwhelmingly debated in light of potential interracial intimacy between black men and white women, which were always assumed to involve rape or sexual violence, with white women invariably portrayed as passive victims of predatory black male lust. There is thus a direct contrast between the foregrounding of sexual violence in US discourses about mixture, and Latin American portrayals

of mestizaje as a process of harmonious fusion between European founding fathers and willing black and indigenous women.[7] A key element of
any analysis of racial mixture in Du Bois's political thought thus requires
interrogating the gender politics that shaped his representations of interracial intimacy, as narratives of mixing tend to privilege heterosexual
reproduction and patriarchal family relationships.[8]

Because racial mixture was one of the fulcrums of state policy on race
in the United States during this era, Du Bois and the National Association
for the Advancement of Colored People (NAACP), founded in 1909, were
directly involved in resisting the adoption of bans on interracial marriage
in northern states between 1913 and 1929.[9] At the same time, romances
of white supremacy inspired by racist science depicted interracial intimacy as monstrous and deviant, and were popularized in novels and
films such as the hugely popular *Birth of a Nation* released in 1915. As
Reginald Horsman has argued about the nineteenth century in remarks
that are equally applicable to the period during which Du Bois's writings
about mixture were produced: "One did not have to read obscure books to
know that the Caucasians were innately superior, and that they were responsible for civilization in the world, or to know that inferior races were
destined to be overwhelmed or even to disappear. These ideas permeated
the main American periodicals and . . . formed part of the accepted truth
of America's schoolbooks."[10] Du Bois, like other African American (and
Latin American) thinkers writing about race in the first half of the twentieth century, thus had to engage directly with eugenics and other strands
of racist science, as well as with the popular forms through which anti-
mixing tenets were disseminated.

Du Bois's attempts to contest both the politics of white supremacy (including the racial terror of the nadir era) and its ideological underpinnings
in racial science led to important experiments with genre. Du Bois's writings about mixture challenged the scientific racism of his day. But contesting the authority of science as well as the affective reach of romantic
narratives of white supremacy required moving beyond the detached em-
piricism of scientific writing to the kind of literary experimentation that
Du Bois pioneered in *Souls*, moving seamlessly between essay, autobiography, verse, and music. As he later explained in *Dusk of Dawn*: "one could
not be a calm, cool, and detached scientist while Negroes were lynched,
murdered, and starved."[11] Du Bois thus engaged in a "deliberate blurring
of boundaries between argument and poetry in the hope of conveying . . .
truths . . . more effectively."[12] As Lawrie Balfour, Susan Gillman, and Alys

Weinbaum have observed, this led Du Bois, in texts such as *Darkwater*, to employ a textual politics of juxtaposition that placed nonfictional and fictional elements alongside each other.[13] I follow Balfour in reading Du Bois's use of juxtaposition as a response to the conundrum that straight-forward philosophical or scientific argument could not adequately convey the full realities of a racialized world or enable his readers to decolonize their imaginations in order to resist the racist white supremacist utopias engendered by scientific racism. As Balfour observes, Du Bois's use of juxtaposition "reveals a conviction that political ideas may exceed the lim-its of analytical expression and that they must be advanced in a way that produces receptivity in the men and women to whom they are directed."[14] This chapter thus interrogates the political utility of Du Bois's various depictions of mixture, which were formulated in response to specific po-litical exigencies during different eras.

I argue that Du Bois's fictional representations of interracial ro-mance, his essays on state policy on race (particularly those about anti-miscegenation law), and his autobiographical reflections on mixture and the scientific concept of race should all be read as forms of what Lourdes Martínez-Echazábal calls "mulatto fictions." She uses the term in the Latin American context to refer to "an array of works, both fictional and nonfic-tional, epistemologically grounded in the various scientific theories of race prevalent from the 1840s to the 1910s."[15] Du Bois and his Latin American counterparts were operating within the same epistemic horizon set by the racial science of the day, even as some tried to imagine a world beyond it. Du Bois sought to contest rather than reflect the racial science of his time, and in the process formulated a political conception of blackness. As he ruefully acknowledged in *Dusk of Dawn*, over the course of his life his ideas about race evolved in a thoroughly nonlinear fashion, reflecting "all sorts of illogical trends and irreconcilable tendencies. Perhaps it is wrong to speak of it at all as 'a concept' rather than as a group of contradic-tory forces, facts and tendencies."[16] Mixture played a key role in Du Bois's evolving understanding of race. This chapter thus argues that Du Bois's "mulatto fictions" should be read as forms of speculative mestizo futurism that nevertheless did not romanticize mixture as the solution to racism.[17]

Specifically, I focus on three moments in Du Bois's oeuvre that bridge his early and later works, as well as his fiction and nonfiction. First, I an-alyze one of his earliest statements on the scientific concept of race, "The Conservation of Races" (1897). This important early text is juxtaposed to Du Bois's essays and editorials against anti-miscegenation law in *The Crisis* (the journal of the NAACP, of which Du Bois served as editor) between 1912 and 1922. The second moment analyzed is the late 1920s, when Du Bois begins to formulate an enlarged sense of solidarity that transcends the United States. This was also a time of ideological radicalization in which Du Bois was increasingly drawn to socialism. I focus, in particular, on the novel *Dark Princess*, an interracial romance that imagines a political alliance of people of color worldwide, in which racial mixture serves as a catalyst for black internationalism and a global anti-colonial uprising. Finally, I analyze Du Bois's extended meditations on mixture, scientific definitions of race, and political blackness in *Dusk of Dawn* (1940). This chapter thus maps the transgressive racial geographies and shifting political commitments of Du Bois's mulatto fictions.

"To See, Foresee, and Prophesy": Du Bois's Mulatto Fictions and Afro-Futurism

Du Bois's most extensive fictional depiction of interracial intimacy, *Dark Princess*, has been described as a "fantastic" text, in reference to its rather implausible plot.[18] I take this characterization of the novel as an invitation to read it and Du Bois's other writings on mixture in light of Afro-futurism. Afro-futurism provides a productive frame for approaching Du Bois's writings on racial mixture because his figurations of transgressions across the color line were indelibly bound up with the question of futurity. As Arnold Rampersad has observed, *Dark Princess* is especially instructive regarding Du Bois's "fears and hopes, on a global scale, concerning the future of race relations."[19] In *Dark Princess* and *Darkwater*, fictional representations of mixture enable Du Bois to imagine (and, he hoped, thereby facilitate the construction of) alternate, better worlds. Du Bois's writings about mixture directly challenged US prohibitions against miscegenation; they also promoted and extolled the potential of international political alliances among people of color, most of whom were still colonial or semi-colonial subjects at the time. As Dora Ahmad has observed, in his "portrayal of a consolidated global South ... [Du Bois] offers a prehistory of the region which would come to be conceptualized as the third world."[20] It is thus particularly appropriate to read Du Bois's writings on mixture in light of Afro-futurism, as racial utopias that dare to imagine a world not dominated or defined by whiteness. An Afro-futurist frame allows us to probe issues of temporality and spatiality in Du Bois's writings about mixture, and to consider how his depiction of political alliances across the color line were informed by the expansion of his political concerns beyond the borders of the United States.

Afro-futurism is an aesthetic and literary movement that aims to counter the overwhelming absence of people of color and concomitant assumptions of racelessness in dominant conceptions of futurity. As Alondra Nelson argued in her introduction to a seminal essay collection on the subject: "Forecasts of a race-free (to some) utopian future and pronouncements of the dystopian digital divide are the predominant discourses of blackness and technology ... racial identity, and blackness in particular, is the anti-avatar of digital life. Blackness gets constructed as always oppositional to technologically driven chronicles of progress."[21] As a result of such "raceless future paradigms" in which race and gender distinctions are assumed to disappear, the utopian future is imagined as both (implicitly) white and race-free. In science fiction and other sites where visions of futurity are generated, blacks and other people of color are thus generally absent or viewed as mired in the past and bound by tradition. Yet African American thinkers have wrestled with similar questions as those raised by the technological advances that define many visions of futurity.[22] Drawing on black political thought's probing of the nature of the self, identity, history, and memory, Afro-futurism seeks to generate visions of the future that center black characters and black experience. It also aims to supplement or displace futurisms that portray Africa (and other non-European locales) only as sites of dystopia. As Kodwo Eshun explains, Afro-futurism seeks to intervene "within the dimension of the predictive, the projected, the proleptic, the envisioned, the virtual, the anticipatory and the future conditional."[23] Afro-futurism also aims to unsettle dominant representations of the past in order to reconceive the future. It engages with "histories of the past, present and ... future that deny the black Atlantic experience" in order to "generate counter-histories that reweave connections between past, present and future."[24]

Taking Afro-futurism as a starting point for reading Du Bois's writing on racial mixture thus foregrounds the place of futurity in his work. By centering his "mulatto fictions," Du Bois can be characterized as an Afro-futurist thinker whose depictions of transgressions across the color line sought to destabilize the existing racial order and imagine a future beyond racism. Du Bois had a sophisticated understanding of the uses of the past, and of the histories of evasion surrounding foundational racial wrongs such as slavery. As exemplified in *Black Reconstruction*, he viewed recovering the black past as central to imagining a postcolonial future.[25] At the same time, however, it is important to consider whether Du Bois posited interracial intimacy itself as a kind of racial utopia, or, if his vision of the racial politics of mixture was more complex. His writings on mixture might thus forestall the seeming tendency to assume the necessarily positive qualities of futurity that are suggested, at least in part, by Afro-futurism.

Du Bois's preoccupation with temporality, and futurity in particular, is evident throughout his oeuvre. Du Bois continually played with temporal categories in order to signal that his writings sought to envision a future world that did not yet exist. The penultimate chapter of *Darkwater*, for example, is the science fiction short story "The Comet," which recounts a dystopian future in which much of New York City is destroyed.[26] Similarly, in the evocatively titled *Dusk of Dawn*, Du Bois explained that in his view race continued to be "the Problem of the future world." Looking back on his life at the age of seventy-two, Du Bois described his work as having been "to see, foresee and prophesy."[27] That Du Bois would see himself as a prophet is not surprising, but his invocation of prophecy speaks to his preoccupation with futurity, even as he was directly involved in the political struggles of his day. In 1926, for example, he described the NAACP as "a group of radicals trying to bring new things into the world." He also suggested, consonant with Afro-futurism, that the impetus behind the work of black artists should be to provide counter-histories of the black experience that could generate alternate futures. "Suppose the only Negro who survived some centuries hence was the Negro painted by white Americans in the novels and essays they have written. What would people in a hundred years say of black Americans?"[28] For Du Bois literature could serve as a vehicle for imagining historical change.

Dark Princess is precisely such a proleptic text. It envisions an alternate history of peoples of color worldwide in order to chart a different course for African American politics as part of a postcolonial world that was yet-to-be. The novel has been described as an exercise in "prophetic messianism," in which Du Bois turned to fiction to portray what could not be achieved through political activism at the time.[29] According to Rampersad, the impetus for *Dark Princess* was Du Bois's frustration with the failure of the various Pan-African Congresses he had organized and participated in "to influence the future of colonialism in Africa." Having "become largely disillusioned with these efforts . . . he turned to fiction and the imagining of a different world."[30] Du Bois's turn to fiction allowed him to take imaginative leaps beyond existing realities and to engage in a more expansive politics of the possible. Indeed, as Ahmad has observed, Du Bois's stylistic shift away from the social realism that characterizes the section of *Dark Princess* set in Chicago also represents a move beyond the pragmatic politics of compromise and acquiescence advocated by Booker T. Washington, toward a more utopian form of African American politics.[31] Du Bois's fictional representations of interracial intimacy are thus emblematic of the link between political imagination and futurity in his work.

In trying to envision an alternate world not defined by the color line, Du Bois also had to figuratively move beyond the United States to chart an alternate political and racial geography.[32] Nicole Waligora-Davis, for example, points to the term "Transcaucasia"—a space "not on the map," in "the fourth dimension beyond the color line"—to suggest that Du Bois charted a "new political cartography" in his writings on mixture that belongs within the tradition of black fugitive thought.[33] In seeking a future place beyond the color line in which black freedom could be envisioned, Du Bois moved beyond the nation-state in ways that resonate with the black fugitive search for alternative, autonomous black spaces. As Waligora-Davis observes, "the contours of African American utopian discourses are marked by this imperative to rearticulate space, to reimagine black futures which are otherwise denied by racisms."[34]

Paying attention to space and geography in Du Bois's mulatto fictions shows a gradual expansion of the terrain of black politics in his work. Mirroring the movement of black bodies during the Great Migration, Du Bois moved away from the South as the center of US black life in *Souls* as well as beyond a black–white racial binary. In later texts such as *Darkwater*, *Dark Princess*, and *Dusk of Dawn*, the terrain of black politics shifts to northern cities, to a cosmopolitan understanding of the black South as part of a Global South, and away from the United States to Europe, India, and Africa.[35] In *Dark Princess*, Chicago, and by extension the United States, is depicted as a dystopian, grim site of black unfreedom, of joyless material accumulation for the black bourgeoisie and mindless exploitation for black workers. In the novel Du Bois's search for an alternate political space beyond the rigidities of the US color line, the empty moralism of black respectability, and the strategic dead-ends of various projects of black liberation (such as violent insurgency and machine politics), eventually led him to India and the possibility of an Afro-Asian international that was central to the political projects of many black radicals at the time.[36] Du Bois thus mapped a decolonizing geopolitical imaginary in his mulatto fictions in which transgressions of the color line were emblematic of the possibility of forging transnational political alliances among people of color in the Global South. Like prior black fugitive spatial dreams, such as Delany's (and briefly, Douglass's) vision of African American emigration to Central America in the nineteenth century, however, Du Bois's black internationalism was also rife with contradictions, tensions, and challenges.

Du Bois's Afro-futurism was also inflected by his growing radicalism and attraction to Marxism. His sense of historical movement was future-oriented, but not necessarily teleological. According to Herbert Aptheker, by 1911 Du Bois "thought of himself as a socialist."[37] The future world Du Bois envisioned in his mulatto fictions combined an analysis of domestic racism and colonial domination with a critique of global capitalism. In fact, Marxism and antiracism were closely linked in the eyes of their opponents. Defenders of Anglo-Saxon racial superiority such as Madison Grant and Lothrop Stoddard equated "Bolshevism" and antiracism, and viewed Bolshevism "as the cause for the militancy marking the colored people of the world." Stoddard attacked Du Bois by name in *The Rising Tide of Color against White World-Supremacy* (1920). This link between black militancy and suspected communism was a driver of the first Red Scare. During the Red Summer of 1919 multiple race riots broke out in cities across the United States "in which pogromists systematically sought to slaughter as many Black men, women, and children as they could, from Chicago to Washington, to Elaine, Arkansas."[38] The influence of Marxism is evident in many of Du Bois's mulatto fictions. There is a searing critique of the black bourgeoisie in *Dark Princess*, and in *Darkwater*'s "The Comet," Wall St. is destroyed by a meteor strike. One of the few survivors is the black male protagonist, a working-class messenger who feels "invisible" to the wealthy white bankers around him. Tragically, it was the wealthiest black community in the US, known as the "Black Wall Street," which was destroyed by a white race riot in Tulsa, Oklahoma, a year later in 1921. Du Bois's mulatto fictions thus reflected not only the growing influence of Marxism on his political thought, but also the way in which debates about mixture served as proxies for deeper anxieties about race and class during this era (the Tulsa riot was sparked by the accusation that a black man had raped a young white female elevator operator).

One of the concrete political imperatives for Du Bois's mulatto fictions was thus the need to counter dystopian narratives about the dangers posed by mixture affirmed by scientific racism as well as white utopias of global Anglo-Saxon racial domination.[39] These white supremacist fictions were grounded in the hegemonic racial science of the time. Du Bois's mulatto fictions thus sought to contest the authority of scientific racism by exposing it as a form of "science fiction." As Du Bois made clear, race science was protean. Different strands of scientific racism appeared and coexisted with each other throughout the late nineteenth and early twentieth century without apparently undermining the scientific validity of race science. Du Bois, however, was unpersuaded.

> The first thing which brought me to my senses in all this racial discussion was the continuous change in the proofs and arguments advanced. I could accept evolution and the survival of the fittest, provided the interval between advanced and backward races was not made too impossible ... But no sooner had I settled into scientific security here, than the basis of race distinction was changed without explanation, without apology. I was skeptical about brain weight; surely much depended upon what brains were weighed. ... When the matter of race became a question of comparative culture, I was in revolt.[40]

Ideas of white superiority–black inferiority were widely believed to be scientifically valid, however, especially at the popular level, not just among elite intellectuals. Romantic fictional narratives of white superiority and racial purity had a profound impact on the white unconscious.[41] Du Bois was thus forced to abandon his early belief that science was sufficient to change white hearts and minds. He turned instead to literary and political experimentation—producing nonfiction, fiction, and multi-genre texts, as well as moving out of the academy to engage in journalism and direct political activism with the founding of the NAACP in 1909—in order to reveal the truth about race and advance the cause of racial justice. As he explained in his well-known "Criteria of Negro Art" essay: "Whatever art I have for writing has been used always ... for gaining the right of black folk to love and enjoy. ... I do care when propaganda is confined to one side while the other is stripped and silent."[42] Via his mulatto fictions Du Bois thus sought to present a contrasting vision of the future to counter romantic narratives of white racial purity and dystopian mixing that devalued black life.

While Du Bois's positive portrayals of interracial intimacy sought to counter dystopian narratives of mixing, it is important not to overstate their optimism.[43] Du Bois did not simply engage in an uncomplicated celebration of mixture. The racial utopias depicted in his mulatto fictions were rife with internal contradictions. According to Paul Gilroy, in *Dark Princess* Du Bois "offers an image of hybridity and intermixture that is especially valuable because it gives no ground to the suggestion that cultural fusion involves betrayal, loss, corruption, or dilution. This is not the fusion of two purified essences but rather a meeting of two heterogeneous multiplicities . . . entirely appropriate to troubled anti-colonial times."[44] Yet close engagement with the breadth of Du Bois's mulatto fictions shows that they offer a complicated account of mixture. Du Bois did depict a non-racist future in which mixture was reframed as neither monstrous nor deviant. Yet, as the episodes of foreclosed black–white mixing on US soil in "Criteria" and *Darkwater* reveal, Du Bois was highly aware that interracial intimacy could result in violence, especially in an era of pervasive racial terror. Du Bois did not seek to glorify mixture per se. Rather, it was a politically useful symbol of a hoped-for global anti-colonial uprising against white supremacy. As Du Bois explained in the publicity notes he prepared for the publisher, "*Dark Princess* is a romance with a message." In addition to telling the story of its protagonists's "search for a way of rebuilding the world across the color line . . . the second and deeper aim of the book is to outline the reaction of the difficulties and realities of race prejudice upon many sorts of people."[45] At a time when fear of mixture drove opposition to racial egalitarianism, Du Bois's mulatto fictions sought to unsegregate his readers's imaginations in the hope that they too would be moved to struggle to rebuild a freer future world.

"I Am Not a Slave": Miscegenation, Eugenics, and US Race Policy during the Nadir

Centering Du Bois's mulatto fictions challenges readings of Du Bois as wedded to a rigid, essentialist conception of race that militated against any acknowledgment of mixture. According to this view, Du Bois understood racial identities as homogeneous, fixed, and permanent features of human life as opposed to the heterogeneous, variable, and transitory historical phenomena that we now understand them to be. Appiah, for example, has argued that Du Bois continued to espouse a biological conception of race despite his stated commitments to a socio-historical notion of race in his 1897 essay on "The Conservation of Races."[46] According to Appiah, Du Bois failed to "transcend" race altogether by not taking his critique of the various definitions of race proposed by racial science to its logical conclusion.[47] Du Bois's involvement in public debates about state codification of race in the United States in the early decades of the twentieth century, specifically the inclusion of a mulatto category in the census and his political activism against proposed bans on interracial marriage, are also viewed as evidence that he was a thinker who was antagonistic to mixture. At a time when there was a strong public consensus against mixture and when the specter of it was used to legitimate racial terror, Du Bois's defense of the right to intermarriage in the 1910s and 1920s involved a denial of the frequency of mixture and a critique of the silence about sexual violence against black women that characterized historical processes of mixing. Yet there were also moments when Du Bois depicted mixing as more than just a red herring for efforts to prevent black equality, such as when he pointed to Brazil's supposed racial egalitarianism as a counter example to US fears of mixture. Du Bois's arguments about mixture early in his career thus reflect the political exigencies with which he was grappling: how black politics should be organized to simultaneously preserve black life and challenge the legal codification of white supremacy and racial terror of the nadir era. Du Bois's writings on mixture in the 1910s and 1920s can thus only be understood in light of the complicated racial politics of interracial intimacy in the United States prior to World War II, when miscegenation was a key site of struggle over the institutionalization of racial segregation or "social equality."

In "Conservation," Du Bois sought to provide a vision of African American politics that could preserve black life in the context of the increasingly violent forms of white supremacy that characterized the nadir era; in the process, he grappled with dominant scientific definitions on race. Du Bois rejected racial science's biological account of race and proposed an alternate definition based on cultural and historical factors. He argued that a "race" was "a vast family of human beings, generally of common blood and language, always of common history, traditions, and impulses, who are both voluntarily and involuntarily striving together for the accomplishment of certain more or less vividly conceived ideals of life."[48] Yet Du Bois paired this definition with a list of eight existing "races" that reflected classifications derived from different strands of racial science, such as those based on phenotype (negroes, Mongolians, etc.) and the historical school's focus on "civilizations" (the English and "Romance nations").[49] But Du Bois's aim in "Conservation" was not to debunk prevailing scientific definitions of race. Rather than a critique of race science per se, the essay proposes a specific vision of African American politics that reflects

what Robert Gooding-Williams has called Du Bois's "political expressiv-
ism."[50] Du Bois's preferred antiracist strategy was not color-blindness or
the "self-obliteration" of African Americans as a group via either cultural
assimilation or biological mixture. He disagreed with African Americans
who believed that the "sole hope of salvation lies in our being able to lose
our race identity in the commingled blood of the nation; and that any other
course of action would merely increase . . . race prejudice."[51] He argued
instead that African Americans should enact a distinct form of black politics built on separate institutions or "race organizations."[52] But Du Bois
also suggested that his embrace of essentialism was tactical. For example,
the second clause of the creed of the American Negro Academy stated
that "we believe it is a duty of the Americans of Negro descent, as a body,
to maintain their race identity *until* this mission of the Negro people is
accomplished, and the ideal of human brotherhood has become a practical
possibility."[53] Based only on "Conservation," it is thus certainly possible to
describe Du Bois as having downplayed "miscegenation" in the service of
black unity.

Du Bois has indeed been read as having formulated a conception of
black politics that reduced or minimized the political salience of interracial identities. Greg Carter, for example, has argued that Du Bois was
largely responsible for fixing mono-racial notions of racial identity in the
United States during the early twentieth century. The definition of race
and modes of antiracist struggle Du Bois advocated in "Conservation,"
Carter argues, "set the basis for minority collective identities as distinctive and antagonistic to mixture." In his view, Du Bois "set the model for
minority anti-racist thinking ever since. Asian Americans, Latinos, and
Native Americans adapted his ideas, substituting their own label where
Du Bois mentioned blacks. This was the foundation for minority groups's
antipathy toward racial mixture in the twentieth century."[54] Du Bois's early
political activism is thus usually read as promoting a homogeneous notion
of black identity that could serve as the basis of antiracist struggle.

Du Bois's role in the debate over the elimination of mixed-race categories from the US census in 1930, for example, is often cited as evidence
of his antagonism to mixture. Categories to measure black–white interracial mixing appeared and were eliminated at various points in the US
census between 1850 and 1930. "Mulatto" appeared in 1850 and was joined
by "quadroon" and "octoroon" in 1890. All three categories disappeared
in 1900, but "mulatto" reappeared in 1910 and 1920, before being permanently eliminated in 1930. As Jennifer Hochschild and Brenna Powell

have observed, the reasons for the inclusion and elimination of racial categories were complex and followed both racist and antiracist motivations,
such as the desire for data that would show the degenerative effects of
mixture or for information about the enslaved population for abolitionist
purposes.[55] While it is not clear precisely which prominent black intellectual was responsible for persuading the US Census Bureau to eliminate
the mulatto category in 1930, Du Bois's main concern seems to have been
the compilation of statistical data about African Americans that could be
easily disaggregated from that of other groups.[56] In an essay on the census
published in the magazine of the Hampton Institute, Du Bois suggested
that the census of 1910 should: "class those of African descent together
and not confound with them groups socially so diverse as the Japanese
and Indian . . . above all the Negro statistics should be so collected as to be
easily segregated and counted by themselves."[57] Later Du Bois suggested
that his qualms about the mulatto category were related to the difficulties
with measuring race. In an unpublished encyclopedia entry on "miscegenation" prepared in 1935, for example, he wrote:

> The attempt to study the size and growth of the mulatto group
> through the United States census has not been very successful . . .
> the attempt was given up probably because the plan . . . to make
> a distinction between persons of different degrees of white and
> Negro blood was officially acknowledged to have been a failure. In
> all the census figures, the method of ascertaining the presence of
> Negro and white blood is left almost entirely to the judgment of the
> enumerator.[58]

Despite his qualms about the imprecise nature of "race," Du Bois also
argued that the importance of scientific research on racial mixing "cannot be too strongly urged." Ultimately, however, the political positions Du
Bois adopted vis-à-vis various public policy questions (such as the mixed-
race census category and intermarriage bans) were driven by his understanding that race mixture "is, in many respects, the crux of the so-called
Negro problem in the United States."[59] Indeed, at this time white attitudes
toward racial equality were closely bound up with hostility to mixture.

Ironically, Du Bois's statements about mixture in the context of the
NAACP's successful activism against legal bans on interracial marriage
in the 1910s–1920s have also been fodder for the claim that he was a
thinker who was antagonistic to mixture. During the era of consolidation

of Jim Crow in the United States at the beginning of the twentieth century, interracial intimacy and political agency were more than just symbolically and rhetorically linked, and not just because the myth of the black rapist became an excuse for lynching and the maintenance of segregation. The right to intermarriage was a symbol of freedom for black men, as eloquently illustrated by the boxer Jack Johnson's response to requests from other prominent blacks that he cease trying to marry white women in 1913: "*I am not a slave*. . . . I have the right to choose who my mate shall be without the dictation of any man."[60] Du Bois made the same connection in 1920, when he sarcastically observed that the "newly discovered crime of sex equality . . . is the impudence of a man of Negro descent asserting his right to marry any human being who wants to marry him." Intermarriage, he argued, was an "elementary right."[61]

Du Bois was an early opponent of anti-miscegenation law, at a time when this was not a widely shared position. Yet in the numerous essays he published opposing legal bans on interracial marriage, Du Bois defended intermarriage as a right, not interracial intimacy itself. For strategic reasons, he also downplayed the frequency of mixture. In an essay responding to questions about the advisability of intermarriage in 1910, for example, Du Bois wrote, "I believe that a man has a right to choose his own wife," but immediately added, "I believe that in general the best results follow when people marry in their own social group." Echoing eugenicist terminology, Du Bois argued that "race blending may lead, and often has led, to new gifted and desirable stocks." Yet despite this rejection of racial science's condemnation of mixture, Du Bois cautioned against intermarriage at this time. "I believe that intermarriage between races is apt to unite incompatible personalities, irreconcilable ideals and different grades of culture. In so far as they do this they should be discouraged." Du Bois's qualms about mixing were historically contingent rather than absolute, however. "I believe that a wholesale intermarriage of races during the present generations would be a social calamity. . . . Whether or not this will be true a hundred or a thousand years from now I do not know." He concluded that absent the distorting effects of white supremacy intermarriage would become a matter of individual judgment and would remain a fairly unusual occurrence rather than the norm.[62]

Du Bois's denials of the frequency of mixture in his articles for *The Crisis*, in contrast to his portrayal of it as thoroughly quotidian in later texts, reflected the NAACP's national strategy of "opposing the laws without endorsing the practice." The NAACP was initially reluctant to publicly oppose anti-miscegenation legislation; in fact, the organization initially disavowed Du Bois's defense of the right to intermarriage in 1910, calling it "a statement of individual opinion." As Peggy Pascoe explains, the NAACP's hesitance to take on such a controversial issue was partly a result of the fact that many of the organization's major white financial donors opposed intermarriage, as did potential (black and white) middle-class supporters who wanted to distance themselves from the allegations of illicit sexuality that were a key feature of the debate about anti-miscegenation law.[63] The NAACP eventually settled on a three-pronged strategy in its campaign against bans on interracial marriage: a refutation of notions of black inferiority, a defense "of marital freedom of choice, and a critique of the sexualization of miscegenation law."[64] In an editorial in *The Crisis* in 1913, for example, Du Bois described intermarriage as "about the last of the social problems about which they [African Americans] are disturbed, because they so seldom face it in fact or theory." Both blacks and whites, he argued, were "practically in complete agreement. Colored folk marry colored folk and white marry white, and the exceptions are very few."[65] Yet, in response to President Warren G. Harding's dictum against racial amalgamation in 1921, Du Bois asked: "What does the President mean? Does he mean that the white and Negro races in this land have never mixed? There are by census reports over two million acknowledged mulattoes in the United States today. . . . Does he mean that there is no amalgamation today? Between 1850 and 1921 the mulattoes have increased over 400 percent. Does he mean there will be no future amalgamation? How does he know?"[66] Du Bois's caution about acknowledging the frequency of mixing (even as he attacked anti-miscegenation law), thus reflected a complicated context in which white opposition to black equality was framed in terms of fear of mixture, and many African Americans also opposed interracial intimacy for different reasons.

In fact, Du Bois was viewed as a proponent of mixture by some of his black contemporaries because of his stance against anti-miscegenation law. African Americans faced with the racial terror and violence of the nadir era tended to focus on black solidarity, and both Du Bois and the NAACP faced significant backlash for their activism against intermarriage bans. For example, Marcus Garvey (the founder of the Universal Negro Improvement Association), criticized Du Bois and the NAACP's activism against anti-miscegenation law. He called the NAACP a "miscegenationist organization." While there was certainly no love lost between Garvey and Du Bois, Garvey claimed that "Du Bois and his National Association for the 'Advancement' of 'Colored' People . . . advocate racial amalgamation or general miscegenation with the hope of creating a new type of colored race by wiping out both black and white." Garvey thus framed Du Bois's opposition to anti-miscegenation law as a project for the creation of a new mestizo type akin to Mexican philosopher José Vasconcelos's argument in *The Cosmic Race*. In fact, this perception of Du Bois was so strong that the UNIA leadership "regarded the NAACP as the penultimate symbol of race mixture."[67] Read in its proper historical context then, Du Bois's defense of the right to interracial intimacy does not support the claim that he was antagonistic to mixture, even if at this time (pace Garvey), he did not celebrate its emancipatory possibilities as he would in later texts.

Even during this era there are moments when Du Bois portrayed mixture as more than an abstract right to be defended. In 1922, for example, Du Bois unequivocally stated that mixture was ubiquitous. Scientific racism's claim that it led to degeneration was "false. From earliest records racial mixing has been the rule and not the exception and there are today no pure races and no scientific line can be drawn between races."[68] Du Bois did not view amalgamation as a solution to racism, however. He insisted that racial mixing would only have positive effects outside the distorting context of white supremacy. In 1935 Du Bois reiterated that racial mixing had always existed, that there "is no hard and fast dividing line between" races, and that existing global conditions favored "miscegenation on a broad scale." The problem was that interracial intimacy had for the most part occurred in the context of institutionalized white supremacy. When racial egalitarianism became the norm, he wrote, "either amalgamation will take place gradually and quietly by mutual consent, or by equally peaceful methods the groups will seek separate careers and separate dwelling places, either in the same or different lands."[69] Du Bois viewed racial equality as a prerequisite for successful interracial intimacy; he did not claim that mixture itself was an antidote to or a bulwark against racism.

Du Bois did at times point to sites outside the borders of the United States, specifically in Latin America, where the pervasiveness of mixture could be usefully deployed to critique claims about the deleterious effects of miscegenation drawn from racist science that were marshaled in support of racial segregation. In 1914, for example, Du Bois waded into a public, bi-national conversation about race relations in the United States and Brazil. His intervention was sparked by "North American champion of eugenics" Theodore Roosevelt's article about "The Negro in Brazil," and specifically the comments of an unnamed white Brazilian statesman he met during his travels there contrasting the two countries's distinct approaches to race: stricter adherence to racial purity in the United States had resulted in rapid material progress accompanied by greater racial conflict, while mixing in Brazil had led to slower progress but more harmonious race relations.[70] As Micol Seigel has observed, this "generative exchange" between Roosevelt and his Brazilian interlocutor served to reinforce existing racial hierarchies in both countries. "The contrast between racial harmony in Brazil and purity in the United States helped explain and defend exceptionalisms on both sides ... [they] served to prove Jim Crow segregation appropriate and necessary in North American contexts, and to validate proposals for the whitening of Brazil."[71] Du Bois stepped in to disrupt Roosevelt's use of the US–Brazil comparison to legitimize racial segregation in the United States.

While he also echoed the Brazilian myth of racial harmony, Du Bois utilized it in service of antiracist ends to intervene in US debates about mixture.[72] In an editorial in *The Crisis* he argued that Roosevelt had studiously avoided sharing certain "simple facts" about Brazil with his readers: that the country had a large black population, and that whites, blacks, and Indians were "fusing into one light mulatto race." Du Bois's corrective to Roosevelt challenged the erasure of blackness in many US depictions of Brazil. After detailing the outstanding contributions of Brazil's mixed-race population in various fields, Du Bois drew the following conclusion:

> And what is all this? Is it not a plea for intermarriage of whites and blacks in the United States? It is not. ... Most white people in the United States prefer to marry white people. That is perfectly proper and defensible. Most colored people prefer to marry colored people. That is perfectly logical and commendable. ... But a vast number of people are not satisfied with such bare facts. They want to bolster them up with scientific lies and social insult ... the result is that they not only accomplish what they wish, but they also accomplish poverty, crime, prostitution, ignorance, lynching, mob violence and the ruin of democratic government for the unfortunate victims of their lies.[73]

The adjectives Du Bois utilized to describe white and black reasons to eschew mixture are telling: the former were "proper and defensible," the latter were "logical and commendable." For Du Bois, blacks who chose not to intermarry were making a reasonable choice in the face of a context in which even social contact across the color line could lead to violence. More than that, however, they were also making a superior ethical choice, by remaining part of a stigmatized group rather than trying to escape it through absorption into whiteness. Yet Du Bois, like Douglass before him, also deployed a romanticized vision of Latin American racial egalitarianism to challenge US racism. Juxtaposing the accomplishments of mixed-race Brazilians with US prejudice served to debunk the "scientific lies" used to bolster segregation (i.e., the claims of racist science that mixture hampered progress and led to degeneration). Du Bois's use of Latin American mestizaje to challenge racial segregation in the United States reflects the centrality of "the other America" to the formulation of racial theories and racial politics in both regions, especially where mixture was concerned.

As the reference to "prostitution" in his condemnation of anti-miscegenation law above illustrates, however, the gender politics of some of Du Bois's arguments about mixture in the 1910s and early 1920s reified patriarchal gender norms and erased the sexual agency of black women, even as black women played a key role in the NAACP's mobilization against anti-miscegenation law. Sexuality and gender were at the core of debates about interracial intimacy during "the nadir," as the sexualization of miscegenation by proponents of segregation served to justify various forms of racial terror (including lynching), and rendered the sexual abuse of black women by white men invisible. Du Bois and the NAACP reframed the debate about interracial intimacy to highlight sexual violence by white men. This was a necessary intervention against the portrayal of black men as predators used to legitimize racial terror and segregation, but it resulted in a paternalistic portrayal of black women solely as victims. In his editorials against anti-miscegenation law, Du Bois repeatedly contested the myth of black men as sexual predators by making the point that historically most mixture had been the result of sexual violence enacted by white men against women of color. It was thus white men who were the real sexual predators. In 1921, for example, Du Bois observed: "We have not asked for amalgamation; we have resisted it. It has been forced upon us. ... It is the white race, roaming the world, that has left its trail of bastards and outraged women and then raised holy hands to heaven and deplored 'race mixture.'"[74] For Carter, the problem with this argument is that it casts all mixture as negative. "Du Bois's analysis populates all mixture in the past ... [and] all interracial intimacy takes on the specter of rape."[75] This is not the case in Du Bois's later texts, where mixture is portrayed as both consensual and linked to futurity. The more problematic consequence of highlighting sexual violence against women of color in order to expose white hypocrisy about mixing, however, was that black women appeared only as victims of white male lust. For example, in 1910, Du Bois criticized white parents in the South who "seek to save their own daughters by making other men's daughters helpless prostitutes before their sons." Intermarriage bans, he argued, were "wicked devices designed to make the seduction of [black] women easy and without penalty."[76] Du Bois's inversion of the predominant gendering of debates about miscegenation in the United States resulted in a paternalistic depiction of black women: they were black men's wives, daughters, and sisters, in need of protection by both black men and the state.

As Pascoe has rightly argued, by framing their critique of anti-miscegenation statutes as "a defense of marriage and plea for the protection of [black] womanhood," Du Bois and the NAACP's "argument operated to uphold conventional notions of sex and gender."[77] Du Bois's affirmation in 1913 that such laws: "leave the colored girl absolutely helpless before the lust of white men ... [they] create in the United States 5,000,000 women, *the ownership of whose bodies no white man is bound to respect*," is emblematic of the problem. Black men, he argued, should oppose intermarriage bans "not because we are anxious to marry white men's sisters, but because we are determined that white men shall let our sisters alone."[78] This critique of bans on interracial marriage raises the question of who precisely Du Bois envisioned as having rightful ownership over black women's bodies: Was it black women themselves, or black men? A feminist analysis of Du Bois's critique of the "sexual component to the structures of white supremacy" thus has to grapple with his failure to contest conventional gender norms about female sexuality.[79] In other words, what are the gender politics of Du Bois's mulatto fictions? Did they simply envision replacing white male control over black women's sexuality with black male patriarchal power, or did they also portray black women's sexual agency? *Dark Princess* is an important counterpoint to the editorials and essays against miscegenation law in this regard. The novel is emblematic of Du Bois's embrace of black internationalism, a black fugitive shift beyond the nation-state that enabled his mulatto fictions to exceed the political exigencies of US debates about mixture, both in its gender politics and geographically enlarged political vision.

"A Romance with A Message": *Dark Princess*'s Mixed-Race Utopia of the Global South

Dark Princess has become a central text in queer and feminist scholarship on Du Bois, yet political theorists have had little to say about it. Literary critics have approached *Dark Princess* as a depiction of black internationalism and disagreed about its gender politics. Some claim that it ultimately reifies traditional gender norms because of the centrality of idealized maternity and reproduction in the text and the recentering of a black male savior narrative at the end of the novel.[80] Others have emphasized the radical conjoining of erotics and politics in Du Bois's fiction and argued that *Dark Princess* did not necessarily reproduce patriarchal conventions about sexuality.[81] Yet the gender politics of *Dark Princess* cannot be analyzed outside of the context of the sexualization of debates about anti-miscegenation law and segregation in the first half of the twentieth century that shaped Du Bois's arguments against intermarriage bans as part of the NAACP. To argue against the view popularized by racial science that mixture led to degeneration was to take a radical stance at the time. This is illustrated by the outraged reaction in 1944 to Du Bois's contribution to the *What The Negro Wants* anthology edited by Rayford Logan. Du Bois's frank depiction of a romance with a white German woman in his essay for the volume ("My Evolving Program for Negro Freedom") challenged the white South's "pathological" fear of interracial marriage. It was deemed so incendiary that the editor at the press initially claimed the manuscript was unpublishable.[82] Read in juxtaposition to the texts on anti-miscegenation law, then, *Dark Princess* challenged conventional beliefs about mixture in the United States, including how notions of black respectability constrained black women's sexuality. The novel's vision of a Global South that could contest the racism of the colonial center was also emblematic of Du Bois's growing disillusionment with the United States, and his desire to transcend the black–white racial binary that constrained conceptions of racial justice and anti-colonial liberation.

As Weinbaum has observed, depictions of interracial intimacy were a central feature of Du Bois's writings in the 1920s. She suggests that "a discourse on interracial romance . . . became constitutive to the substance and success of his antiracist, anti-imperialist, internationalist politics in the 1920s."[83] Yet the narratives of black–white mixing that appear in "Criteria" and *Darkwater* are all foreclosed or unconsummated. In one instance, the attempt to pass as white to protect a hidden interracial marriage leads to suicide, and in another a white woman uses the threat of a false rape accusation to extort a successful black lawyer. In "The Comet" a potential interracial romance is thwarted by the reassertion of racialized patriarchal power. In a dystopian future, a white woman and a black man (believing themselves to be the only survivors of a meteor strike) turn to each other, only to be separated by the reappearance of her white male relatives who re-establish racial boundaries.[84] Following Balfour's suggestion that the question of how "genre shapes the reading and writing of political theory" is central to Du Bois's use of juxtaposition, it is important to understand *Dark Princess* in light of the political implications of privileging tragedy or romance.[85] Reading "The Comet" as tragedy (with its "attention to reversal, paradox, and the power of contingency") highlights Du Bois's turn to romance in *Dark Princess* to depict utopian political aspirations that sought to transcend the constraints of the nadir era. *Dark Princess* was a tale of successful interracial intimacy beyond the black–white US racial binary that challenged conventional gender norms around female sexuality. Yet "The Comet" and other narratives of foreclosed mixing were fictional depictions of Du Bois's argument in his essays against anti-miscegenation law that mixing in the context of institutionalized white supremacy often led to disaster and violence because racial segregation distorted the moral capacities of whites. The existence of both romantic and tragic narratives of mixing in his mulatto fictions reflects Du Bois's refusal to fetishize the positive political implications of mixture.

Briefly, *Dark Princess* tells the story of the political development and romantic partnership of an African American male, Matthew Townes, and Kautilya, a female Indian princess. The novel is divided into four sections, each of which depicts a different moment in Matthew and Kautilya's political evolution. We first meet Matthew in "The Exile," when he has been barred from concluding his medical studies by Jim Crow racial segregation (he is not allowed to practice obstetrics on white women). This leads him to go to Europe, where he meets Kautilya, who introduces him to her allies, the members of the "Council of the Darker Peoples of the World," who are planning a world revolution led by people of color. The members of the Council, who are mostly of aristocratic backgrounds, doubt the readiness of African Americans to join in their struggle but are persuaded by Matthew and Kautilya. In the second section Matthew returns to the United States at the Council's direction to foment a black uprising, and meets Perigua, a West Indian leader reminiscent of Marcus Garvey. Matthew works as a Pullman porter, and joins Perigua in planning the bombing of a train carrying leaders of the Ku Klux Klan, from which he retreats at the last minute upon the princess's reappearance. In "The Chicago Politician," Matthew is rescued from jail by an ambitious black political boss and his mulatto assistant, Sara Andrews. They make Matthew a part of their corrupt black political machine, and he enters into a loveless marriage with the cold and respectable Sara. The princess, who has been working at various menial jobs in the United States and has become a labor organizer, then reappears; Matthew leaves Sara, and Matthew and Kautilya consummate their relationship. The novel ends with the birth of their son, Madhu, at the cabin of Matthew's mother, a former slave, in rural Virginia. Madhu is crowned "The Maharajah of Bwodpur" and is presented as the mixed-race savior and future leader of the darker peoples worldwide.

Dark Princess thus reflects Du Bois's political commitment to black internationalism and Marxism during the 1920s.[86] Dark Princess fictionalized actual international political developments, including the emergence of a nationalist, anti-colonial movement for Indian liberation and the debates in the international communist movement about the "Negro Question" and the "National Question." As Bill Mullen has argued, Dark Princess "predicts a series of political decisions and maneuvers by black and Asian radicals . . . toward a deliberately miscegenated internationalist politics that anticipated, among other things, the shape of anticolonial movements of the 1930s, 1940s, and 1950s."[87] Du Bois's experience organizing the Pan-African and Universal Races Congresses served as an inspiration for the events in Dark Princess. As he later wrote, his immediate hopes for the congresses were not "spectacular nor revolutionary," but "if in decades or a century they resulted in such world organization of black men as would oppose a united front to European aggression, that certainly would not have been beyond my dream . . . what I wanted to do was . . . to sit down hand in hand with colored groups and across the council table to learn of each other."[88] Dark Princess allowed Du Bois to envision a future in which the real challenges to his emerging political vision of a global political movement of people of color founded on a joint commitment to Marxism and black internationalism could be surmounted. Black internationalism, as Brent Edwards has observed, is constitutively marked by "unavoidable misapprehensions and misreadings, persistent blindnesses and solipsisms, self-defeating and abortive collaborations."[89] The global anti-colonial alliance of people of color prefigured in Du Bois's novel could not escape these tensions. They are evident, for example, in

the social class divisions and skin-color hierarchies that led the aristocratic members of the Council of Darker Peoples to express doubts about
the capacity of African Americans to contribute to their struggle.

The "Afro-orientalism" that mars *Dark Princess* is emblematic of the
disjunctures that accompany attempts to forge global political solidarities among people of color in Du Bois's hoped-for postcolonial utopia.
The novel suffers from clear orientalist overtones, including its reproduction of problematic colonial tropes like the feminization of the orient.
According to Mullen, Du Bois was part of "a tradition of what might be
called Afro-orientalism ... [that] generally depended on an exotic essen-
tializing of Afro-Asian vitality, usually associated with the feminine, and
an uncritical glorification of black antiquity." The idealized depictions of
India and Kautilya in the novel reflect Du Bois's "romantic conceptions
of the Asiatic."[90] Yet this was not the only challenge to attempts to bridge
anti-racist struggles in the United States, exile Indian nationalism, and
Pan-Africanism. As Ahmad has shown, Du Bois's principal Indian interlocutor, the Hindu nationalist and Indian National Congress member Lala
Lajpat Rai, whom he asked to review the novel's sections on India for ac-
curacy, in fact, did not share Du Bois's view that black Americans suffered
from internal colonialism. Instead, Rai viewed their position as analogous
to India's untouchables or its Muslim minority and tended to downplay
racial violence against African Americans in his writings on the United
States. As Ahmad rightly observes, Du Bois and Rai's selective depictions
of Indian and US racial politics, respectively, are emblematic of how "concurrent movements for self-determination romanticize and exploit each
other as often as they genuinely empower."[91]

In addition to trying to envision black internationalism, in *Dark Princess*
Du Bois set out to create a widely accessible text that could counter dystopian visions of mixing in the United States popularized by romances of
white supremacy (such as the film *Birth of a Nation*) inspired by the anti-
miscegenation dictates of eugenics.[92] In "Criteria of Negro Art" (1926),
Du Bois clearly articulated the need for art that could counter depictions
of interracial intimacy that reinforced white supremacy. He recalled a current magazine story in which: "A young white man goes down to Central
America, and the most beautiful colored woman there falls in love with
him. She crawls across the whole isthmus to get to him. The white man
says nobly, 'No.' He goes back to his white sweetheart in New York." The
problem, Du Bois argued, was the absence of counter-narratives that
could challenge such blatantly self-serving representations of interracial

intimacy. "I object," he wrote, to "the denial of a similar right of propaganda to those who believe black blood human, lovable."[93] Yet, despite the essay's call for unabashedly politicized art, in it Du Bois also defended black artists's need for artistic freedom, particularly vis-à-vis taboos about sexuality. "The young and slowly growing black public still wants its prophets almost equally unfree. ... We are ashamed of sex and we lower our eyes when people will talk about it. ... In all sorts of ways we are hemmed in and our new young artists have got to fight their way to freedom. ... We can afford the Truth. White folk today cannot."[94]

Du Bois's frank depiction of sexuality and interracial romantic relationships in *Dark Princess* was consistent with his arguments in "Criteria." Most of Du Bois's contemporaries were puzzled by the novel's explicit sexual content and interracial romance when it was published in 1928. Black readers "found the novel disconcerting," while to white reviewers "this outrageously optimistic novel about black messianic liberation had to have seemed implausible."[95] The fact that the novel's two protagonists were nonwhite did not prevent *Dark Princess* from being rejected as an unacceptably positive portrayal of miscegenation by white reviewers. According to the review of the novel that appeared in the *New York Times*, for example, "the theme of miscegenation is so decidedly controversial that to those who believe in the preservation of racial purity the book will fail to lessen their prejudice."[96] But *Dark Princess* did not merely depict mixture in a positive light, it also challenged conventional gender norms about female sexuality.

In the novel, Du Bois critiques the politics of respectability practiced by the black middle classes in response to the hyper-sexualization of blackness that was a constitutive feature of white supremacy. One of the recurring themes in *Dark Princess* is the contrast between repressed, cold, respectable middle-class black women, and warm, sensual, and empathetic working-class or aristocratic women. While working as a Pullman porter and conspiring with Perigua to carry out violent revolt, for example, Matthew has two significant romantic/sexual encounters with black women. One is with a potential romantic partner, a possibility that is foreclosed by their different class positions. Miss Gillespie is described as a young colored woman, "a bit prim," who was "afraid to be familiar with a porter. He might presume. She was not pretty ... had a cold half-defiant air," and avoided any show of solidarity with Matthew, despite the fact that he protected her from racist treatment on the train. In contrast, Matthew's other significant encounter is with an unnamed prostitute in Harlem, with whom he finds solace. She fulfilled his "yearning for some touch of sympathy and understanding."[97] Troublingly, however, the sex worker is never named in the text and scarcely speaks. The reader's understanding of their encounter is thus based entirely on Matthew's perceptions of it.

Du Bois's critique of the politics of black respectability in *Dark Princess* is most evident in the contrast drawn in the novel between Sara Andrews, the representative middle-class black woman, and other women who transgress conventional gender norms and strictures on female sexuality, such as the unnamed prostitute and Kautilya herself. During his sexless marriage to Sara, for example, Matthew more than once compares her un-favorably to the unnamed prostitute: "he had never forgot—shamefaced as it made him—the way that girl in Harlem had twisted her young, live body about his and soothed his tired harassed soul. . . . Always he had dreamed of marriage as like that, hallowed by law and love . . . [Sara] did not repress passion—she had no passion to repress."[98] Matthew later reiterated that Sara "lacked . . . human sympathy. Now if she had had the abandon, that inner comprehension, of the prostitute who once lived opposite Perigua—but no, Sara was respectable."[99] Sara is thus not only depicted as sexless, she is also lacking in empathy. Indeed, Sara is described as the quintessen-tial bourgeois person who appears to abide by conventional morality yet fails to be truly ethical. She "had no particular scruples or conscience," yet was "personally honest and physically 'pure' almost to prudery."[100] After Matthew leaves her for Kautilya, Sara herself reifies the virgin–whore di-chotomy used to discipline female sexuality: "Haven't I been decent? . . . What did he want? . . . A whore instead of a wife?" Kautilya was "a com-mon slut stealing decent women's husbands."[101] Sara, the embodiment of the respectable black middle class in the novel, views decency and sexual pleasure as incompatible.

As in *Darkwater*'s "The Damnation of Women" (1920), *Dark Princess* reflected Du Bois's complicated gender politics: on the one hand, both texts idealize black maternity, yet, on the other hand, both also argued for the right of black women to exercise political and sexual agency.[102] In contrast to the foreclosed or tragic black–white couplings in *Darkwater*, "Criteria," and the essays against anti-miscegenation law, the specter of sexual violence does not haunt *Dark Princess*'s central narrative of (non-white) interracial intimacy. Both the unnamed sex worker and Kautilya defy conventional morality. And while the degree of agency of the sex worker in Harlem is unclear, she is not merely a victim. Kautilya, mean-while, is portrayed as capable of deeper and truer emotion than Sara, combined with embodied sexuality. As they are about to part to carry out their respective political missions, for example, Matthew tells Kautilya: "I suppose that all this feeling is based on the physical urge of sex between us. . . . But the magnificent fact of our love remains. . . . It rises from the ecstasy of our bodies . . . to the resurrection of the spirit."[103] The connection between Matthew and Kautilya is portrayed as both sexual and spiritual, it is a result of both erotic desire and their joint commitment to political activism. Despite featuring a primary romance that culminated in heterosexual reproduction, *Dark Princess* therefore also contested black respectability and its strictures on female sexuality.

The crucial enabling factor of the successful interracial romance in *Dark Princess* was that it transcended the black–white racial binary and US-centric versions of African American politics. The only (potential) interracial encounter in *Dark Princess* involving a traditional white–black US pairing was the false rape accusation by the white female companion of a Ku Klux Klan leader who tried to seduce Matthew on the train, which led to the lynching of Jimmy, another black porter. Interracial intimacy thus appears to triumph in *Dark Princess* because it bypasses the black–white dyad and transgresses national borders. Matthew and Kautilya fulfill Du Bois's prerequisites for successful mixing: they were intellectual equals, and insofar as they were not social equals, it was not because of a dichotomous racial order, but because of her royal status. Matthew and Kautilya's relationship also exceeded the traditional US black–white binary not only because she was Asian (Indian) and he was African American, but because they are both described as simultaneously mixed and black. For example, when being introduced to the representatives of the Darker World, Matthew was told that he appeared mixed. He replied: "My grandfather was [black], and my soul is. Black blood with us in America is a matter of spirit and not simply of flesh. 'Ah! Mixed blood,' said the Egyptian. 'Like all of us, especially me,' laughed the Princess. 'But, your Royal Highness—not Negro,' said the elder Indian in a tone that hinted at protest. 'Essentially,' said the Princess."[104] This passage highlights both the universality of mixture and the persistence of racial hierarchies even among "the darker races." Du Bois recognized that blackness could not be reduced to biology; it was "a matter of spirit and not simply of flesh." Racial identities were not just colonial impositions, they were also the result of self-making. The consequence of this, however, illustrated by the elder Indian nobleman's attempt to distance India from blackness, was that there could be no presumption of unproblematic solidarity even in the Global South, with its shared commitment to resisting European colonialism and global white supremacy.

While the internal politics of Du Bois's hoped-for revolutionary anti-colonial movement are thus rather murky, *Dark Princess*'s Afro-Asian alliance reflected his conclusion that African Americans needed to move beyond focusing solely on the struggle against racial segregation in the United States to a "robust black internationalism" that could challenge the global color line.[105] Matthew's flirtation with various types of black politics in the novel, only to discard each in turn, reflects Du Bois's own political evolution. Before his departure for Europe, Matthew was a classic assimilationist. He believed in US meritocracy and adhered to black respectability. After his return, he briefly adopted Perigua's brand of Black Nationalism, in which violence was the only reasonable response to white violence and racial terror. As he prepared to carry out the plan to blow up a train transporting Ku Klux Klan leaders to a national convention in Chicago, Matthew mused that "all the enslaved, all the raped, all the lynched, all the 'jim-crowed' marched in ranks behind him. . . . He was going to fight and die for vengeance and freedom."[106] In the second half of the novel, however, a disillusioned and nihilistic Matthew becomes part of Chicago's black political machine. He is finally rescued when he re-embraces black internationalism and rejoins the alliance led by Kautilya and the Council of Darker Peoples. The novel's hope thus ultimately resides with a global antiracist and anti-colonial political movement, that is nevertheless riven by internal fissures and tensions.[107]

The version of mixed-race futurism that Du Bois offered in *Dark Princess* reflected his growing disappointment with US democracy. In the novel, Du Bois envisioned transnational alliances of people of color, united by shared experiences of racial and colonial domination, that transcended the nation-state. By the 1940s Du Bois had become convinced that African Americans could not wage the struggle for racial justice in isolation. In a 1946 memorandum on the future direction of the NAACP, for example, Du Bois forcefully declared his commitment to black internationalism:

> Above all, we American negroes should know that the center of the colonial problem is today in Africa; that until Africa is free, the descendants of Africa the world over cannot escape chains. . . . The NAACP should therefore put in the forefront of its program the freedom of Africa . . . the complete abolition of the colonial system.

A world which is One industrially and politically cannot be nar-
rowly national in social reform.[108]

In *Dark Princess*, through the character of Matthew, Du Bois prefigured his
own political evolution. He traced his disappointment with different strands
of US black politics, and his grim assessment of the possibilities inherent
in alternative forms of inclusion into existing racial orders represented by
violent insurgency and electoral politics. In this context, Du Bois's representations of interracial intimacy, by turns apocalyptic and utopian, serve as
metaphors for the move from a national to a transnational vision of black
politics, for his eventual black fugitive refusal to confine the struggle for
racial justice to the nation-state. If the tragic or foreclosed instances of US
black–white mixing in "Criteria" and *Darkwater* are emblematic of Du Bois's
disappointment with the nation, the successful transnational interracial romance in *Dark Princess* represents his growing conviction regarding the in-
sufficiency of the domestic realm of politics as a source of political change.
In the final chapter of *Dusk of Dawn*, Du Bois described this shift, which led
him to urge African Americans to look beyond the United States and to "put
behind your demands, not simply American Negroes, but West Indians and
Africans, and all the colored races of the world."[109] Du Bois thus moved decisively beyond the US and its black–white racial binary in his mulatto fictions.

Given the novel's privileging of an Afro-Asian alliance, it is entirely
plausible to read *Dark Princess* as thoroughly exceeding an American
hemispheric space. *Dark Princess* shares *The Cosmic Race*'s global expanse
of mixture. Vasconcelos's text also thoroughly centers Latin America as
the cradle of a new mestizo subjectivity, however. Similarly, there are
moments in *Dark Princess* when Du Bois re-centers the Americas. For
example, after Matthew abandons Perigua's plan to blow up the train carrying the Ku Klux Klan leaders, Kautilya assures him that "your dream
of the emancipation of the darker races will come true in time, and you
will find allies and helpers everywhere, and nowhere more than in black
America."[110] Kautilya resolves the dilemma posed by the fact that a global
alliance of people of color would inevitably have to contend with internal
power dynamics and imperial hierarchies by positing the US South as an
always-already-transnational space. "Here in Virginia you are *at the edge
of a black world*. The black belt of the Congo, the Nile, and the Ganges
reaches by way of Guiana, Haiti, and Jamaica, like a red arrow, up into
the heart of white America. Thus I see a mighty synthesis: you can work
in Africa and Asia right here in America if you work in the black belt."[111]

This geographic reordering of the Global South within the US South points to an alternate reading of *Dark Princess*'s political cartography that locates the Americas as a thoroughly miscegenated space. Indeed, this reading is especially suggestive given the Caribbean's large Asian/Indian diaspora, of which Du Bois was certainly aware. Writing about Jamaica in 1915, for example, he offered a description that prefigures Kautilya's invocation of a black world in the US South: "There in Jamaica the world is met. African and Asia and Europe all meet. . . . In Jamaica for the first time I lived beyond the color line—not on one side of it but beyond its end." In utopian sentiments reminiscent of *Dark Princess*, Du Bois would laud Jamaica's "gift of racial peace . . . the most marvelous paradox of this paradoxical western world."[112] Yet, at the same time as he lauded the transcendence of the color line in the Caribbean, Du Bois acknowledged the region's poverty as a result of colonial exploitation, belying the temptation to succumb to overly rosy accounts of hemispheric mixture as antiracist futurity. Racial justice required more than the trespassing of the color line.

The challenges to concerted political action against global anti-black racism that Du Bois wrestled with in *Dark Princess* and his other mulatto fictions continue to be as relevant today as they were in his time. His call to envision creative forms of black internationalism, for all the limitations of his particular figurations, have a resonant urgency in our present moment. At a time when radical disregard for black life in the form of police killings of unarmed black persons in the United States leads to inevitable comparisons to the racial terror of previous eras, the pressing need to find black lives "human, lovable" remains a vital imperative. Du Bois's speculative mulatto fictions remind us of the futility of waging de-colonial and antiracist struggles in isolation, even as the difficulties of translating and articulating disparate struggles remain as sharp and clear as ever.

"What Is Africa to Me?": Revisiting Mixture in *Dusk of Dawn*

Four decades after the publication of "Conservation," Du Bois would return to the question "what is race?" in *Dusk of Dawn* (1940). Written two decades before his death, *Dusk* is one of Du Bois's later mulatto fictions. It is an extended meditation on racial science and the constitutive elements of a shared "grammar of blackness." In *Dusk*, racial mixture emerges as a key trope through which Du Bois articulates (in the sense in which Brent

Edwards suggests we understand the term) how racial identity can be conceived and diasporic solidarity enacted.[113] *Dusk* is ostensibly an account of Du Bois's life, but it is also more than that. As its subtitle announces, it is "an essay toward an autobiography of a race concept." As he explained in the preface: "I have written then what is meant to be not so much my autobiography as the autobiography of a concept of race, elucidated, magnified and doubtless distorted in the thoughts and deeds which were mine."[114] *Dusk* maps the dominant scientific definitions of race that prevailed during Du Bois's long life, as well as his own evolving racial thought. Mixture features prominently within the personal and intellectual genealogy of race that Du Bois offers in *Dusk*. The connection between the social fact of mixture and antiracism is shown to be complex in the text. If recognition of mixture abounds in *Dusk*, Du Bois also suggests that the constructed character of race could be fully acknowledged without abandoning a positive notion of collective racial identity.

In *Dusk*, Du Bois described racial mixing as ubiquitous in the United States and suggested that he had always been interested in studying mixture.[115] He observed that, contrary to the denials of both whites and blacks, racial mixing was widespread in the United States. Sounding very much like his Latin American counterpart, Vasconcelos, Du Bois described the Americas as a space of mixing par excellence:

> Here in America and in the West Indies, where we have had the most astonishing modern mixture of human types, scientific study of the results and circumstances of this mixture has not only lagged but been almost non-existent. We have not only not studied race and race mixture in America, but we have tried almost by legal process to stop such a study. It is for this reason that it has occurred to me just here to illustrate the way in which Africa and Europe have been united in my family. There is nothing unusual about this interracial history. It has been duplicated thousands of times; but on the one hand, the white folk have bitterly resented even a hint of the facts of this intermingling; while black folk have recoiled in natural hesitation and affected disdain in admitting what they know.[116]

Du Bois's language here, describing mixture as the process by which Africa and Europe were "united" in his family, is striking because of its romanticized portrayal of interracial intimacy. This harmonious depiction of mixture is in sharp contrast to the emphasis on rape and sexual violence against black women and women of color in his essays on anti-miscegenation law in the 1910s and 1920s.

In *Dusk*, Du Bois presents his family's interracial history and the quotidian nature of mixture as epistemological resources that allowed him to contest the various definitions of race proffered by racial science. He recalled the constant refrain that mixture led to degeneration that was part of his "scientific" training. "When the matter of mixed races was touched upon their evident and conscious inferiority was mentioned. I can never forget that moment in the class of the great Heinrich von Treitschke in Berlin ... 'Mulattoes,' he thundered, 'are inferior.' I almost felt his eyes boring into me."[117] The disjuncture between Du Bois's lived experience of race and the tenets of the racist science of the day could not have been clearer. He described intermarriage as common in his family and within the black community of his hometown. In Great Barrington, "the color line was manifest and yet not absolutely drawn. I remember a cousin of mine who brought home a white wife. The chief objection was that he was not able to support her."[118] It was precisely such unions that the proposed bans on interracial marriage opposed by the NAACP were intended to prevent. In Europe, Du Bois also experienced the absence of racial segregation. He recalled the same incident that had provoked such consternation in his essay for the *What the Negro Wants* anthology. During his stay in Germany:

> an American husband and wife from the West came, and were so alarmed about my social relations with German girls that they solemnly warned the Marbach family against racial intermarriage. The warning was quite unnecessary. I had already told the daughter, Dora, with whom I was most frequently coupled, that it would not be fair to marry her and bring her to America. She said she would come 'gleich!' [anyway] but I assured her that she would not be happy, and besides, I had work to do.[119]

In *Dusk*, Du Bois thus presents interracial intimacy as ubiquitous, despite being socially and legally proscribed in the United States.

Du Bois used his family's interracial history to illustrate the arbitrariness of the US color line and the malleability of race. He recounts the story of his paternal grandfather, the light-skinned son of a white Bahamian plantation owner who might have been able to pass for white in the United States had he not lost his inheritance. As a result, Alexander

Du Bois "resented being classed as a Negro and yet [was] implacable in his attitude toward whites." Du Bois connected this story of descent into blackness, so to speak, to hidden stories of ascent into whiteness among the founding fathers. In an especially sacrilegious move from the perspective of those committed to white supremacy and racial purity, Du Bois compared Alexander Du Bois's trajectory across the color line to Alexander Hamilton's, whom he had previously included in a list of famous mulattoes in *Darkwater*. "If Alexander Du Bois, following the footsteps of Alexander Hamilton, had come from the West Indies to the United States, stayed with the white group and married and begotten children among them, anyone in after years who had suggested his Negro descent would have been unable to prove it and quite possibly would have been laughed to scorn, or sued for libel."[120] Like the story of the two Johns in *Souls*, the two Alexanders of this vignette take two diametrically opposed paths, in which the enormous material difference in their fates was determined by the vagaries of the color line. Du Bois in *Dusk* shows racial segregation to be perverse and arbitrary, resting as it did on the assumption that there were fixed and identifiable "races."

If mixture rendered the notion of separate and distinct races untenable, as Du Bois suggests in the story of the two Alexanders, it also challenged the idea of a homogeneous black identity. Du Bois acknowledged the wide phenotypical spectrum of blackness in *Dusk*. He described feeling thrilled upon going to Fisk at being "for the first time among so many people of my own color or rather of such various and such extraordinary colors, which I had only glimpsed before, but whom it seemed were bound to me by new and exciting and eternal ties."[121] This passage is typical of Du Bois's contradictory approach to race in *Dusk*: he simultaneously recognized that a sense of shared black identity did not occur naturally (it was "new and exciting"), and nevertheless also writes as if it was pre-ordained (it reflected "eternal ties"). Du Bois's equivocal racial essentialism is on full display here, as racial group solidarity is paradoxically described as both novel and eternal simultaneously. Indeed, Du Bois explained in detail how he came to question and eventually abandon the idea of a biological concept of race.

When I went South to Fisk I became a member of a closed racial group, with rites and loyalties ... so that when I came to Harvard the theory of race separation was quite in my blood. ... Nor again was there any idea of racial amalgamation. I resented the idea that we desired it. I frankly refused the possibility while in Germany and even in America gave up courtship with one 'colored' girl because she looked quite white, and I should resent the inference on the street that I had married outside my race.

But Du Bois was forced to question his adherence to "a closed racial group" by the tactile reality of mixture. "All this theory, however, was disturbed by certain facts in America, and by my European experience. Despite everything, race lines were not fixed and fast. Within the Negro group especially there were people of all colors." This led him to question the idea that there was any biological underpinning to race: "In Europe my friendships and close contact with white folk made my own ideas waver. The eternal walls between races did not seem so stern and exclusive. I began to emphasize the cultural aspects of race."[122] Du Bois preserved the radical possibilities of blackness by detaching it from biology and reconceiving it as political blackness.

Du Bois's subsequent reflections on the nature of his tie to Africa, which follow this personal, familial, and intellectual genealogy of interracial intimacy in *Dusk*, help to elucidate how his evolving ideas about race led to the formulation of a political conception of blackness. First, Du Bois recognized that his direct links to Africa were tenuous: "This then is my racial history and as such it was curiously complicated. With Africa I had only the one direct cultural connection and that was the African melody which my great-grandmother Violet used to sing."[123] Growing up as he did in the United States, far removed (in space and time) from the original site of diasporic dispersal, Du Bois acknowledged that "my African racial feeling was then purely a matter of my own later learning and reaction. ... *But it was none the less real* and a large determinant of my life and character. I felt myself African by 'race' and by that token was African and an integral member of the group of dark Americans who were called Negroes. At the same time I was firm in asserting that these Negroes were Americans."[124] Du Bois's claim that his identification with Africa was a reaction to lived experiences of anti-black racism that led him to develop positive feelings of collective belonging anticipates the insights of more recent scholarship on the power of "invented traditions" and "imagined communities."[125] The scare quotes around race in the sentence "I felt myself African by 'race'" are a clear acknowledgment of the disputed status of both the concept and the claim to racial connection. And just as he seems to be falling into the trap of racial essentialism, Du

Bois pivots back to a clear acknowledgment that US blacks are Americans, not Africans.

In *Dusk* Du Bois explicitly moved away from the initial race concept he espoused in "Conservation." In place of common blood, language, traditions, impulses, and voluntary and involuntary strivings, he invoked a notion of collective racial identity based primarily on shared socio-historical experiences of anti-black racism. Citing the first stanza of the poem "Heritage" by his erstwhile son-in-law Countee Cullen, Du Bois reflected:

> What is Africa to me? Once I should have answered the question simply: I should have said 'fatherland' ... because I was born in the century when the walls of race were clear and straight; when the world consisted of mutually exclusive races; and even though the edges might be blurred, there was no question of exact definition and understanding of the meaning of the word. One of the first pamphlets that I wrote in 1897 was on 'The Conservation of Races.' ... Since then the concept of race has so changed and presented so much contradiction that as I face Africa I ask myself: what is it between us that constitutes a tie which I can feel better than I can explain?

Du Bois's answer to Cullen's question is revealing. He points to the links of phenotype and (remote) kinship only in order to dismiss them. He also notes the lack of scientific consensus on whether there were any biological aspects of race. Instead, Du Bois's understanding of his link to Africa is tied to a specific political project, the "normative imagining of a moral-political vision of black diasporic community." As David Scott suggests, for many black diasporic communities shaped by slavery, which is a living past that has yet to be overcome, Africa represents "the name of a difference, of a refusal, and therefore of a horizon of hopes at once moral and historical, aesthetic and political."[126] It is precisely in this sense that Du Bois speaks of his relationship to Africa in *Dusk*.

> Africa is, of course, my fatherland. Yet neither my father nor my father's father ever saw Africa or knew its meaning or cared ever much for it ... still my tie to Africa is strong. On this vast continent were born and lived a large portion of my direct ancestors. ... The mark of their heritage is upon me in color and hair. These are obvious things, but of little meaning in themselves; only important as

they stand for real and more subtle differences from other men. Whether they do or not, I do not know nor does science know today.[127]

Du Bois could hardly have been unaware of the irony of referring to Africa as his "fatherland" given his paternal ancestry (i.e., the forced-to-be-black Alexander Du Bois), hence the immediate subsequent acknowledgment that neither his father nor grandfather identified much with Africa. African ancestry, then, did not guarantee a sense of connection to Africa. Instead, Du Bois's gestures to Africa in *Dusk* can be read as instances of the production of counter-memory: of the ethical commitment, central to black internationalism, to remember against the grain of a shared, if disparate, history of subjection and exclusion.

Indeed, the crux of Du Bois's argument about race in *Dusk* is that a collective black identity could develop among differently situated (geographically, nationally, linguistically, etc.) individuals as a result of similar experiences of anti-black racism. The antiracist politics that such experiences might give rise to could also enable connections with other subaltern groups, as evidenced by Du Bois's broadening of his analysis to include other forms of global colonial and racial exploitation. His concluding thoughts on his connection to Africa reflect just such an understanding:

> But one thing is sure and that is the fact that since the fifteenth century these ancestors of mine and their other descendants have had a common history; have suffered a common disaster and have one long memory. The actual ties of heritage between the individuals of this group, vary. . . . But the physical bond is the least and the badge of color relatively unimportant save as a badge; the real essence of this kinship is its social heritage of slavery; the discrimination and insult; and this heritage binds together not simply the children of Africa, but extends through yellow Asia and into the South Seas. It is this unity that draws me to Africa.[128]

It is precisely because Du Bois's rejection of racial essentialism is so emphatic in this passage that the extremely romanticized account of his first visit to Africa that follows it is so jarring. Du Bois's equivocations about the nature of black identity in *Dusk* stem in part from his continued belief that a collective racial identity delineated in positive terms was necessary in order to wage antiracist and anti-colonial struggle.

If the Du Bois of *Dusk* did not conclude that the correct antiracist strategy was to transcend race, he was nevertheless aware of how restrictive conceptions of collective racial identity could impinge on individual autonomy. Explaining the outlook developed by those "entombed" and imprisoned by racism, Du Bois observed that "this group imprisonment within a group has various effects upon the prisoner. He becomes ... centered upon the problems of his particular group. ... He thinks of himself not as an individual but as a group man, a 'race' man." Du Bois also acknowledged that many of those classified as black in the United States believed that color-blindness, rather than a separate collective racial identity, was the best solution to anti-black racism. "There were plenty of my colored friends who resented my ultra 'race' loyalty. ... They pointed out that I was ... a mulatto ... that race distinctions must go. I agreed with this ... as an ideal, but I saw it leading to inner racial distinction in the colored group. I resented the defensive mechanism of avoiding too dark companions in order to escape ... discrimination in public."[129] Here Du Bois shows how the acknowledgment of mixture is often connected to arguments for transcending race, while also demonstrating that such strategies could function to reinforce, rather than challenge, white supremacy and anti-black racism. Rather than taking blackness as a given in *Dusk* then, Du Bois depicts it as a self-conscious choice resulting from opposition to anti-black racism and racial solidarity with darker-skinned black persons.

Despite Du Bois's emphasis on interracial intimacy in his mulatto fictions, he did not postulate mixture as a utopian color-blind, post-racial future. Du Bois understood that white supremacy and colonialism could continue to shape global power relations even after notions of biological racial inferiority were ostensibly abandoned. In the chapter on "The White World" in *Dusk*, for example, he analyzed white ethical orientations, not merely in terms of a cultural understanding of whiteness, but rather as something akin to the idea of whiteness as property or as a mode of structuring the political. Du Bois began by noting that "there has been an understandable determination in the United States among both Negro and white thinkers to minimize and deny the realities of racial difference." He agreed that a "scientific definition of race is impossible." But he then went on to trace the ways in which this ostensibly antiracist position was perverted by white moral pathology (what Charles Mills has called "the epistemology of ignorance") into a denial of the accrual of unearned advantages as a result of white supremacy, and of any responsibility on the part of individual whites for its perpetuation.[130] Breaking down the question of "social guilt" using the example of British colonialism, Du Bois argued that while it was true that not all Britons were directly involved in colonial activities and that some opposed the slave trade, based on this fact "we cannot jump to the opposite and equally fallacious conclusion that there has been no guilt, that the development of the British Empire is a sort of cosmic process with no individual human being at fault."[131] In Du Bois's view affective attachment to white supremacy functioned to render most white persons incapable of appreciating black beauty and recognizing black intellectual capacity. It also led them to measure their own self-worth in terms of their superior position vis-à-vis various undeserving "others." As a result, even liberal white persons failed to understand how Du Bois could simultaneously reject racial hierarchy while valuing blackness. As he attempted to explain to one of his hypothetical white interlocutors: "Race is a cultural, sometimes an historical fact. And all that I really have been trying to say is that a certain group that I know and to which I belong ... bears in its bosom just now the spiritual hope of this land."[132] As Du Bois observes, the problem with color-blindness is that it requires historical amnesia about racism and precludes any positive conception of collective racial identity.

More than half a century after the publication of Du Bois's *Dusk of Dawn*, mixed-race futurisms with dubious antiracist commitments, if not implicit anti-black racisms, continue to define the horizon of possibility for attempts to envision a world beyond racism.[133] If Du Bois's mulatto fictions were a response to the dystopian vision of mixing popularized by the scientific racism of his time, multiracialism is the twenty-first century's romantic narrative of racial hierarchy. As Jared Sexton has observed, various forms of contemporary multiracial discourse perform "ideologically restorative work [that] serves to counteract the overlapping critical interventions of black freedom struggle, feminist movement, sexual liberation, and queer activism."[134] For Sexton, contemporary multiracialism is both a symptom of and a crucial ideological component of the "refortified antiblackness" characteristic of the post–Civil Rights Era in the United States. Contemporary multiracial politics follows a profoundly neoliberal logic as it does not seek to dismantle structural racism or economic inequality through collective action. Instead, it privileges individual practices, romantic love, and the heteronormative nuclear family as preferred modes of antiracist struggle and sites of racial transformation.[135] Unlike *Dark Princess*, in which it serves as an avatar for global anti-colonial, antiracist revolutionary politics, in many contemporary multiracial discourses mixture appears to be *the* end in itself.

Du Bois did at times succumb to the temptation to equate multiracialism with racial egalitarianism, as in his reification of the myth of Brazil as a racial paradise in the 1910s and 1920s. By the 1940s, however, he had developed a more nuanced view of Latin American race relations. As Seigel observes, he formulated an early critique of the myth of Brazilian racial democracy. Du Bois "acknowledge[d] Brazilian racism by the early 1940s, far earlier than most."[136] By the 1940s, African Americans writing in the US black press were telling their readers that despite the absence of legal segregation, the color line continued to operate in Brazil. They also noted the creation of several "racial organizations ... similar to the NAACP ... established ... to fight signs of racism in Brazilian life."[137] Du Bois published a number of articles on Brazil in *The Crisis* because he believed it was important to "challenge the view implicit in most books on Brazil that it was a white country." By the 1940s, however, Du Bois "reversed his previous position and presented a hard-hitting critique of Brazilian race relations and ideology." As David Hellwig has shown, at that point Du Bois argued that African Americans needed to abandon the belief that mixture in Latin America had eliminated racism. "Racial amalgamation had meant neither 'social uplift' nor greater power and prestige for mulattoes and mestizos in Latin America. While 'dark blood' ran through the veins of many whites, dark people continued to experience social barriers, economic exploitation and political disenfranchisement. White immigration was encouraged at all costs."[138] This shift in Du Bois's reading of mixture in Latin America was possible because he was not wedded to a naïve form of mestizo futurism. In the 1940s, Du Bois presciently articulated elements of Sexton's critique of how ideologies of mixture can function as anti-blackness. Taken together, Du Bois's mulatto fictions offer a rich archive of his thinking about the political valences and ethical implications of mixture, which generally avoid the conceptual trap of equating multiracialism with antiracism.

Most centrally, rereading Du Bois as a theorist of *mestizaje* serves to undermine one of the foundational tropes of comparative analysis of racial thought in the Americas: that it is only Latin American thinkers who have seriously grappled with mixture as a means of critiquing white supremacy and resisting colonial domination. Remapping Du Bois studies to highlight the role of mixture in his political thought thus allows us to begin to rethink conventional comparisons between US and Latin American racial thought in which Du Bois and Vasconcelos are positioned as polar opposites. Instead, this chapter has shown that they should be juxtaposed as hemispheric interlocutors who both formulated important, albeit flawed, accounts of mixture as futurity.

4

"A Doctrine that Nourished the Hopes of the Nonwhite Races"

VASCONCELOS, MESTIZAJE'S TRAVELS,
AND US LATINO POLITICS

IN HIS MOST famous text, *La Raza cósmica: misión de la raza Iberoamericana* (1925/1948), the Mexican philosopher José Vasconcelos formulated a utopian vision in which racism would be overcome by the unfolding of a universal Latinidad defined by mestizaje. He boldly declared that since its founding moments Latin America had been "concerned with the liberation of the slaves, with the declaration of the equality of all men by natural right, and with the civil and social equality of Whites, Blacks and Indians." Latin America, Vasconcelos argued, had been assigned a "transcendental mission. . . . The mission of fusing all peoples ethnically and spiritually."[1] At the time Vasconcelos's "*mestizofilia,* that is *mestizaje* as thoroughly desirable," directly challenged the dominant view, derived from scientific racism, that mixed-race populations were inferior. In the process, he also undoubtedly overstated Latin American racial egalitarianism and obscured anti-black and anti-indigenous racism. Yet Vasconcelos's iconic theory of mestizaje remains a foundational reference point for certain strands of Latin American thinking about race.[2] More surprisingly, Vasconcelos's ideas have been deeply influential in the United States.[3] In particular, the narrative of Latin American racial harmony grounded in mestizaje popularized by Vasconcelos in the early twentieth century has been appropriated by late-twentieth- and early-twenty-first-century US Latino thinkers.[4] This chapter is thus concerned with mestizaje's travels. What happens when race theory trespasses borders and moves across time and space?

How is it reconfigured in response to specific historical conditions and political conjunctures? How do ideas about race mutate as they cross from one America to the other America, with their different racial logics?

Like US African American thinkers who viewed the region as a racial paradise, Vasconcelos presents a flattened and romanticized account of mestizaje in Latin America. As scholars of racial politics in Latin America have shown, Latin American racial systems have been characterized by extra-legal forms of racial discrimination that produced racially hierarchical societies with differential access to citizenship, wealth, and so on.[5] Yet the reality of racial hierarchy has coexisted with political thinking on race that has presented the region as racially harmonious. Specifically, ideologies of mestizaje such as Vasconcelos's make a number of key claims about the relationship between mixture and racial egalitarianism: (1) that Latin American identity has been defined by long-standing and widespread practices of cultural and biological mixture; (2) that the principal result of a process of mixing that began in the colonial era has been a national population that is homogeneous in its mixed-ness, to the point that the various groups that contributed to the mixing process (Spaniards, Indians, and Africans) disappeared as separate racio-cultural groups per se; and (3) that as a result of a racial system that blurred the boundaries between races and did not include legally encoded racial segregation, Latin America avoided the problems with racial stratification and discrimination that plagued other countries, particularly the United States. These claims, which were a staple of national narratives of mestizaje in Latin America, influenced intellectual debates in many countries in the region for much of the twentieth century and were reproduced in official state discourses. Yet ideologies of mestizaje have always been contested, precisely because they were produced in the midst of social conflicts and political upheavals.

As the excellent recent scholarship on race in Latin America has shown, mestizaje as state policy and as a multifaceted social practice has operated in complex ways in different countries in the region. Precisely because lived experiences of mixture have differed, there has been a rich contestatory history around state discourses of mestizaje. Much of the scholarship on Latin American mestizaje points to the fact that social experiences of mixing should not necessarily be equated with the absence of a hierarchical racial order. Indeed, mixture does not necessarily dismantle racial essentialism per se, because ideas of mixture depend on, and constantly reconstitute, notions of racial origins (i.e., the pre-existing identities that contribute to the mixing process). Even within the context of a dominant national ideology of mestizaje, there can be constant reference to blackness and Indian-ness. Discourses of mestizaje might likewise eschew racial binarism and replace it with multiple categories ostensibly conceived in cultural terms, but they do not necessarily thereby avoid racialism or racial essentialism.[6] At the same time, discourses of mestizaje also narrowed elite choices by rendering legally encoded racial exclusion anathema in Latin America. This meant that in countries such as Cuba and Brazil, for example, marginalized groups such as people of African descent were able to deploy discourses of mestizaje to open spaces for certain forms of political inclusion.[7] In the twentieth century, vocal black and indigenous movements launched full-frontal critiques of Latin American ideologies of mestizaje. They also successfully mobilized to obtain recognition from the state as distinct groups and won public policies to redress the effects of racial discrimination, such as affirmative action.[8] Latin American race relations are (and were) thus significantly more complex than Vasconcelos and other theorists of mestizaje tended to acknowledge.

Yet, in an example of how ideas about race travel and are reshaped hemispherically and temporally, late-twentieth- and early-twenty-first-century US Latino political theorists have drawn inspiration from Vasconcelos's celebration of mixture. Vasconcelos has been an important reference point for Latino thinkers, particularly Chicano activists. He became "an ideological standard-bearer for the Chicano movement that began in [the 1960s] . . . and for pan-Latino thinkers through the 1990s."[9] In 2014, for example, the popular National Public Radio program "Latino USA" devoted an episode to Vasconcelos's ideas. After describing his argument that the world was destined to become more and more mixed, the announcers concluded that in the twenty-first century "the cosmic race seems to be emerging," and it was embodied by US Latinos.[10] Latino political theorists and philosophers as diverse as Gloria Anzaldúa, Jorge J. E. Gracia, and Eduardo Mendieta have argued that because of the legacy of Latin American mestizaje, Latinos disrupt the binary (black–white), static, and overly biological conceptions of race that have historically prevailed in the United States.[11] It is important to note that Latino theorists have repurposed Latin American mestizaje in the service of different racial projects, however. Early Chicano activists viewed "*The Cosmic Race* as a hallmark text of cultural and racial vindication."[12] In contrast, current invocations of Latin American mixture in US Latino political thought tend to be in service of endorsing a notion of color-blindness in which mestizaje is equated with the destruction of race.[13] Latino political theorists have thus repurposed Vasconcelos's flattened account of Latin American mestizaje in the service of intervening in US racial politics to different ends.

Of course, political theorists routinely engage in selective reading in order to recuperate useful theoretical tools from texts whose conclusions they might not fully endorse; yet it is still necessary to pay careful attention to the concrete historical and political contexts in which ideas emerge. When US Latino theorists have drawn on Latin American mestizaje, they have overlooked the fact that US racial politics helped shaped Vasconcelos's ideas about race. For instance, the notion of mixture as racial harmony in Latin America was framed by a consistent practice of comparison with racial segregation and prohibitions against miscegenation in the United States. Even more than Sarmiento, Vasconcelos was deeply versed in US racial politics, given that he lived in the country for extended periods of time at various points in his life.[14] More centrally, however, Latin American ideologies of mestizaje were consolidated in many countries in the first half of the twentieth century, an era of direct US military intervention in the region. The notion of mestizo identity formulated by Latin American intellectuals such as Vasconcelos sought to facilitate regional unity and oppose US dominance in the hemisphere. The trope of Latin America's racial advantage vis-à-vis the United States thus emerged at a specific historical moment and served an anti-colonial function for Latin American elites.

Vasconcelos's ideas about mixture should therefore be read as part of an anti-colonial strand of Latin American political thought for which comparisons to the United States on race were a central feature of the response to US imperialism. Like other twentieth-century thinkers, his notion of Latin America's superior race relations as a result of mestizaje was part of an anti-colonial project to counter US imperialism. Twentieth-century Latin American thinkers concerned with resisting US intervention in the region felt the need to refute the idea that their countries were doomed to racial inferiority (and hence political and economic subordination) because of their large multiracial populations. The aim of Vasconcelos's theory of mestizaje was to vindicate Latin America and defend Latin American political capacity. His arguments about mestizaje are thus best understood by situating them within a hemispheric intellectual lineage in which comparisons between US and Latin American race relations were a key rhetorical feature of anti-colonial discourses.[15] Like Sarmiento, who was an unlikely precursor to this tradition, Vasconcelos's ideas about race were shaped in key ways by the United States. Unlike Sarmiento, however, Vasconcelos did not seek to emulate US racial politics. The hemispheric intellectual frame developed in this book is thus doubly appropriate for understanding Vasconcelos's ideas about race. Not only was his theorization of Latin American mestizaje framed in dialogue with domestic racial politics in the United States and in response to US imperialism, it has also been subsequently appropriated by contemporary Latino thinkers.

Despite the claim by one of his contemporaries that Vasconcelos "worked mightily to decolonize Mexico,"[16] Vasconcelos's political thought (like that of most other anti-imperial Latin American thinkers) was selectively decolonial. Juxtaposing Vasconcelos's mestizo futurism to contemporary theories of decolonization in Latin America is thus instructive because it reveals some of the limits of his critique of global white supremacy. Initially coined by the Peruvian sociologist Aníbal Quijano and later taken up by others, contemporary Latin American decolonial thought argues for a simultaneous "decolonization of knowledge" and "decolonization of power." Latin American decolonial thinkers have critiqued Latin American states as "colonial nation-states" that were constituted on the basis of "whiteness" and reproduced colonial forms of racial subordination after independence. According to Quijano, for example, after nominal independence from Europe, Latin American states controlled by a white-identified Creole elite rearticulated the colonial matrix of power and developed a form of "internal colonialism" that continued to subordinate mestizo, black, and indigenous populations.[17] Contemporary decolonial thought thus critiques post-independence racial hierarchies and Latin American Euro-centrism. It highlights Latin America's reproduction of the dominant geopolitics of knowledge that casts European ideas as universal scientific "truth." Catherine Walsh, for instance, critiques the tendency of Latin American political thought "to reproduce the meta-narratives of the West while discounting or overlooking the critical thinking produced by indigenous, Afro, and mestizos whose thinking finds its roots in other logics, concerns, and realities that depart not from modernity alone but also from the long horizon of coloniality."[18] Vasconcelos's theory of mestizaje is a case in point, as it continued to operate within an epistemic logic that privileged European ideas and sources. Despite challenging the scientific racism of his day emanating from Europe and the United States, Vasconcelos did not develop a consistent critique of the reification of colonial racial hierarchies in post-independence Latin America. Indeed, Vasconcelos was part of an anti-colonial strain of Latin American political thought for which opposition to US imperialism operated fundamentally in the grammar of race. His project was thus anti-colonial only in a limited sense, insofar as it challenged US imperialism. The question of whether Vasconcelos formulated a critique of global white supremacy that could dismantle Latin America's domestic racial hierarchies is much more complicated.

Most analyses of Vasconcelos's political thought on race are based almost exclusively on *The Cosmic Race*, which was first published in 1925 and reissued in 1948. More specifically, they tend to focus on its opening essay, "Mestizaje."[19] *The Cosmic Race* is undoubtedly Vasconcelos's most famous and enduring text. Yet focusing only on it results in incomplete accounts of Vasconcelos's arguments about race. In texts published after *The Cosmic Race*, such as *Indología* (1926) and *Bolivarismo y Monroísmo* (1934), for example, Vasconcelos formulated a more radical critique of Latin American elites's aspirations to whiteness. Vasconcelos's many interpreters have thus missed the most radical elements of his political thought, and the most potentially recuperable aspect of his ideas about race. In *Indología* and *Bolivarismo y Monroísmo*, Vasconcelos at times articulates a critique of global white supremacy and Latin American racism. The Vasconcelos of these texts is thus a better candidate for recuperation in service of egalitarian racial projects than the celebrator of mestizaje. Precisely because Vasconcelos is an unlikely source of a critique of Latin American elites's identification with whiteness, his arguments in these texts merit careful attention.

My reading of Vasconcelos thus juxtaposes *The Cosmic Race* with the lesser known *Indología* and *Bolivarismo y Monroismo*. These texts (which have not been translated into English) expand the arguments about hemispheric racial politics and Latin American regional identity initially formulated in *The Cosmic Race*, and in certain key ways revise and amend them. *Indología* and *Bolivarismo y Monroísmo* both include critiques of the internalized racism of Latin American elites. *Indología* also contains passages that recognize black and indigenous contributions to Latin American identity, while *Bolivarismo y Monroísmo* directly addresses racial discrimination against Latinos during the nadir era of US race relations. Finally, I turn to an example of mestizaje's hemispheric travels, specifically Anzaldúa's selective borrowing from Vasconcelos. Anzaldúa's account of mestiza subjectivity in the US–Mexico borderlands highlights Vasconcelos's relative silence about gender and sexuality. By centering a feminist, female, queer mestiza subject, Anzaldúa "queers" Vasconcelos's theory of mestizaje. Yet she was not able to escape the problematic racial and gender inheritances of his mestizo futurism.

Like his contemporary Du Bois, Vasconcelos's theory of mestizaje situated mixture in both the past and the future (i.e. the future past). Contemporary appropriations of Vasconcelos which claim that US Latinos are the embodiment of an unfolding multiracial future illustrate not only mestizaje's travels, but the resilience of mestizo futurisms that are repurposed to new ends in different historical contexts. In the 1920s and 1930s, Vasconcelos turned to the iconography of mixture to envision the inversion and transcendence of hemispheric racial hierarchies.

"A Philosophy Conceived by Our Enemies": Vasconcelos and Scientific Racism

In Mexico, Vasconcelos was part of a generation that politically opposed the thirty-five-year-old Porfirio Díaz dictatorship (which lasted until 1911) and supported the Mexican Revolution (1910–1920), and intellectually rebelled against Positivism.[20] As a student, he encountered the Uruguayan José Enrique Rodó's influential formulation of a hemispheric opposition between the two Americas, contrasting Latin America's greater aesthetic capacities to US greed and materialism.[21] As was the case with Du Bois's turn to Pan-Africanism and Marxism, the 1920s was also an era of radicalization for Vasconcelos, when he was influenced by socialism and the anti-colonial international intellectual trends of the interwar period. In 1927, for example, he participated in an international anti-imperialist congress in Brussels, which called "for the right of the darker nations to rule themselves," passed resolutions on the freedom of Puerto Rico and against US imperialism, and raised the issue of African liberation.[22] In later years (after his loss in the Mexican presidential election of 1929, which was considered fraudulent by many observers), Vasconcelos became decidedly more conservative ideologically, but he remained firm in his critique of US imperialism.

Vasconcelos's writings of the 1920s and 1930s were driven by an anti-colonial urge to counter US intervention in Latin America.[23] This in turn required direct engagement with the racial science of his day, and specifically its negative views about mixture. In Latin America, the question of anti-colonial resistance to US imperialism was inextricably bound up with scientific "theories of Negro inferiority, mulatto degeneration, and tropical decay."[24] The political disorder that plagued the region after independence was attributed to widespread mixture, while the supposed superiority of Anglo-Saxon civilization which made world domination an inevitability also served to justify US intervention. Latin American intellectuals were deeply influenced by European and US scientific racism, but they did not simply uncritically adopt racial theories produced abroad.[25] While some believed that the solution to the region's racial dilemma was whitening, others altered the tenets of racial science to serve their own ends. Vasconcelos exemplified the latter trend. He inverted the dominant racial hierarchy that valued "pure" over mixed races, and further lauded mixture as proof of Latin America's greater racial harmony in comparison to the United States.

Like his contemporary Du Bois, Vasconcelos had a fraught relationship to science. Vasconcelos and Du Bois adopted different strategies to challenge racist science, however. In contrast to Du Bois, who despaired about the capacity of detached scientific prose to expose the horrors of racial violence and who as a result turned to experiments with genre, Vasconcelos continued to seek the imprimatur of science for his mestizo futurism, even as he exposed racial science as an ideological fiction. He told his Latin American readers that "this [racist] science, which invaded us ... is fought as all imperialism is fought, by confronting it with a superior science."[26] In contrast to Du Bois's strategy in his mulatto fictions, particularly *Dark Princess*, Vasconcelos did not acknowledge the fantastic and futuristic elements of his own text. *The Cosmic Race*, he argued, would "attempt explanations, not with the fantasy of the novelist, but with an intuition supported by the facts of history and science."[27] As Nancy Leys Stepan has argued, in late-nineteenth-century Latin America "science became a rallying cry for the modern, secular elite ... science was widely recognized as essential to Western material and cultural authority—to the very definition of modernity and civilization." In Mexico, in particular, "evolutionism and scientism were popular among intellectuals."[28] In fact, the version of Positivism that dominated Mexican educational institutions during the *Porfiriato* was propagated by a group of intellectuals known as "*los científicos*" (the scientists), some of whom attributed Mexican political disorder to racial causes and argued that dictatorship was necessary because the country was not ready for democracy. "Science was seen as the panacea, able to end the chaotic situation of Mexico."[29] Unlike some of the *científicos*, Vasconcelos did not attribute Mexican post-independence chaos to the country's racial makeup, but like other Latin American intellectuals he was very cognizant of the power of science as ideology. Vasconcelos approached science as a key field of contestation that he was unwilling to cede. Following a presentation of the lecture on race "El hombre" in Puerto Rico, for example, a local intellectual praised the scientific soundness of Vasconcelos's theory of mestizaje.[30] He replied: " 'Doctor, it is just as arbitrary and as fragile as the idea of white supremacy.' Scientific knowledge, at least certain types of it, is still that, a tool of combat, and our obligation is to make use of it."[31] This statement captures a key assumption underlying Vasconcelos's writings about race: while "race" may have been an arbitrary scientific construct, it was nevertheless absolutely necessary to not only challenge and debunk racist ideas of white supremacy, but to formulate positive conceptions of racial identity that Latin Americans could embrace.

Throughout *The Cosmic Race* and *Indología*, Vasconcelos simultaneously disputed the validity of various tenets of US and European scientific racism—such as notions of tropical decay and deleterious mestizaje—and presented his defense of racial mixture as scientifically valid. Vasconcelos's attempt to imbue his theory of mestizaje with the imprimatur of science was emblematic of the way Latin American intellectuals "opened up racist science to their own political projects."[32] In an epistemological inversion, Vasconcelos positioned his defense of mestizaje as historically accurate and scientific, in contrast to biased claims about European superiority. For instance, referring to the designation of the Americas as the "new" world, he wondered: "How can we continue to accept the fiction, invented by our European fathers, of the novelty of a continent that existed before the appearance of the land from where the discoverers and conquerors came?"[33] He also forcefully disputed theories of Anglo-Saxon racial superiority, arguing that they were: "nothing but the illusion of each fortunate people during the period of their power." Supposedly scientific arguments about race and colonialism were inextricably linked, Vasconcelos argued, because: "The official science itself is, in each period, a reflection of the pride of the dominant race. . . . Every imperialistic policy needs a philosophy to justify itself. . . . We have been educated under the humiliating influence of a philosophy conceived by our enemies. . . . In this manner, we have come to believe in the inferiority of the mestizo, in the unredemption of the Indian, in the damnation and the irreparable decadence of the Black."[34] Vasconcelos thus positioned his mestizo futurism as a more valid alternative to the scientific racism of his time.

Despite how anachronistic his terminology appears to us today, Vasconcelos's theory of mestizaje was quite radical in the 1920s, as it directly contradicted almost universally held views about the deleterious effects of mixture. He explicitly engaged with various strands of racial science. *The Cosmic Race* is suffused with references to eugenics and to the notion of Anglo-Saxon superiority derived from the arguments of the historical school of scientific racism. Vasconcelos agreed that the problem of the twentieth century (to borrow from Du Bois) was the "conflict of Latinism against Anglo-Saxonism; a conflict of institutions, aims and ideals." But he also engaged in various strategic racial inversions. He argued that "Latin predominance was unquestionable at the beginning" of the colonization of the Americas, and—contradicting claims that tropical climates led to indolence and decay—he claimed that South America's Latin colonizers had "seized the best regions ... while the English had to be satisfied with what was left to them by a more capable people."[35] The conflict between Latins and Anglo-Saxons in the twentieth century was now "set entirely in the New World," he argued, between the United States and Latin America. And one of the key differences between the two Americas was their attitude toward mixture. Whereas the United States practiced genocide and sought "exclusive dominion by the Whites," Latin America was "shaping a new race, a synthetic race."[36] Thoroughly inverting accepted racial hierarchies, Vasconcelos positioned mestizaje, which from the perspective of racial science was Latin America's Achilles heel, as the source of its superiority vis-à-vis the United States.

As a result of its widespread influence in Latin America, Vasconcelos (like Du Bois) was also forced to contend with eugenics, and he took on the arguments of US eugenicist Madison Grant, in particular. In *The Cosmic Race*, Vasconcelos repeatedly incorporates the language of eugenics, while altering its meaning. As Stepan has shown, Latin Americans took different approaches to the question of how to apply eugenics to their various national contexts; some argued that mixture would lead to whitening, while others resorted to a notion of "constructive miscegenation" (i.e., that mixtures between certain racial types, namely those that were not too distant, were productive).[37] Mexicans tended to adopt the second approach, but this did not mean "that Vasconcelos repudiated eugenics per se. On the contrary, Vasconcelos in keeping with his education as a man of science and letters, adopted the language of eugenics; but as with racial theory, he redesigned it to suit his own ends."[38] In *The Cosmic Race*, for example, Vasconcelos contrasted "scientific eugenics" to "aesthetic eugenics." The former led to condemnations of mixture, while the latter would proceed under the "law of personal taste." Yet Vasconcelos's aesthetic eugenics replicated existing racial rankings by incorporating the language of deliberate social selection characteristic of "scientific" eugenics. Thus, he argued that when aesthetic eugenics came to prevail: "The very ugly will not procreate, they will have no desire to procreate."[39] Under Vasconcelos's aesthetic eugenics then, anti-miscegenation statutes and forced sterilization of the unfit would be unnecessary because the less desirable would somehow cease to procreate of their own accord. There were thus limits to the extent to which racist science could be reimagined.

Vasconcelos was less equivocal in his refutation of US eugenicist Madison Grant's theory that the dominance of the superior "Nordic" race in the United States was being threatened by nonwhite immigration and mixture with inferior races. Vasconcelos read the French translation of *The Passing of the Great Race* published in 1926, after he had completed lecture tours in Puerto Rico and the Dominican Republic in which he presented the essays collected in *Indología*.[40] He discussed Grant's book in an appendix to the essay "El hombre," which sketched his theory of mestizaje and refuted the dominant view in racial science of mixture as degeneration. Vasconcelos explained that "as I was just about to complete the writing of this book, I have come across the one by Madison Grant, with a prologue by [Georges Vacher de] Lapouge, who, as I understand it, is one of the most respected skull-measurers [*midecráneos*] of those who have made the pseudo-science of anthropology."[41] Having dealt with Lapouge, Vasconcelos proceeded to debunk Grant's evidence for Nordic superiority. Yet he added that "despite it all, Grant's book is interesting, because it sets forth the antithesis to the doctrine that I formulate as the gospel for Latin America."[42] Vasconcelos argued that what really worried Grant was the fact that white dominance was being threatened in the United States: "in a fair fight Gobineau and Grant's providential blonds cannot always defeat, either the Jews ... or the Irish ... or blacks, whose music and dance prevail. ... Not only will they [whites] not dominate the planet, they will not even triumph in the United States." There was only one point on which Vasconcelos found himself in agreement with Grant, and this was the eugenicist insistence on limiting the reproduction of "inferior and degenerate types," although in his view these were not determined by race but by "economic situation and education." Moreover, this problem could only be truly solved, according to Vasconcelos, by "raising the social level of the masses."[43] In a subsequent essay, "La supremacia de los blancos"

(The supremacy of the whites) published in *La Prensa* (a Spanish-language newspaper in San Antonio, Texas), Vasconcelos observed that "there is not a single one of Grant's arguments that can withstand serious examination." Yet it was nevertheless necessary to pay attention to Grant's arguments, he explained to his US Latino and Latin American readers, because they served as the foundation for public policies such as: "blacks being concentrated in the South, leaving them together with us Mexicans" as a result of whites being supposedly unsuited for tropical climates. Indeed, such views had already led to the implementation of more restrictive US immigration policies. The relevant lesson that Latin America should derive from these debates about race in the US, Vasconcelos argued, was that "any race ... under just and free conditions, progresses immediately and becomes the equal of the highest human types. Grant's book and the history of the United States have convinced me of the opposite thesis to Grant's ... that we are all equal."[44] Vasconcelos concluded that Latinos and Latin Americans needed to recognize "once and for all, that our problem does not lie in being mestizos."[45] The need to counter white supremacist racist science, and US eugenics in particular, was thus a key impetus for Vasconcelos's theory of mestizaje.

Vasconcelos's theory of mestizaje was also part of an anti-colonial strand of Latin American political thought of which Sarmiento was an unlikely intellectual precursor. Vasconcelos viewed Sarmiento as a model. Gabriella De Beer, one of Vasconcelos's biographers, suggests that "in Sarmiento, Vasconcelos saw what he would have liked others to see in him ... Sarmiento symbolized the educated leader diametrically opposed to ... the military chieftain."[46] In an essay in *La Prensa* entitled "Sarmiento as Statesman," Vasconcelos lauded him as an example of a Latin American who fulfilled Plato's vision of a republic led by the wisest and most educated. According to Vasconcelos, Sarmiento's presidency had provided Latin America with "an argument against the tutelage of [the] Monroe [doctrine] and in favor of the full sovereignty of the [Latin] American nations."[47] In a hemispheric linkage that Sarmiento would have found enormously flattering given his admiration for Lincoln, Vasconcelos claimed that "America's glory days ... were the presidencies of Sarmiento ... in Argentina ... and Lincoln's administration in the United States."[48] Vasconcelos's admiration for Sarmiento is surprising precisely because of their deep disagreements on questions of race and Latin American identity, the impact of the Spanish legacy, and their stance vis-à-vis the United States.

Vasconcelos admired certain elements of Sarmiento's political thought, especially his critique of *caudillismo* and promotion of public education.[49] Like Sarmiento before him, Vasconcelos was deeply critical of *caudillismo*, and more specifically of the way political disorder threatened Latin American independence by facilitating US intervention. These issues were extremely pertinent in Mexico, which had already lost half its national territory to US expansion, and as its closest Latin American neighbor was the most vulnerable to US meddling. Additionally, political instability had been followed by the Díaz dictatorship. In a clear reference to Sarmiento, Vasconcelos condemned "those barbarous dictatorships that ... do nothing more than continue the tradition of *facundism* [facundismo] in a continent that generally lags in civilization."[50] He argued that if Latin America were able to "cast off the yoke of those barbarous caudillajes that are the reproach of some of our countries we will have eliminated at least half of the causes that threaten our destinies."[51] Vasconcelos thus viewed twentieth-century Latin American dictatorships, whether right- or left-wing, as the modern legacy of *caudillismo*. Moreover, for Vasconcelos the dangerous localism of *caudillismo* was an expression of the kind of shortsighted nationalism that prevented Latin American hemispheric political unity. Latin America, he argued, had not overcome European nationalism, and in so doing had exposed itself to US imperialism. "The founders of our new nationalism were, without knowing it, the best allies of the Anglo-Saxons."[52] While Sarmiento and Vasconcelos shared a critique of *caudillismo*, the latter went much farther in calling for Latin American regional unity than the former.

In fact, Vasconcelos and Sarmiento had totally inverted assessments of Spain and the United States. Sarmiento wrote at a time when the threat of US expansionism was beginning to be perceived but had not yet fully manifested itself, whereas during Vasconcelos's lifetime US intervention in Latin America was at its height. While Sarmiento criticized the effects of Spanish colonization and saw the United States as a political model for Latin America, Vasconcelos (being much further removed from the struggles for independence) valued the Spanish legacy and viewed the United States as a cautionary tale rather than a model. He noted, for example, that Sarmiento: "did not have a clear vision of the unity of the [Latin American] race. ... The Anglo-Saxon model weighed too much in his judgment."[53] Vasconcelos also vehemently disputed Sarmiento's view that the Spanish legacy was to blame for Latin American political problems. Instead, he argued, US intervention in Latin America had been furthered by "the cultural doctrine propagated throughout the continent of the uselessness of whatever is Spanish. Not even our best have escaped this anti-Spanish phobia. Sarmiento falls prey to it, even though he does not want to be taken for an Indian either."[54] For Vasconcelos, the nineteenth-century critique of the Spanish legacy opened the doors to US domination in the twentieth, encouraged by the "foreign-izing, Pan-Americanizing, Monroeist current fomented, without realizing its risks, by men of such eminent capacity as Sarmiento."[55]

The differences between Vasconcelos and Sarmiento's views of hemispheric relations are also evident in the shift from the discourse of "Ambas Américas" (both Americas), which was concerned with establishing horizontal ties between the United States and Latin America, to the notion of "Our America" (Latin America), which sought to unite the region against the United States.[56] There were moments when Vasconcelos formulated a notion of egalitarian coexistence in the Americas reminiscent of Sarmiento's "Ambas Américas" trope. In *Indología*, for example, he argued that Latin America and the United States were "the two cultures of the New World. That is why it is urgent … to find a way that these two cultures[,] rather than becoming spent and exhausted in conflict[,] reach an understanding and collaborate in progress."[57] In order for the United States to regain Latin American "friendship," however, Vasconcelos also argued that it needed to end its "illegitimate occupation" of Puerto Rico as well as Panama. If this were to come to pass, he argued: "True amity, which existed in the continent during the era of our independence, when all of our liberals turned to the United States in search of wisdom and advice, would be reestablished in an instant, to the advantage of both Americas."[58] In general, however, Vasconcelos emphasized the need for cultural and ethno-racial unity and Latin American Pan-Americanism in order to counter US hegemony.

Vasconcelos also rejected the United States as a political model, especially where race relations were concerned. If Sarmiento's travels to the United States showed him an ideal that he wished to emulate, Vasconcelos found in South America the hope for the future. In the travel sections of *The Cosmic Race* on his voyage to Brazil and Argentina, for example, he argued that "civilization has failed in North America and is transplanting itself, as always, to the South." Playing on one of the Spanish words for future, *porvenir*, whose literal translation is "to come," he argued that "Brazil is the future."[59] Sarmiento's model was the United States, Vasconcelos's was Latin America. In fact, contrary to Sarmiento's arguments in *Conflicto y armonías de las razas en América,* Vasconcelos exalted mixture as positive, not negative, and argued that Latin America should embrace its mestizo identity. He emphatically warned Latin Americans not to follow imported racial theories: "Let us take care not to imitate other peoples who create barriers based on color. ... Destiny has decreed that the races that live in Latin America should not be kept separate, but rather that they should continue to unite."[60] In contrast to Sarmiento's pessimism about mestizaje's effect on Latin American political capacities, Vasconcelos embraced it as a superior model of race relations than the racial segregation practiced in the United States.

In his driving preoccupation with hemispheric relations between the two Americas, Vasconcelos was indeed Sarmiento's heir, even as his prescription for how Latin America could assert itself as the United States's political equal was radically different. Vasconcelos and Sarmiento had thoroughly inverted views about which of the two Americas's racial system was more advantageous, and who was therefore the model where race relations were concerned. Vasconcelos was convinced that Latin America's superior racial politics were crucial to its ability to withstand US dominance in the hemisphere. His aim was thus not to transcend or deconstruct race. Rather, he urged Latin Americans to embrace a conception of their racial identity that would allow them to unite politically and resist US imperialism.

"A Doctrine that Nourished the Hopes of the Nonwhite Races": Latin American Mestizaje

The Cosmic Race (1925) and *Indología* (1926) were both published during the 1920s, an era when Vasconcelos was at his most politically radical; together, they contain the key elements of his arguments about mestizaje and Latin American identity. Yet most analyses of his theory of mestizaje rely almost exclusively on *The Cosmic Race*. Vasconcelos described *Indología* as "in a certain sense only an enlargement" of *The Cosmic Race*, but *Indología* contains significant departures from *The Cosmic Race*.[61] Despite being published only a year apart, there are important differences between the two texts. Juxtaposing *The Cosmic Race* and *Indología* reveals a couple of important ways in which *Indología* diverges from *The Cosmic Race*. First, *Indología* contains a significantly more positive portrayal of black and indigenous Latin Americans than *The Cosmic Race*. Second, *Indología* contains an incipient critique of the identification with whiteness of Latin American elites (which would be more fully articulated later in *Bolivarismo y Monroísmo*). In both *The Cosmic Race* and *Indología*, however, Vasconcelos continued to portray mestizaje as a process of harmonious fusion. As a result, he elided the violence of the conquest, and especially in *The Cosmic Race*, ignored racism within Latin America in the service of formulating a conception of Latin American racial identity as nonwhite that could function as an anti-colonial bulwark against US imperialism.

The Cosmic Race has been described as "a utopian fantasy" that reflected Vasconcelos's preoccupation with futurity.[62] It has become an iconic text, and a stand-in for Vasconcelos's mestizo futurism, which assigned a "providential" role to the Americas, and Latin America specifically.[63] Vasconcelos believed that Europe was "the continent where everything has already been tried ... [America is] the continent where things are being done."[64] Europe was the past, Latin America the future, and that future was mestizo. Vasconcelos thus reconceptualized mixture as beneficial for Latin America. He inverted dominant scientific claims about the negative effects of mixture and repurposed the idea of "constructive miscegenation" to fit a popular trope among early twentieth-century anti-colonial Latin American thinkers: that Latin America had developed a superior approach to race relations than its more powerful northern neighbor, and that the United States (and the world) had something to learn from the region's racial politics, specifically its openness to mixture.

Vasconcelos's theory of mestizaje as sketched in *The Cosmic Race* was that Latin America was at the vanguard of a historical movement toward the creation of a synthetic race that would combine all the best characteristics of all previous races. His theory encompassed three key propositions. First, contrary to the tenets of scientific racism, racial mixing did not lead to degeneration; instead it had positive effects. "In the contemporary period, while the pride of the present masters of the world asserts through the mouth of their scientists the ethnic and mental superiority of the Whites ... [they] are much slower, and almost dull, compared with the mestizo ... The truth is that vigor is renewed with graftings."[65] Second, the twentieth century was an era especially conducive to racial mixing, such that racial amalgamation was becoming the path of the future. He argued that: "The Indian has no other door to the future ... but the road already cleared by Latin civilization. The white man, as well, will have to depose his pride and look for progress and ulterior redemption in the souls of his brothers from other castes."[66] Finally, because Latin America was the region of the globe where mestizaje was most advanced, it was destined to play a key world-historical role. According to Vasconcelos, Latin America's "fundamental characteristic" was that it had produced a "fusion of ethnic stocks," and as a result it was destined to be the "cradle of a fifth race into which all nations will fuse with each other. . . . In this fashion the synthetic race that will gather all the treasures of History . . . shall be created."[67] While Vasconcelos's theory of mestizaje undoubtedly challenged some tenets of scientific racism, *The Cosmic Race* is also a text plagued with internal contradictions.

Positive recuperations of Vasconcelos's theory of mestizaje tend to gloss over the more unsavory moments in *The Cosmic Race*, which reproduced racist stereotypes about nonwhites and obscured Latin American anti-black and anti-indigenous racism.[68] The text contains multiple derogatory descriptions of nonwhites. The following passage regarding the benefits of racial mixing, with its use of the terminology of eugenics, is typical:

> The lower types of the species will be absorbed by the superior type. In this manner, for example, the Black could be redeemed, and step by step, by voluntary extinction, the uglier stocks will give way to the more handsome. . . . The Indian, by grafting onto the related race, would take the jump of millions of years . . . and in a few decades of aesthetic eugenics, the Black may disappear, together with the types that a free instinct of beauty may go on signaling as fundamentally recessive and undeserving, for that reason, of perpetuation.[69]

Vasconcelos included the caveat that it was the new mestizo race, not whites, that occupied the highest rung of his "ascending scale of ethnic improvement," but the existence of a racial hierarchy in which blacks and Indians were at the bottom remained constant. He described other nonwhite groups in similarly unflattering terms, noting the Chinese tendency to "multiply like mice," for example. Perhaps because he believed that "superior types" would absorb "inferior stocks," Vasconcelos celebrated the benefits of incorporating traits from all racial groups into the new synthetic race. Describing the various elements that composed the Latin American mestizo, he wrote:

> His soul resembles the old Mayan cenote. . . . This infinite quietude is stirred with the drop put in our blood by the Black, eager for sensual joy, intoxicated with dances and unbridled lust. There also

appears the Mongol, with the mystery of his slanted eyes that see everything according to a strange angle. . . . The clear mind of the White, that resembles his skin and his dreams, also intervenes. Judaic striae hidden within the Castilian blood since the days of the cruel expulsion now reveal themselves, along with Arabian melancholy, as a remainder of the sickly Muslim sensuality. Who has not a little of all this, or does not wish to have all?"[70]

Given this litany of negative traits ascribed to nonwhite racial groups, it is difficult to believe that Vasconcelos found much to value in them. These kinds of "racial eruptions" recur throughout *The Cosmic Race*.[71] They demonstrate the kind of selective reading entailed in depictions of Vasconcelos's iconic text as racially egalitarian.

In fact, the key factor that lends the appearance of plausibility to Vasconcelos's contentions about Latin American racial harmony is his continuous recourse to hemispheric comparison in *The Cosmic Race*. Comparisons between US and Latin American racial politics pervade the text. They function to vindicate Latin America's supposedly superior race relations. For instance, Vasconcelos drew a stark contrast between "spontaneous mixing" in Latin America and "the inflexible line that separates the Blacks from the Whites in the United States, and the laws, each time more rigorous, for the exclusion of the Japanese and Chinese from California."[72] While he was forced to acknowledge that Latin American countries (including Mexico) had also adopted immigration restrictions against Asians at the time, Vasconcelos claimed that they had done so for economic reasons, not because they were also motivated by anti-Asian racism.

> If we reject the Chinese, it is because man, as he progresses, multiplies less, and feels the horror of numbers. . . . In the United States Asians are rejected because of the same fear of physical overflow . . . but also because Americans simply do not like Asians, even despise them, and would be incapable of intermarriage with them. The ladies of San Francisco have refused to dance with officials of the Japanese navy, who are men as clean, intelligent, and, in their way, as handsome as those of any other navy in the world.[73]

This explanation of the supposedly different motivations for restrictions on Asian immigration in the two Americas is entirely in keeping with how comparative references to US racism function in *The Cosmic Race*. In it mestizaje is continually juxtaposed to racial segregation in the United States, and the mere existence of mixture serves as proof of Latin America's supposed lack of racism.

Despite the brief allusion above to the aesthetic preferences of US (white) women, Vasconcelos's theory of mestizaje is striking in its silence about gender and sexuality. This is a noteworthy omission given the fact that, as we saw with Du Bois, public and scientific debates about mixture during this era were overdetermined by questions of gender and sexuality. Vasconcelos's account of mestizaje is masculinist in two ways: women are rarely mentioned in his texts and when they do appear it is mainly as objects of the male sexual gaze. There are numerous examples of this in the travel sections of *The Cosmic Race* and *Indología*. In his account of his tour of Brazil in *The Cosmic Race*, for example, "beautiful women" are a recurring element of the landscape for Vasconcelos. His descriptions of Rio de Janeiro are peppered with references to "an abundance of beautiful women."[74] Women also rarely appear in *Indología*, and then only as sexualized objects of Vasconcelos's gaze. For example, he described the women at a party he attended in the Dominican Republic as follows: "The women dance, the young girls dance. There is an inciting little blond teacher, who has all the men swooning . . . the tender and virtuous matron is [also] present, as are the seductive mulatta and the sentimental young girl."[75] Yet, for a theorist of mixture, Vasconcelos generally has little to say about who is involved in making the new mestizo race and how mixing is supposed to occur. This absence of explicit discussions of gender and sexuality in Vasconcelos is in stark contrast to the way sexualized patriarchal gender relations overdetermine the work of the other major twentieth-century Latin American theorist of mestizaje, the Brazilian Gilberto Freyre.[76] It is also one of the ways in which Vasconcelos's mestizo futurism differs from Du Bois's mulatto fictions.

In contrast to Du Bois, who emphasizes the theme of sexual violence against black women and women of color, Vasconcelos tended to sidestep the question of differential power relations in mestizaje. He glossed over the issue of how racism shaped experiences of mixture by turning it into a question of aesthetic preferences, even as he acknowledged that notions of beauty were shaped by prevailing ideas about race. For example, in a moment of either extreme naiveté or willful ignorance, given his extensive knowledge of racial science's negative views of mixture, he suggested: "At present, partly because of hypocrisy, and partly because unions are made between miserable persons in an unfortunate state, we see with profound horror the marriage of a black woman and a white man. We would feel no repugnance at all if it were the union of a black Apollo and a blond Venus."[77] Madison Grant and other eugenicists were unlikely to have been persuaded of the benefits of mixing with even the most beautiful specimens of "inferior races." In fact, one of the rare exceptions to Vasconcelos's silence about the fact that historically mixture was most often the result of sexual violence occurs in his discussion of "scientific" versus "aesthetic" eugenics in *The Cosmic Race*. He believed that there were three stages of human development, in the first "material or warlike" stage, he acknowledged that "the mixing of bloods has also been imposed by material power. . . . There can be no selection where the strong take . . . the vanquished female." As humanity evolved to the higher stages, however, he argued that "racial mixing . . . obeys the fancy of free instinct."[78] Silences are often as instructive as that which is explicitly stated in a text.[79] Vasconcelos's silence about gender and sexuality is partially explained by the imperatives of a theory that wished to situate Latin American mestizaje as indicative of racial egalitarianism. This required erasing both the sexual violence of the colonial era, as well as glossing over the continuation of colonial racial hierarchies into post-independence Latin American societies.

While there are significant continuities between *The Cosmic Race* and *Indología*, there are also important differences between the two texts. *Indología* is composed of essays on various topics, including: racial science, education, Latin American thought, and so on. The essays were delivered as lectures on a speaking tour by Vasconcelos to the Dominican Republic and Puerto Rico. *Indología* also contains a travel section, as the lengthy prologue, instead of a standard introduction, is more of a travelogue describing his experiences delivering the lectures. Like *The Cosmic Race*, *Indología* is not entirely devoid of racist stereotypes about blacks or negative assessments of indigenous cultures. On balance, however, the "racial eruptions" in *Indología* are minimal compared to those in *The Cosmic Race*. In *Indología*, black and indigenous Latin Americans are depicted as more active co-contributors in the development of the region's mestizo identity. When Vasconcelos laments his lack of black ancestry or refers to elements of pre-conquest indigenous peoples's cultures admiringly in *Indología*, there is less cause for skepticism than in *The Cosmic Race*.

In contrast to *The Cosmic Race*'s relative silence about black and indigenous Latin Americans, Vasconcelos described the African presence as a key component of the region's identity in *Indología*. In the prologue, he rebuked those who were ashamed of Latin America's African ancestry. Replying to a local interlocutor who observed that a prominent Puerto Rican nationalist whom he had praised was a mulatto, Vasconcelos reflected:

> As if being a mulatto was not the most illustrious citizenship card in America! I believe even Bolívar was one. He was, if we are to believe the English descriptions, notwithstanding that today they would have him be the descendant of blue-blooded ancestors from I don't know which strain of pure Basque stock. Unfortunately I don't have black blood, but I have a small fraction of indigenous blood, and I think that it is to this that I owe a greater breadth of feeling than most whites, and a kernel of a culture that was already enlightened when Europe was still savage.[80]

There are thus moments in *Indología* when Vasconcelos criticized the tendency of Latin American elites to deny their black and indigenous heritage. This is an implied acknowledgment of internal racism in Latin America. Such moments of consistency in the application of his critique of white supremacy to Latin America lend a certain credence to Vasconcelos's claim (made in reference to Puerto Rican nationalism, but adapted here to refer to his theory of mestizaje) that it was: "a doctrine that nourished the hopes of the nonwhite races."[81]

There are other moments in *Indología* when Vasconcelos condemns the pretensions to whiteness of Latin American elites and contrasts it negatively to the lesser degree of internalized racism among their darker-complexioned co-nationals. Describing the reception to his lectures on race in the Dominican Republic, for example, he claimed that it was black Dominicans who had been most receptive to his argument:

> Such a mixed-race country would have to welcome such a talk with interest. ... I do not exaggerate when I say that in certain sites where people of color are plentiful I was received like a kind of Messiah. ... I noticed the most interest among the faces of the blacks, because they, in contrast to the mulatto, do not try to hide a truth that cannot be denied, nor do they renege of a color that was the aristocracy of the earth possibly five thousand years ago. ... The white [man] was then like an albino rat, hidden in burrows or covered by the trees.[82]

The interest black Dominicans evinced in Vasconcelos's critique of racial science's condemnation of mestizaje could be read as indicative of their desire to whiten by identifying as mixed rather than black, however.[83] But as his reference to the internalized racism of mulattoes demonstrates, at the time this was not how Vasconcelos understood the implications of his critique of scientific racism's negative view of mixture. At certain moments in *Indología*, then, he claims not to have envisioned mestizaje as a form of whitening.

Indología is also more positive in its depiction of indigenous peoples than *The Cosmic Race*, although on this point the text is more equivocal. Vasconcelos decried the despotism of the Aztecs and the Incas, for example, even as he expressed admiration for other indigenous peoples. Of the Mayas and Quechuas, he wrote:

> the great cities, the prodigious architecture, the splendid decorative art, the full arrangement of the constructions demonstrate that, when the Spaniards arrived in America calling themselves the bearers of civilization, in reality civilization, or at least one of the greatest manifestations of human civilization, not only had already manifested itself, but had already decayed in America . . . before the existence of Europe as a cultured region, there had already flourished in Central America and the Yucatan, empires and civilizations whose architecture, at least, has nothing to envy of and indeed in many aspects surpasses European architecture proper.[84]

Elsewhere in the text Vasconcelos's passionate defense of the legacy of Spanish colonization in Latin America led him to belittle or dismiss the accomplishments of indigenous peoples, however. He praised the educational efforts of the Spanish missionaries, for example, and disputed the notion that the destruction of indigenous cultures that accompanied the conquest represented a loss. Contradicting his previous recognition of the existence of advanced indigenous cultures in some areas of pre-conquest Latin America, Vasconcelos claimed that Spanish Catholic missionaries had inducted willing Indians into a superior culture:

> Not a few Indians, as they became educated, entered fully to take advantage of social life in a civilization like ours, which never established barriers of color or blood. . . . The missionaries have been accused of . . . extirpating the beliefs of the conquered people. . . . In

our continent, material conquest was accompanied by the destruction of indigenous ideology; but the ideology that was destroyed was replaced [by another], and I do not believe anyone will seriously deny that the replacement was advantageous.[85]

Vasconcelos's denial of the claim that the conquest represented a loss for indigenous peoples was entirely consistent with the imperatives of a conception of Latin American mestizaje as harmonious fusion that sought to erase the violence of Spanish colonization.

Indeed, Vasconcelos was a critic of *indigenismo*, which he viewed as promoting false narratives about the splendor of pre-conquest indigenous cultures that unfairly maligned the Spanish conquest and led indigenous peoples to delude themselves into believing that autochthonous cultural renewal was possible.[86] He presented indigenous integration into mestizo national identities and cultures in Latin America as preferable to the US model of creating reservations, which he described as "the path of death by isolation."[87] In contrast, via mestizaje, indigenous Latin Americans were able to become the "ally and at times co-author of a great culture."[88] Vasconcelos made these claims in defense of his decision as Minister of Education to reject a proposal to create separate schools for indigenous students. In a jab at elite mestizos influenced by *indigenismo*, he suggested that implementing US style-racial segregation in Mexico would be impossible because it would be difficult to "specify who should fall within it and who should not, as many of those who favor the American system would have been interned as Indians, if they were to present themselves in the United States."[89] Here hemispheric comparison between US and Latin American racial politics operated to buttress Vasconcelos's rejection of the desire to preserve a distinct indigenous identity, such that indigenous education could be delegitimized by being equated with racial segregation.[90] Vasconcelos believed that the Spanish legacy was the most crucial component of Latin American identity. He was thus unwilling or unable to envision indigenous Latin Americans as anything except (at best) co-contributors to mestizaje.

Indología also contains a critique of the propensity of Latin American elites to deny the region's black and indigenous ancestry, however. For example, Vasconcelos acknowledged that *mulataje* and Afro-indigenous mixture had been part of Latin American mestizaje:

Let us continue with our mestizaje. ... Let us also pay attention to the fact that alongside the older indo-Hispanic one another humbler mixing process has occurred, that is also important as a factor ... and is also endowed with rare virtues: the mixing of Spaniard and black and of Portuguese and black, the mulatto, which has given so many illustrious sons to our nations. ... Add to these mixtures ... indigenous mixture, black mixture, and the combination of these two types. ... For the first time so many and such diverse peoples have united in the same vast region of the world on equal footing.[91]

The implication of this call to recognize black and indigenous participation in Latin American mestizaje was that the region's elites should cease trying to deny or distance themselves from a nonwhite regional identity. At the same time, however, Vasconcelos still described *mulataje* and Afro-indigenous mestizaje as "humbler" mixtures, and they are both presented as part of a harmonious process of fusion. Vasconcelos's theorization of mixture in *Indología* thus encompassed both: (1) the valorization of a homogeneous mestizo subject that precluded recognizing the existence of black and indigenous Latin Americans as distinct peoples, and (2) an incipient critique of Latin American elites's tendency to identify with whiteness.

Vasconcelos's critique of the racial self-hatred of Latin American elites is clearest in the appendix refuting the ideas of US eugenicist Madison Grant. There, Vasconcelos articulated a scathing critique of Latin American elites who failed to accurately perceive their location within global white supremacy.

Because of the little white blood we have, we think as if we were an outpost of colonization among the Indians. ... This spiritual servility is what leads me to renege of some of our own and *to say once and for all that we are not white*. This assertion is particularly scandalous to the semi-whites who gad about Europe pretending to be Parisian. Very well, let them hide behind the door of any of the luxury hotels they tend to frequent off of the sweat of the enslaved Indian and they will see how they, who lord it over the Indians, are treated by any of these citizens of France; immediately they will hear themselves being called mixed. The white Argentinean ... as much as the dark Mexican or the Dominican or the Cuban. ... We belong to a colonial, semi-independent population threatened by the white imperialisms of Europe and the United States.[92]

This moment is notable for a number of reasons. Vasconcelos's frustration with the aspirations to whiteness of Latin American elites is palpable. The passage also recognizes the existence of Latin American racial hierarchy, something that is almost entirely absent from *The Cosmic Race*. This is evident in the reference to "semi-whites" who view themselves as "an outpost of colonization among the Indians," "lord it over the Indians," and live "off of the sweat of the enslaved Indian." Not only did Vasconcelos at certain moments acknowledge Latin American racism in *Indología*, like Du Bois he connected his analysis of racism in the Americas to an anti-colonial critique of global white supremacy. Despite the differences between their mestizo futurisms, then, Vasconcelos and Du Bois's ideas about race were not as fundamentally at odds as they are often understood to be.[93]

In fact, Vasconcelos's aim was not so much to deconstruct or disavow race, but rather to encourage Latin Americans to embrace a particular conception of their racial identity as nonwhite, mixed-race peoples, which would in turn allow them to unite politically in order to confront US imperialism. He argued that Latin America was "a perfectly homogeneous ethnic group. ... *We constitute a homogeneous racial whole*, as homogeneous as any other homogeneous race on earth."[94] It was this sense of common racial identity which would enable the region's "spiritual fusion and political confederation."[95] Vasconcelos was thus highly critical of other Latin American intellectuals who claimed that race did not exist. This critique would later be fully developed in *Bolivarismo y Monroísmo*, which contains Vasconcelos's most extensive and direct discussion of the theme of Latinos's position in US racial politics. In contrast to *The Cosmic Race*, in the 1930s Vasconcelos's analysis of racism against Latinos in the United States during the racial terror of the nadir era served to demonstrate how global white supremacy continued to shape the lives of Latin Americans.

"We Live Deceived": Latinos and US Racial Politics during the Nadir

Despite his promise? threat? in *Indología* that he would no longer write about "these trite issues of race and Iberoamericanism," Vasconcelos continued to do so.[96] This is especially true of *Bolivarismo y Monroísmo*, which was published in 1934, during Vasconcelos's second period of exile in the 1930s, a significant portion of which was spent in the United States.[97] The ostensible theme of *Bolivarismo y Monroísmo* was the struggle between

US imperialism (Monroe-ism) and Latin American Pan-Americanism (Bolivarism), but it contains Vasconcelos's most extensive analysis of US racial politics, and of anti-Latino racism specifically. While there are numerous references to US racism in *The Cosmic Race*, they function as a foil in comparison to which Latin America's superior racial harmony is revealed. Notably, the examples of US racism in *The Cosmic Race* are not instances of racial discrimination against Latinos; instead Vasconcelos pointed to xenophobic attitudes toward the Japanese and Chinese in California or the existence of racial segregation against blacks. In contrast, *Bolivarismo y Monroísmo* contains multiple references to racial discrimination against Mexican Americans in the Southwest and toward Latin American immigrants.

Writing to a Latin American audience prone to dismiss the significance of race, Vasconcelos sought to demonstrate the continued salience of racism. Against both liberals, for whom race was not a legitimate political category, and Marxists, who believed that the relevant category was international class struggle, Vasconcelos argued that globally there was a "policy firmly rooted in the fact of the inequality between men on the basis of color and race. ... Race may be debatable as a biological thesis, but that does not render any less true the fact that race produces important and notable socio-economic consequences everywhere."[98] The aim of Vasconcelos's analysis of domestic US racial politics in *Bolivarismo y Monroísmo* was thus not so much to assert Latin America's superior approach to race relations as it had been in *The Cosmic Race*, but rather to persuade the region's intellectuals of the continued salience of race.

The open adherence to white supremacy and ubiquitous racial terror that characterized the nadir of US race relations during the early twentieth century also affected Latinos. Not only was this an era of heightened anti-immigrant sentiment, like African Americans, Latinos were also targets of racial violence. In addition to the passage of restrictive immigration laws aimed at curbing the flow of nonwhite immigrants, during the 1930s anti-immigrant campaigns resulted in tens of thousands of Mexicans and Mexican Americans being pressured, through raids and job denials, to leave the United States. Latinos were also targets of racial terror, especially Mexican Americans in the Southwest, hundreds of whom were lynched during this era. The US Spanish-language newspapers that Vasconcelos published in, and no doubt read, documented these *linchamientos* (lynchings) of Latinos.[99]

Unlike Sarmiento, who lived in the United States during Reconstruction, a period during which the United States seemed committed to racial justice, Vasconcelos wrote and resided in the United States during "the nadir," when white supremacy was explicitly adhered to as official ideology and racial violence was commonplace. *Bolivarismo y Monroísmo* demonstrates that Vasconcelos was well-aware of the heightened racial terror and anti-immigrant sentiment in the United States during this era. The text contains multiple references to the Ku Klux Klan and lynching. "Black freedom is a myth in the US South," he wrote, "and the killings due to racial hatred, the lynchings, tell us that our Indians would have nothing to gain" by being incorporated into such a system.[100] Vasconcelos's descriptions of US racism showed the contradiction between its self-conception as a democracy and the reality of racial subordination.

The almost offhand way in which Vasconcelos incorporated information about lynching in *Bolivarismo y Monroísmo* speaks to how ubiquitous racial terror was during this era and to how widespread knowledge of it was. For example, in a passage about an entirely different subject (US ability to influence coverage in Latin American newspapers), he observed that were the US media to do the same, the company in question: "Would last as long as a lynching does, that is two or three hours."[101] The casual insertion here of the approximate duration of a lynching, an event that Vasconcelos presumably never attended, speaks to how normalized racial terror was during this era. Vasconcelos also made it clear in *Bolivarismo y Monroísmo* that racism was not restricted to the South. He noted that segregation operated in the entire country. He explained to his Latin American readers that there is a "chasm that in North America separates the white Methodist from the black Methodist. Not even to pray do Anglo-Saxons and blacks gather together in the same church."[102] In *Bolivarismo y Monroísmo* references to racial terror in the United States during the nadir era thus functioned to convince Latin Americans of the continued salience of race, not to absolve Latin America of racism (as was the case in *The Cosmic Race*).

Indeed, Vasconcelos reiterated and amplified *Indología*'s critique of elite Latin American intellectuals's tendency to identify with whiteness in *Bolivarismo y Monroísmo*. In order to rebut Latin American arguments "against race," he pointed to racial discrimination against Latinos in the United States:

> Tell us then, messieurs theorists, that the problem of race does not exist in America; tell that to the Mexicans expelled after they had forged patrimonies in territories such as Texas and California

that used to be theirs and where a treaty guarantees them asylum. Preach it to the South American workers who to find a decent job in the United States would have to join Unions that *do not admit them*, because, despite their socialist ideology, they do not reserve places within their ranks neither for blacks nor negroids nor Mexicans or South Americans. That is reality as it exists.[103]

He also suggested that too many Latin American intellectuals were willing adherents to doctrines of white supremacy. In Latin America, he argued: "The doctrine of the Ku-Klux-Klan has been broadcast with the endorsement of our intellectual heroes. ... Preaching the survival of the fittest was satisfying to many of our brown professors, as if by proclaiming it they could escape the supposed penalty of their color."[104] Instead, Vasconcelos sought to remind his fellow Latin American intellectuals that race relations needed to be understood within the context of global white supremacy:

Race does not exist, habitually shouts the [Latin American] pariah forced to serve as a wage laborer, now to the English, tomorrow to the French. But the French, the English, the Germans, the oppressors, practice caste within their territories ... [we can believe race does not exist] when we see the English sharing a table with the Hindus, their co-nationals within the [British] Empire, or the day that the Yankees share a railroad car with their black compatriots. The warning I am formulating does not seek to establish among us petty distinctions, but rather to demonstrate the extent to which we live deceived.[105]

This and other passages like it in *Bolivarismo y Monroísmo* point to a recognition on Vasconcelos's part of the way racism shaped global colonial relations that was absent from *The Cosmic Race*'s vision of mestizaje as proto-color-blindness.

It is important to keep in mind that Vasconcelos was speaking to other elite Latin Americans who were the beneficiaries of racial privilege, however. It was proto-white, elite Latin Americans who experienced a loss of privilege when they were racialized as nonwhite outside the region. Black and indigenous Latin Americans did not need to cross the US–Mexico border (or travel to Europe) to experience racialization or realize the existence of racism. His analysis thus prefigures contemporary discourses about Latinos "discovering" race upon their arrival in the

United States that overlook how race and social class stratification shape the experience of migration.

Vasconcelos was emphatic about the fact that Latin American elites were often blind to their subordinate position within global white supremacy. The racialization of all Latin Americans as nonwhite, and the low position they occupied within US domestic racial hierarchies once they crossed the border served as key evidence for his argument.

> The super-white criollos of our continent tend to smirk at North American racial distinctions, believing that they are beyond the reach of the metric that is applied to the Indians, the rule that affects the Chinese and the blacks. If the occasion allows, they will learn right away that light skin bestows a rank that lasts only as long as their pesos. The instant they search for work, they will learn that racism places the Spaniard . . . in a similar category as the Berber.[106]

Because even light-skinned Latin Americans were viewed as at best "pseudo-whites" in the United States and Europe, Vasconcelos argued, the region's elite should abandon its futile aspirations to whiteness. Latin American denials of race functioned as pleas for inclusion into whiteness, not as a challenge to it: "Our snobbery points in the direction of the strong . . . it obscures the servile desire to reject the ethnic reality that constitutes us. The timidity and mimicry of an inferior species leads our Europeanizers and Saxon-izers to view themselves bovaristically as different from what they are. But such a false, ineffective, posture precipitates ruin instead, it does not prevent it."[107] Comparisons between US and Latin American race relations in *Bolivarismo y Monroísmo* thus did not function to demonstrate Latin America's more egalitarian racial politics (as they had in *The Cosmic Race*), but rather as the basis for a critique of mistaken elite Latin American racial self-conceptions.

Bolivarismo y Monroísmo also contains Vasconcelos's most extensive discussion of racial discrimination against US Latinos. He argued that Latin American populations that had become part of the United States as a result of imperial expansion, such as Puerto Ricans and Mexican Americans in the Southwest, represented a warning for what awaited the rest of Latin America.

> The example of Texas, conquered forty years ago, shows us what the Latin American could expect from such an advance of racial

imperialism. The entire Mexican population, that is Hispanic-
American, of California and Texas, a population the majority of
which is as white as the whitest Argentinean criollo, as the whitest
Spaniard from Castile, now finds itself subordinated, dispossessed
of its property, its language bastardized, proletarianized in body
and soul.[108]

Vasconcelos observed that Mexican Americans were subjected to forcible
assimilation, and all Latin American immigrants, regardless of skin color,
faced racial discrimination in employment. "Every worker from Argentina
or Mexico that offers his labor in the sweatshops of Yankeeland discovers,
right away, that the nature of his blood bars him from the best jobs." And
this could not be attributed simply to a language barrier, as "Jews and
blacks speak good English," but they were also denied the best jobs.[109]
Because of Latinos's place in the US racial order, Vasconcelos argued, all
Latin American immigrants were subjected to racial discrimination:

> There is no race, we think, until the day that crossing the US border
> reveals that we have already been classified, and before being given
> the opportunity to define ourselves. And it will be totally pointless
> at that moment to recall the vague lineages and literary opinions
> that want to situate us in the Mediterranean or Scotland . . . the fool-
> ish and naïve Latin American who in his country believed that race
> had been abolished and that all men are equal discovers, shortly
> after moving to the United States, that there is a rigid unwritten hi-
> erarchy that determines one's place in society and also one's salary.
> And if he digs a bit more deeply he will verify that the highest posi-
> tions in the land . . . all are in the hands of the aristocracy of the
> pure bloods of New England.[110]

In the case of Latinos, this strict racial hierarchy manifested itself in
particular in employment discrimination, according to Vasconcelos. In
the United States, he argued, there was a salary scale that matched "the
racial classifications of the Department of Immigration," with Northern
Europeans at the top followed by Southern Europeans and the Irish,
"blacks with US or British citizenship, the Chinese, and at the bottom of
the scale, South Americans and Mexicans."[111] While Vasconcelos's claim
that Latinos were at the bottom of the US racial order during the nadir era
is highly debatable, he painted a picture of systematic racial discrimination

against Latinos that was intended to persuade Latin Americans at home to abandon their futile aspirations of inclusion into whiteness.

Vasconcelos's Latin American contemporaries did not necessarily share his view that Latin Americans needed to embrace a nonwhite mestizo identity in order to successfully confront US imperialism, however. Neither did many US Latinos at the time. The early twentieth century was an era of heightened anti-imperialism in Latin America, but this did not necessarily mean that other intellectuals in the region shared Vasconcelos's critique of global white supremacy. Some Latin American intellectuals, especially those on the right, continued to deny the salience of race and embraced a project of whitening.[112] Leftist intellectuals, meanwhile, critiqued Vasconcelos as insufficiently radical; they viewed him as too attached to Spain's colonial legacy and lacking a social class analysis. In a review of *Bolivarismo y Monroísmo* published in the New York City Spanish-language newspaper *La Nueva Democracia*, for example, Luis Alberto Sánchez, a Peruvian intellectual and member of the APRA party (*Alianza Popular Revolucionaria Americana* or American Popular Revolutionary Alliance), lauded Vasconcelos's anti-imperialism. At the same time, in line with the *indigenismo* of the APRA, Sánchez critiqued Vasconcelos's "Hispanic-American ideal" as privileging a shared Spanish legacy while being insufficiently attentive to the indigenous legacy that was also an integral part of mestizaje.[113] According to Sánchez, to embrace Bolivarism as defined by Vasconcelos (i.e., the unity of all Latin American nations that shared a "Spanish culture") would imply acceptance of "the triumphal survival of the Colonial over the autochthonous organizations . . . forgetting indigenous resistance . . . and the actual existence of a Pre-Hispanic indigenous culture."[114] As Sánchez's astute critique demonstrates, despite its noteworthy challenge to the identification with whiteness of Latin American elites, Vasconcelos's conception of mestizo regional identity in *Bolivarismo y Monroísmo* continued to subordinate black and indigenous Latin Americans in significant ways.

During the 1930s, US Latinos, and especially Mexican Americans, also did not necessarily adopt Vasconcelos's suggestion to embrace a nonwhite racial identity given the realities of white supremacy and US racial politics. Instead, many Mexican Americans sought to avoid the heightened racism of the nadir era by seeking legal inclusion into whiteness. One of the clearest examples of this strategy was the response to the introduction of "Mexican" as an option in the "race or color" category in the census of 1930. This was the first and only time that "Mexican" appeared as a separate racial category in the US census. It contravened a historical pattern of counting Mexican Americans as "white"; between 1850 and 1920 Mexican Americans were included in the "white" category. According to sociologist Laura Gómez:

> The classification of Mexicans as a racial group coincided with the Great Depression, and with increased economic competition between whites and Mexicans, both native-born and immigrant. This negative economic climate fomented anti-Mexican racism, violence, and government hostility, including mass deportation (to Mexico). More than 400,000 Mexican-origin persons, including many American citizens were rounded up by police and deported during this period. In Los Angeles fully one third of the Mexican American population returned to Mexico during the 1930s, either forcibly or voluntarily (in anticipation of the round-ups). ... The racist, violent events of the 1930s were a sharp reminder to Mexican Americans of their marginal status. Although they were formally U.S. citizens, their Mexican American racial status kept them in a second-class position.[115]

Mexican American organizations such as the League of United Latin American Citizens (LULAC), supported by the Mexican government and its representatives in the United States, protested the creation of the separate "Mexican" racial category and succeeded in having Mexican Americans reclassified as white in the next census.[116] As Gómez observes, the strategy of legal inclusion into whiteness did not safeguard Latinos from the racial violence of the nadir era. As Vasconcelos warned, it also did not challenge the prevailing racial order.

By the 1960s, however, US Latinos embraced Vasconcelos's ideas and adapted them to serve their own political needs. US Latino invocations of Vasconcelos from the 1960s onwards have primarily drawn on *The Cosmic Race*. For example, Vasconcelos's arguments have been used to defend a pan-national conception of US Latinidad. An editorial entitled "La raza cósmica" published in a Chicago-based Spanish language newspaper in 1960, drew on Vasconcelos in order to challenge the creation of a local organization only for Mexican Americans that would have excluded the city's Puerto Rican population.[117] Similarly, the more radical Latino organizations that were founded after LULAC, especially those associated with the Chicano movement of the 1960s, embraced Vasconcelos's theory of mestizaje. The National Council of La Raza, founded in 1968, for example, which bills itself as "the largest national Hispanic civil rights and advocacy organization in the United States," derives its name from Vasconcelos's work. The organization's website explains that the term "la raza":

> was coined by Mexican scholar José Vasconcelos to reflect the fact that the people of Latin America are a mixture of many of the world's races, cultures, and religions . . . the full term coined by Vasconcelos, 'la raza cósmica,' meaning 'the cosmic people,' was developed to reflect not purity but the mixture inherent in the Hispanic people. This is an inclusive concept, meaning that Hispanics share with all other peoples of the world a common heritage and destiny.[118]

Chicana/o organizations in the 1960s thus did eventually adopt positions similar to Vasconcelos's call in the 1930s to embrace mixture, not as a form of whitening, but as a pan-Latin American (and pan-Latino) non-white racial identity that could challenge Anglo dominance.

Yet the question of whether Latinos should view themselves, and act politically, as a group with a collective racial identity grounded on shared experiences of racialization and discrimination in the United States, regardless of skin color, remains a contested one to this day.[119] As was the case in the 1930s, this debate, which is partly about the racial politics of US Latinidad, is once again playing out on the terrain of census categorization. The Census Bureau's decision to convert Hispanic or Latino into a racial category in the 2020 census, as opposed to allowing Latinos to check one or more of the existing racial categories (black, white, multiracial, etc.) as has been the case since 1980, has generated significant controversy. Some Latinos view this as the imposition of a US notion of race that is at odds with the fact that Latin Americans view their identity in cultural and ethnic, rather than racial, terms.[120] Others fear that shared racialization under a "brown" or pan-ethnic Latino category will obscure the fact that "there are very distinct social outcomes in terms of intermarriage, housing segregation, educational attainment, prison sentencing, labor market outcomes and so on that vary for Latinos according to racial status."[121] Vasconcelos's arguments in *Bolivarismo y Monroísmo* appear to have been directed more at Latin Americans than US Latinos, but as exemplified in the current debate about whether Latino/a should be a racial category on the census, his call for Latin Americans to embrace a racial identity as nonwhite to counter US imperialism and Anglo dominance is also relevant to late-twentieth- and early-twenty-first-century debates about the racial politics of US Latinidad.

Vasconcelos's analysis of Latinos's subordinate location within the US racial order in the 1930s in *Bolivarismo y Monroísmo* contains a potentially more radical critique of the racial politics of US Latinidad than the iconic mestizo futurism of *The Cosmic Race*. It is thus ironic that subsequent Chicano/a appropriations of Vasconcelos would selectively draw upon the more problematic aspects of his political thought on race. By adopting *The Cosmic Race*'s myth of mestizaje as racial egalitarianism without paying sufficient attention to the problematic way discussions of US racial politics function within the text, Vasconcelos's Chicano appropriators bypassed other moments in his oeuvre, such as *Bolivarismo y Monroísmo*, that directly contend with anti-Latino racism in the United States.

"The Future Will Belong to the Mestiza": Anzaldúa and Mestizaje's Travels

Given the anti-imperial function of its celebration of Latin America's supposedly more harmonious race relations vis-à-vis the United States, the appeal of Vasconcelos's theory of mestizaje to Latin Americans is clear. As Nicandro F. Juárez argued in the Chicano Studies journal *Aztlán* in 1973, however, "It is less easy to understand why Vasconcelos is heralded as a revolutionary by some present-day Chicano leaders."[122] Indeed, reflecting the hemispheric travels of Vasconcelos's theory of mestizaje, what is today the most widely read version of *The Cosmic Race* was published in 1979 by the Department of Chicano studies at UCLA. It is a bilingual edition that reproduced only a part of the original Spanish text. In addition to the essay, "Mestizaje," it includes the brief prologue Vasconcelos appended to the 1948 Spanish edition (which included the travel essays) but omits the lengthy travel sections on Brazil and Argentina. As Vasconcelos's work has traveled north it has thus done so in truncated form. Even more puzzling than Chicano activists drawing on Vasconcelos in the 1960s and 1970s, however, is the continued influence of his theory of mestizaje on later generations of US Latino thinkers. Chicana feminist Gloria Anzaldúa, for example, who was a critic of the previous generation of male Chicano nationalists, nevertheless also invoked Vasconcelos.[123] That Anzaldúa would cite *The Cosmic Race* is surprising given the contrasting accounts of mestizo lived subjectivity that she and Vasconcelos formulated. For Anzaldúa, mestiza consciousness was fluid, fractured, hybrid;

for Vasconcelos, mestizaje was a seamless process of harmonious synthesis. Moreover, in contrast to Vasconcelos's silence on gender and sexuality, Anzaldúa "queers" mestizaje by highlighting queer, female Chicanas as the pre-eminent US Latino subject.[124] Anzaldúa thus provides a corrective to the heteronormativity of most mestizo futurisms, including those of Du Bois and Vasconcelos. Yet her repurposing of mestizaje in the service of a feminist Chicana/Latina political project depended on a selective reading of Vasconcelos that reified the myth that Latin American mixture equaled racial egalitarianism. This in turn precluded the articulation of a full feminist critique of the patriarchal gender politics of mestizaje.

Anzaldúa explicitly situates her project within a philosophical lineage in which Vasconcelos was a key source. He is one of the few thinkers mentioned by name in *Borderlands/La Frontera*, her most widely read text.[125] Anzaldúa cited *The Cosmic Race* in the opening sentences of the chapter where she develops her conception of mestiza subjectivity, "*La conciencia de la mestiza*: Towards a New Consciousness." She describes his notion of the cosmic race as affirming racial mixing, as inclusive, and as the harbinger of a new US Latina hybrid subject:

> Jose Vasconcelos, Mexican philosopher, envisaged *una raza mestiza, una mezcla de razas afines, una raza de color—la primera raza síntesis del globo*. He called it a cosmic race, *la raza cósmica*, a fifth race embracing the four major races of the world. Opposite to the theory of the pure Aryan, and to the policy of racial purity that white America practices, his theory is one of inclusivity. At the confluence of two or more genetic streams, with chromosomes constantly "crossing over," this mixture of races, rather than resulting in an inferior being, provides hybrid progeny, a mutable, more malleable species with a rich gene pool. From this racial, ideological, cultural and biological cross-pollinization, an 'alien' consciousness is presently in the making—a new *mestiza* consciousness, *una conciencia de mujer*. It is a consciousness of the Borderlands.[126]

Already in this initial invocation of Vasconcelos, Anzaldúa reframes his ideas to highlight the experience of US Latinos, and Chicana women and queer subjects in particular. As she explained in a footnote, in the only other direct reference to him in *Borderlands/La Frontera*, her notion of mestiza consciousness "is my own 'take off' on Jose Vasconcelos's idea."[127] Anzaldúa's account of Latino hybrid subjectivity thus mixed elements derived from Vasconcelos and others that were specific to US Latinidad. She drew on his claims about Latin American mestizaje as a process of racial and cultural mixing, but she also grounds her analysis in Chicanos's hybrid position as a people who straddle the US–Mexico border, with a dual identity caught between Mexican and Anglo cultures in the United States.

Anzaldúa described the mestiza as a subject defined by contradiction and multiplicity, not as a synthetic whole as Vasconcelos envisioned the cosmic race:

> La mestiza constantly has to shift out of habitual formations; from convergent thinking, analytical reasoning that tends to use rationality to move toward a single goal (a Western mode), to divergent thinking, characterized by movement away from set patterns and goals toward a more whole perspective, one that includes rather than excludes. The new mestiza copes by developing a tolerance for contradictions, a tolerance for ambiguity. ... She learns to juggle cultures. She has a plural personality, she operates in a pluralistic mode ... nothing rejected, nothing abandoned. Not only does she sustain contradictions, she turns the ambivalence into something else.[128]

For Anzaldúa the in-between-ness and multiplicity characteristic of Latinidad were embodied by (female) Chicana inhabitants of the border in particular: "Cradled in one culture, sandwiched between two cultures, straddling all three cultures ... la mestiza undergoes a struggle of flesh, a struggle of borders, an inner war."[129] Anzaldúa's notion of a fractured Latina subjectivity is thus quite distinct in some ways from Vasconcelos's homogeneous conception of the Latin American mestizo. Anzaldúa relocated the pre-eminent site of mestizaje away from Latin America (as it was for Vasconcelos), to the US–Mexico borderlands, which she portrayed as the archetypal site of racial and cultural encounter where hybrid, fractured subjectivities could emerge.

Anzaldúa's Chicana futurism drew inspiration from Vasconcelos's theory of mestizaje, but it also departs from his ideas in significant ways, particularly by incorporating feminist and queer concerns.[130] For example, she argued that "en unas pocas centurias, the future will belong to the mestiza."[131] Borderlands/La Frontera thus positions women, who are rarely mentioned in Vasconcelos's texts, and queer Latinos, who are entirely absent, as the preeminent US mestizo/Latino subjects. She writes: "As a mestiza I have no country, my homeland cast me out, yet all countries are mine because I am every woman's sister or potential lover. (As a lesbian I have no race, my own people disclaim me; but I am all races because there is the queer of me in all races)."[132] Setting aside for a moment the biological essentialism (which echoes Vasconcelos) of Anzaldúa's conception of race in this passage, it is emblematic of her displacement of upperclass, fair-skinned, straight men as the normative subject of US Latinidad. In contrast, Anzaldúa's Chicana futurism privileges a mestiza subject that critically engages with history and reinterprets it in order to differentiate "between *lo heredado, lo impuesto, lo adquirido.* . . . She adopts new perspectives toward the darkskinned, women and queers."[133] Anzaldúa's intersectional analysis here connects race, gender, and sexuality. "As long as woman is put down, the Indian and the Black in all of us is put down. The struggle of the mestiza is above all a feminist one."[134] Anzaldúa's *Borderlands/La Frontera* thus begins to provide a feminist critique of the traditional gender politics of mestizaje. Her "queering" of mestizaje corrects the default heteronormativity of Vasconcelos's (and most other) mestizo futurisms.

Anzaldúa also inverted Vasconcelos's cultural hierarchy by giving a privileged role to indigeneity in her conception of the mestiza, not to the Spanish legacy as he did.[135] *Borderlands/La Frontera* is suffused with references to indigenous symbols and deities. Anzaldúa draws upon elements from pre-Cortesian thought to develop concepts such as "nepantilism" and "the Coatlicue state" in the text. Anzaldúa's Chicana futurism thus emphasized different ancestral elements than Vasconcelos's mestizo futurism. The mestiza's cultural ancestry for Anzaldúa was primarily indigenous. Describing the Rio Grande Valley, for example, she wrote: "This land was Mexican once[,] was Indian always, and is. And will be again."[136] Yet, like many Chicano/a intellectuals, including Chicana feminists, Anzaldúa deployed an overly romanticized portrayal of indigeneity that looked to the precolonial past rather than to contemporaneous indigenous movements. Echoing Vasconcelos's more radical moments, however, she also argued that Latinos needed to acknowledge their internal racism. "Before the Chicano can have unity with Native Americans and other groups, we need to know the history of their struggle and they need to know ours . . . each of us must know our Indian lineage, our afro-*mestisaje*, our history of resistance."[137] Anzaldúa thus attempted to reimagine mestizaje in more racially egalitarian terms, yet this project entailed certain inescapable tensions.

Anzaldúa was not able to fully escape the problematic inheritance of Vasconcelos's racial and gender politics. In particular, while she explicitly acknowledged Latin American racial hierarchies in *Borderlands/ La Frontera*, she did not formulate an explicit critique of the way harmonious narratives of mestizaje erased the sexual violence that was an integral part of the cultural and corporeal encounters that gave rise to the new mestizo subject. Anzaldúa did not correct Vasconcelos's silence about the sexual violence of mestizaje. As Afro-Brazilian intellectual Abdias do Nascimento observed about Gilberto Freyre's notion of racial democracy in Brazil, harmonious narratives of mestizaje erase sexual violence against non-European women.[138] The erasure of the sexual violence of slavery in narratives of harmonious mixture was accomplished in part via the hyper-sexualization of black women, whose bodies were then viewed as always willing and available. Rather than victims they became the seducers of their masters. Vasconcelos's brief reference to the "seductive mulatta" in *Indología* illustrates the continued reverberations of the specific gendered racialization of Latin American narratives of mestizaje. This legacy of discourses of harmonious mestizaje continues to shape black and indigenous women's ability to exercise corporal and sexual autonomy. Anzaldúa briefly alludes to gender violence in *Borderlands/La Frontera*, and to the sexual hypocrisy of Chicano culture. For example, she observed that the mestiza needed to distinguish between "the inherited, the acquired, the imposed." Yet *Borderlands/ La Frontera* does not contain any direct analysis of how narratives of mestizaje as harmonious fusion gloss over patterns of forced access to enslaved black and indigenous women's bodies. In fact, Anzaldúa reifies the traditional gendering of mestizaje that posited it as mixture between indigenous women and Spanish men, when she wonders: "which is the baggage from the Indian mother, which the baggage from the Spanish father, which the baggage from the Anglo?" that the mestiza carried on her back.[139] One element of this gendered and racialized burden was undoubtedly the continued silence about the sexual violence of mixture under colonialism and slavery, which Anzaldúa does not explore in this text. Ultimately, despite the important ways in which she "queers" mestizaje, Anzaldúa's adoption of Vasconcelian narratives of harmonious Latin American mixture thus precluded her from formulating a full intersectional feminist critique of his theory of mestizaje.

Anzaldúa's selective reading of Vasconcelos is emblematic of the way Latino political theorists have repurposed the myth of Latin American racial harmony to ground claims of Latino racial exceptionalism in the United States. Mestizaje operates as a marker, a symbol in their accounts of US racial politics and Latinidad. It is invoked to signal an alternate historical racial trajectory that is almost never the subject of serious critical scrutiny. Anzaldúa, for instance, drew on Vasconcelos without placing his claims about mestizaje in any kind of historical, political, or philosophical context, in contrast to the way she carefully plumbed the Chicana/o experience in the United States for insights about subjectivity, racial solidarity, and cultural negotiation. Mestizaje's hemispheric travels thus point to the need to interrogate the racial politics of US Latinidad itself. As Cristina Beltrán has rightfully argued, Latinos are not a monolithic group with shared opinions, and there are multiple strands of Latino politics.[140] There are also multiple Latino racial projects. Indeed, conservative Latino racial projects depict Latinos as an alternative to the US racial order, and to African Americans in particular. Claims about Latino exceptionalism vis-à-vis US racial thought grounded in mestizaje can thus be mobilized ideologically in very different ways, and are not necessarily formulated in service of racially egalitarian political projects.

Vasconcelos was part of an anti-colonial strand of twentieth-century Latin American political thought that envisioned the region as racially mestizo/nonwhite, culturally cohesive, and politically united in order to counter heightened US intervention. Yet his theory of mestizaje was only selectively decolonial, because the notion of Latin America's superior race relations vis-à-vis the United States glossed over internal racial hierarchies in Latin America. It is only by placing Vasconcelos's ideas within a hemispheric intellectual frame that this dual effect is revealed, however. There were moments when Vasconcelos did formulate a more radical critique of Latin American aspirations to whiteness, but it was not in his most widely read and influential text, *The Cosmic Race*. Subsequent appropriations of Latin American mestizaje by Latino thinkers in the United States thus recuperate the least radical or egalitarian aspects of Vasconcelos's racial thought. The point I am making here is not that Latino political theorists should not draw upon Latin American sources, but rather to draw attention to the dangers of selective reading, or more precisely, to the silences and erasures that result when texts are read without paying attention to the historical and intellectual context in which they were produced and to which they were responding. As mestizaje travels from one America to the other, its meanings shift, and it is thus essential to think carefully about the racial politics of narratives of Latino exceptionalism in the United States that rely on Latin American theories of mixture. Vasconcelos's mestizo futurism has had an enduring appeal, but unmoored from the intellectual and historical context in which it was formulated, we risk losing sight of the complexity of his call for elite Latin Americans to dis-identify with whiteness. The version of Vasconcelos's political thought on race that has survived is thus one evacuated of its most potentially radical critique.

Conclusion

IN 1927, THE African American intellectual W. E. B. Du Bois and the Mexican philosopher José Vasconcelos each attended a different international congress that contributed to the formation of what came to be known as the Third World.[1] In February of that year, Vasconcelos participated in the first conference of the League Against Imperialism in Brussels; six months later, in August, Du Bois chaired the fourth Pan-African Congress in Harlem, New York City. Du Bois and Vasconcelos's participation in these important global gatherings of intellectuals and leaders of what Du Bois called "the darker races" illustrates a heretofore underappreciated connection between these two iconic American (in the hemispheric sense) thinkers: their deployment of iconographies of mixture to prefigure anti-colonial struggles against US empire and global white supremacy. This unexpected resonance between Du Bois and Vasconcelos's political ideas is emblematic of how the kind of hemispheric intellectual genealogy undertaken in this book challenges the siloing of Latin American and US African American political thought as two distinct and disparate philosophical traditions. It also transforms prevailing understandings of the political thought of each of the four thinkers analyzed here. Reading Latin American and US African American thinkers alongside each other reveals Frederick Douglass, Domingo F. Sarmiento, W. E. B. Du Bois, and José Vasconcelos as eminently hemispheric thinkers. Sarmiento's nineteenth-century dream of establishing an intellectual dialogue between the two Americas has yet to be fully realized, even in the twenty-first century. The aim of this book has been to "bridge the chasm" that has heretofore separated Douglass and Sarmiento, Du Bois and Vasconcelos.[2] It juxtaposed racial theories formulated in *ambas Américas* (both Americas) during the late nineteenth and first half of the twentieth century, uncovering traces of the hemispheric in the political thought of each of these thinkers. Grappling with the racial thought of Douglass, Sarmiento, Du Bois, and Vasconcelos simultaneously illuminates broader trends within their respective philosophical traditions. Specifically, one of the conclusions of this book is that the hemispheric dimensions of Latin American and African American political thought alike have been obscured in different ways.

While the tendency of Latin American thinkers to engage in comparisons with "the other" America is widely recognized, what has been less noted is the way in which this engagement depended on selective readings of US racial politics refracted through Latin American realities. One of the pitfalls of comparison is that the conceptual logics that underpin it (such as a priori assumptions of sameness or difference), tend to construct illusions of coherence and distinctness in the units being compared. Sarmiento and Vasconcelos both wrote extensively about the United States, and their theories of race were fundamentally shaped by the problem of unequal hemispheric relations between the United States and Latin America. Sarmiento read the US Civil War through the lens of the struggle between civilization and barbarism, and saw Argentina's *gauchos* in the "poor whites" of the South during Reconstruction. Vasconcelos, particularly in *The Cosmic Race*, deployed US racial segregation to prove the superiority of Latin American mestizaje. For Latin American thinkers, the constitutive comparison to the United States has thus served as both a crutch and source of anxiety. Twentieth-century Latin American discourses of harmonious mestizaje served an anti-colonial function vis-à-vis the United States at the expense of obscuring racism within the region. Thus was born a narrative of Latin American racial exceptionalism that has "traveled" and been incorporated into contemporary debates about Latino politics in the United States. In contrast to attempts to derive normative lessons for anti-racist theorizing from Latin American mestizaje, therefore, my analysis points instead to the need to abandon reflexive comparisons between United States and Latin American racial formations, and to historicize them as specific political-theoretical moves that emerged during the first half of the twentieth century in response to US intervention. I suggest that instead of continued investment in a cherished notion of Latin American racial exceptionalism, a more productive emphasis would be to trace the long history of travel, borrowing, and dialogue between thinkers and traditions across the hemisphere, especially where race thinking is concerned.

If dominant understandings of Latin American political thought on race have portrayed it as reflexively outward-looking (i.e., always defined in comparison to the United States), the obverse has been true for African American political thought. If anything, African American political thought has been depicted as more provincial than it actually has been. At various points in their careers, Douglass and Du Bois both deployed claims of racial egalitarianism and black freedom in Latin America as a counterpoint to slavery, racial segregation, and black exclusion in the United States. These comparative arguments relied on what were doubtless romanticized depictions of Latin American race relations in order to intervene in US debates about race, but they illustrate the fact that African American thinkers, like their Latin American counterparts, also looked to "the other America" as model and foil. Instead of reifying a depiction of African American thinkers as primarily concerned with domestic racial politics in the United States, then, this book shows that they were in conversation with black populations in the rest of the Americas. Ironically, the black fugitive dimension of African American political thought has been downplayed in readings of Douglass and Du Bois that situate them solely within the boundaries of US American liberalism. Instead, it is vital to recognize how being able to envision black futures not limited by the boundaries of the nation-state allowed African American thinkers to make more expansive arguments in favor of racial justice and black humanity, especially in the context of slavery and Jim Crow.

Mapping a hemispheric intellectual genealogy of race not only brings into focus the nuances of different currents of race thinking in the Americas, it also transforms our understanding of each of these thinkers. Douglass, who is often read as representative of the assimilationist strand within African American political thought, emerges here as a more geographically capacious thinker whose hemispheric engagement with black populations in the Caribbean was central to his vision of a US multiracial polity transformed via nonwhite immigration. Likewise, a hemispheric reading of Sarmiento decenters Europe and foregrounds the centrality of the Americas to his political thought. By focusing on his writings about the United States in the 1860s, I show that in contrast to readings of him as a thinker who thoroughly embraced Europeanization and rejected American sources, from very early on in his career the center of gravity in Sarmiento's political thought shifted from Europe to the United States, which came to function as both model and emerging imperial threat. A hemispheric reading yields similar insights about Du Bois and Vasconcelos. In contrast to readings of Du Bois as a thinker mired in a static, binary (black–white) US conception of race who emphasized an essentialist notion of black identity in order to facilitate struggles for racial justice, a hemispheric reading highlights the centrality of debates about mixture and futurity to his political thought. It demonstrates the need to engage with Du Bois's mulatto fictions in order to probe his shift away from nation-centric politics to mixed-race utopias of the Global South. Read through a hemispheric frame, Du Bois is revealed as a theorist of mestizaje. Given mestizaje's "travels" and subsequent appropriation by US Latinos, a hemispheric intellectual frame is absolutely essential to gaining an accurate understanding of Vasconcelos's racial thought. Analyzing Vasconcelos's writings about racial discrimination against Latinos in the United States during the nadir era reveals his unexpected formulation of a critique of the aspirations to whiteness of Latin American elites. A hemispheric mode of reading thus alters our understanding of Douglass, Sarmiento, Du Bois, and Vasconcelos.

In addition to advancing new interpretations of each thinker and tradition, the hemispheric juxtapositions enacted in this book plumbs their ideas to sketch key theoretical concepts constitutive of racial thought in the Americas, such as the important ways in which black fugitivity enlarges and revises notions of democratic fugitivity, and the concept of mestizo futurism, which highlights the political utility of imagination that is a key feature of Du Bois and Vasconcelos's writings about mixture. Reading Sheldon Wolin's notion of "fugitive democracy" in light of slave fugitivity gleans new insights for democratic theory.[3] Theorizing the fugitive in the democratic via the experience of black fugitives fleeing slave law alters the temporality of Wolin's concept and moves it beyond the question of the episodic nature of democratic politics to grapple with the permanently uneven reach of democracy and the rule of law. African American and Latin American thinkers writing about race in the late nineteenth and first half of the twentieth century had to contend with a shared corpus of racist ideas that had the imprimatur of science. In a context in which white supremacy, black inferiority, and mestizo degeneracy were widely accepted "truths," thinkers like Du Bois and Vasconcelos had to look beyond existing racial orders to envision a future world that was yet-to-be. I argue that their writings about mixture should thus be understood as mestizo futurisms that served to counter racial science and allowed them to prefigure the emergence of a multiracial, decolonized Global South that is still not yet fully realized.

Reading Douglass, Sarmiento, Du Bois, and Vasconcelos as hemispheric thinkers also yields important methodological insights for political theory. Juxtaposition enables simultaneous analysis of different philosophical traditions while avoiding the pitfalls of comparison. Comparison not only often assumes the a priori existence of stable, discrete units that can then be compared; it can also construct the differences it claims to analyze. This exercise in hemispheric juxtaposition has shown that what we find in the Americas are dialogically formed racial ideas that have been repurposed as they travel across space and time. Charting an intellectual genealogy of racial thought in the Americas thus requires engaging in an interpretive approach that liberates African American and Latin American thinkers from the frame of the nation. It also requires paying attention to the specific historical and political contexts in which these thinkers formulated their ideas, in order to interrogate how the boundaries between traditions are produced as contingent products of varying political and intellectual projects.

Uncovering the traces of the hemispheric in the political thought of Douglass, Sarmiento, Du Bois, and Vasconcelos also requires reading a broader set of texts, and situating all texts in context. The importance of questions of textual selection to the hemispheric juxtapositions enacted in this book also raise broader questions about the kinds of texts and thinkers that are legible as political theory. It is precisely their status as subaltern philosophical traditions—geographically of the West, but marginal to Western political thought—that makes reading African American and Latin American political thought simultaneously such a rich and compelling exercise.

The emergence of the field of comparative political theory has not necessarily resolved the problem of political theory's ethnocentrism.[4] The task of comparative political theory is conceived as either the study of non-Western political thought, or the comparison of Western and non-Western thinkers and traditions. The effect has been additive, however. Non-Western figures (such as Qutb or Confucius) and traditions are appended to the canon of political theory, but the field's epistemological Eurocentrism continues to be reproduced both in who is seen as a major or minor figure, and in the way the discipline's core concerns and areas of study remain unaltered. As a result, comparisons between Western and non-Western thinkers often involve measuring the distance or proximity of non-Western thinkers from dominant Western concepts.[5] Such approaches to comparative political theory tend to both reify "the West" and preclude the kind of juxtaposition between two subaltern traditions enacted in this book.[6] Conceiving comparative political theory in this way fails to interrogate how the boundaries between "Western" and "non-Western" are created and reified in the first place. This book shows how political theory can move beyond centering Western political thought, by considering how the intellectual concerns of various philosophical traditions are shaped by particular geographies. In the case of Latin American and US African American political thought, for example, a hemispheric frame allows us to trace the movement of people and ideas across the Americas, and to highlight political and philosophical questions that may not align with the dominant concerns of Western political thought, even as these traditions drew upon and repurposed European thinkers and ideas.

Finally, this might seem to be a book about the past, given its focus on nineteenth and early twentieth-century thinkers, but the ideas of these iconic figures continue to resonate with the problematics of the present. There are echoes of Douglass, Sarmiento, Du Bois, and Vasconcelos in a number of contemporary debates about race in the United States and Latin America. For example, while scientific notions of nonwhite racial inferiority have been abandoned, the continuity and resurgence of racism today reveals the inadequacy of arguments about race as social construction to dismantle racial power and global white supremacy. At a moment when racism seems reascendant, it is clear that we remain trapped in the grammar of race that Douglass, Sarmiento, Du Bois, and Vasconcelos were grappling with in the nineteenth and twentieth centuries. Traces of nineteenth-century debates about how to dismantle colonial racial orders and build multiracial democracies in the Americas that could decenter whiteness, as well as the legacies of twentieth-century mestizo futurisms that prefigured today's Global South, are sedimented in unexpected ways in the twenty-first century. Douglass, for example, anticipated the anxieties elicited by a project of decentering whiteness in US democracy during Reconstruction. More than a century ago, he imagined a US polity that dared to answer: "*I would,*" when asked to incorporate nonwhite immigrants on terms of full equality.[7] In other words, Douglass dared to envision a US polity willing to transform itself into a nonwhite majority state. He proved more optimistic than prescient in his predictions, but the vision of a multiracial US democracy that he sketched remains powerfully evocative today, as the United States undergoes the throes of the demographic changes he foresaw and the backlash they have engendered. Vasconcelos's mestizo futurism—with its

complex racial politics that combined a critique of Latin American aspirations to whiteness with erasure of internal racial hierarchies via the
trope of comparison—haunts contemporary claims about Latino racial
exceptionalism in the United States. These echoes of the past in the
problematics of our racial present suggest that we still urgently need to
understand the origins and travels of hemispheric racial thought across
the Americas.

Notes

INTRODUCTION

1 The first English translation of *Facundo* was published in 1868 in the United States, as I discuss in detail in chapter 2. The *Narrative* does not appear to have been translated into Spanish, but Caribbean intellectuals were certainly aware of Douglass's life story, as noted in chapter 1.

2 Roberto González Echevarría, "*Facundo*: An Introduction," in Domingo Faustino Sarmiento, *Facundo: Civilization and Barbarism*, trans. Kathleen Ross (Los Angeles: University of California Press, 2004), 1; Lewis R. Gordon, "Douglass as an Existentialist," in *Frederick Douglass: A Critical Reader*, ed. Bill E. Lawson and Frank M. Kirkland (Malden, MA: Blackwell Publishers, 1999), 223–24n3.

3 As far as I am aware, this is the first book to analyze Douglass and Sarmiento's, and Du Bois and Vasconcelos's political ideas simultaneously. Excellent studies of individual or multiple figures in African American or Latin American political thought include: Lawrie Balfour, *Democracy's Reconstruction: Thinking Politically with W. E. B. Du Bois* (New York: Oxford University Press, 2011); Robert Gooding-Williams, *In the Shadow of Du Bois: Afro-Modern Political Thought in America* (Cambridge, MA: Harvard University Press, 2009); Stephen H. Marshall, *The City on the Hill from Below: The Crisis of Prophetic Black Politics* (Philadelphia: Temple University Press, 2011); Jorge J. E. Gracia, ed., *Forging People: Race, Ethnicity, and Nationality in Hispanic American and Latino/a Thought* (Notre Dame, IN: University of Notre Dame Press, 2011); Diego A. Von Vacano, *The Color of Citizenship: Race, Modernity and Latin American/Hispanic Political Thought* (New York: Oxford University Press, 2012).

4 I use the terms "America" and "American" to refer to the continent as a whole, not solely to the United States as is accepted usage in the United States. I thus add the modifier "US" to African American and American political thought in order to flag this distinction.

5 Du Bois is a partial exception to this trend, as his later Pan-African and Marxist commitments and promotion of global anti-colonial alliances are usually acknowledged. Yet readings of his oeuvre centered only on *Souls* often downplay these aspects of his political thought.

6 Douglass, Sarmiento, Du Bois, and Vasconcelos all wrote extensively about a variety of political and philosophical questions. My analysis of their work here is limited to their ideas about race, and in some cases a specific aspect of it, such as their writings about mixture or hemispheric power relations, etc.

7 The terms Global North and Global South have largely supplanted Cold War Era global socioeconomic and ideological divisions between the First, Second, and Third World. The Global North includes the United States, Canada, Western Europe, and developed parts of East Asia, while the Global South spans Africa, Latin America, developing Asia, and the Middle East. The Global South thus encompasses much of what Du Bois called "the darker races."

8 See Neil Roberts, *Freedom as Marronage* (Chicago: University of Chicago Press, 2015); Katherine A. Gordy, "No Better Way to Be Latin American: European Science and Thought, Latin American Theory?," *Postcolonial Studies* 16, no. 4 (2014): 358–73.

9 I am using the term "South" here not in a geographical sense, obviously. For a discussion of the prevalence of East–West and North–South comparisons in political theory, see David Haekwon Kim, "José Mariátegui's East-South Decolonial Experiment," *Comparative and Continental Philosophy* 7, no. 2 (2015): 157–79.

10 The notion of futurism is usually associated with the early twentieth-century avant-garde Italian artistic movement. The Futurists admired speed, technology, youth, and objects that represented the triumph of human technological innovation over nature (such as the car, the airplane, and the industrial city). They were also passionate nationalists who endorsed violence and glorified the hygienic properties of war in their manifestoes. Some of the movement's leading figures were drawn to Italian fascism. I do not use the term to refer to the artistic movement, but its association with authoritarian political projects is an apt reminder that a political embrace of futurity is not normatively neutral.

11 Dohra Ahmad, "'More Than Romance': Genre and Geography in Dark Princess," *ELH* 69, no. 3 (2002): 776.

12 By Latino exceptionalism I mean claims that Latinos challenge the United States's binary racial order and deconstruct race by introducing Latin America's more complex notions of racial identity and superior approach to race relations. See Juliet Hooker, "Hybrid Subjectivities, Latin American Mestizaje, and Latino Political Thought on Race," *Politics, Groups, and Identities* 2, no. 2 (2014): 188–201.

13 David Scott, *Conscripts of Modernity: The Tragedy of Colonial Enlightenment* (Durham, NC: Duke University Press, 2004), 1.

14 George M. Fredrickson, *The Black Image in the White Mind: The Debate on Afro-American Character and Destiny, 1817–1914* (Middletown, CT: Wesleyan University Press, 1987), xvii.

15 Thomas E. Skidmore, *Black into White: Race and Nationality in Brazilian Thought,* 2d ed. (Durham, NC: Duke University Press, 1993), 49–51.

16 Fredrickson, *The Black Image in the White Mind,* 74.

17 Ibid., 75–76.

18 Aline Helg, "Race in Argentina and Cuba, 1880–1930: Theory, Policies, and Popular Reaction," in *The Idea of Race in Latin America, 1870–1940,* by Richard Graham, Thomas E. Skidmore, Aline Helg, and Alan Knight (Austin: University of Texas Press, 1990), 62n6.

19 One clear example of the fact that intellectuals from the Americas felt that they had to counter European and North American scientific racism is the Haitian intellectual Anténor Firmin's response to de Gobineau, which was originally published in French in 1885. See Anténor Firmin, *The Equality of the Human Races,* trans. Asselin Charles (Chicago: University of Illinois Press, 2002).

20 Skidmore, *Black into White: Race and Nationality in Brazilian Thought,* 53.

21 Fredrickson, *The Black Image in the White Mind,* 232–35.

22 Skidmore, *Black into White: Race and Nationality in Brazilian Thought,* 52.

23 Douglass discussed the impact of the American school of ethnology on debates about slavery in Frederick Douglass, *The Claims of the Negro Ethnologically Considered: An Address before the Literary Societies of Western Reserve College at Commencement, July 12, 1854* (Rochester, NY: Lee, Mann, 1854).

24 Fredrickson, *The Black Image in the White Mind,* 147–50.

25 Richard Graham, "Introduction," in *The Idea of Race in Latin America, 1870–1940* (Austin: University of Texas Press, 1990), 2.

26 See Reginald Horsman, *Race and Manifest Destiny: The Origins of American Racial Anglo-Saxonism* (Cambridge, MA: Harvard University Press, 1981).

27 Nancy Stepan, *The Hour of Eugenics: Race, Gender, and Nation in Latin America* (Ithaca, NY: Cornell University Press, 1991), 1–2.

28 Ibid., 31. By the late 1920s, twenty-four US states had passed such laws.

29 Ibid., 55.

30 Ibid., 17.

31 Ibid., 106.

32 See Duncan Bell, "Before the Democratic Peace: Racial Utopianism, Empire and the Abolition of War," *European Journal of International Relations* 20, no. 3 (2014): 647–70.

33 Peggy Pascoe, "Between a Rock and a Hard Place," in *What Comes Naturally: Miscegenation Law and the Making of Race in America,* by Peggy Pascoe (Oxford: Oxford University Press, 2009), 172.

34 There have been extensive debates about method in comparative political theory, and while most scholars would reject the idea that they approach

comparison as a politically neutral method, much of the field continues to proceed from the assumption that stable, discrete traditions exist that can then be compared. Key texts on method in the field include: Fred Dallmayr, ed., *Border Crossings: Toward a Comparative Political Theory* (Lanham, MD: Lexington Books, 1999); Roxanne L. Euben, *Enemy in the Mirror: Islamic Fundamentalism and the Limits of Modern Rationalism* (Princeton, NJ: Princeton University Press, 1999); Farah Godrej, *Cosmopolitan Political Thought: Method, Practice, Discipline* (New York: Oxford University Press, 2011); Leigh K. Jenco, "'What Does Heaven Ever Say?': A Methods-Centered Approach to Cross-Cultural Engagement," *American Political Science Review* 101, no. 4 (2007): 741–55; Andrew F. March, "What Is Comparative Political Theory?," *Review of Politics* 71, no. 4 (2009): 531–65.

35 Micol Seigel, "Beyond Compare: Comparative Method after the Transnational Turn," *Radical History Review* 2005, no. 91 (2005): 62.

36 On travel and political theory, see Roxanne Euben, *Journeys to the Other Shore: Muslim and Western Travelers in Search of Knowledge* (Princeton: Princeton University Press, 2006).

37 This is a play on Cuban nationalist and advocate of Latin American Pan-Americanism José Martí's famous essay, "The Truth about the United States," which sought to disabuse his Latin American readers of their admiration for their northern neighbor. See José Martí, *José Martí: Selected Writings*, trans. Esther Allen (New York: Penguin Classics, 2002), 329–33.

38 Earlier anti-imperial thinkers should be distinguished from the contemporary "decolonial turn" in Latin American political thought, which emerged as a critique of the epistemological links between conceptions of modernity and postmodernity and the European colonial project. Latin American decolonial thinkers argue that even postmodern critiques of modernity formulated from the vantage point of the history of European ideas reproduce Eurocentrism and the "coloniality of power." They also critique the way Latin America has reproduced the dominant geopolitics of knowledge, thus requiring the decolonization of Latin American political thought. See Aníbal Quijano, "Coloniality of Power, Eurocentrism, and Latin America," *Neplanta* 1, no. 3 (2000): 533–80.

39 The point that traditions of thought rely on selective depictions of "the other" as a way of constructing themselves has been brilliantly made by Edward W. Said, *Orientalism* (New York: Vintage Books, 1994).

40 The *Oxford English Dictionary* defines juxtaposition as: "The action of placing two or more things close together or side by side, or one thing with or beside another." http://www.oed.com/view/Entry/102290?redirectedFrom=juxtaposition#eid.

41 Perhaps the most influential use of the idea of counterpoint was Cuban intellectual Fernando Ortiz's borrowing of the term "*contrapunteo*" from popular music to analyze the central role of tobacco and sugar in shaping Cuban history.

See Fernando Ortiz and Harriet De Onís, *Cuban Counterpoint: Tobacco and Sugar* (New York: A. A. Knopf, 1947).

42 Chadwick Allen, *Trans-Indigenous: Methodologies for Global Native Literary Studies* (Minneapolis: University of Minnesota Press, 2012), xix. Juxtaposition is also analogous to the notion of creolization; see Jane Anna Gordon and Neil Roberts, *Creolizing Rousseau* (London: Rowman & Littlefield International, 2015), 2–3.

43 See "Introduction: W. E. B. Du Bois and the Politics of Juxtaposition," in *Next to the Color Line: Gender, Sexuality, and W.E.B. Du Bois*, eds. Susan Kay Gillman and Alys Eve Weinbaum (Minneapolis: University of Minnesota Press, 2007).

44 Lawrie Balfour, "Darkwater's Democratic Vision," *Political Theory* 38, no. 4 (2010): 537–63.

45 Race is one among a number of cleavages within Latin American political thought. For example, in the post-independence era the dominant fault line was between liberals and conservatives (the former favored a secular state, public education, and individual property, while the latter defended the prerogatives of the Catholic Church and a patriarchal social and political order). The early twentieth century saw the emergence of Latin American variants of Marxism and feminism; this was also a high point of anti-imperialism, which cross-cut traditional ideological divisions. Liberation theology and the philosophy of liberation became prominent at the end of the twentieth century, and decolonial thought in the early twenty-first century.

46 See Bernard Boxill, "Two Traditions in African-American Political Philosophy," *Philosophical Forum* 24, nos. 1–3 (1992–93): 119–35; Michael Dawson, *Black Visions: The Roots of Contemporary African-American Political Ideologies* (Chicago: University of Chicago Press, 2001).

47 Indeed, the figures analyzed here are all heterosexual men, all of whom wrote from a masculinist perspective. I address this potential gap in the book through an intersectional, feminist reading of their work that is attuned to the operations of gender and sexuality in their writings. These issues are particularly pertinent to the chapters on Du Bois and Vasconcelos.

48 The unlikely nature of these hemispheric juxtapositions, and the way they destabilize dominant readings of these thinkers are illustrated by the paired epigraphs that precede parts I and II, which are shown to be inadequate representations of their ideas by the end of each chapter.

49 All translations from texts in Spanish are my own.

50 The links between Sarmiento and Vasconcelos are discussed in detail in chapter 4. Gooding-Williams argues that Du Bois explicitly sought to position himself as Douglass's intellectual heir, despite the fact that (in his view) they had deeply contrasting approaches to black politics. See Gooding-Williams, *In the Shadow of Du Bois: Afro-Modern Political Thought in America*, 5.

51 I borrow the term "mulatto fictions" from Lourdes Martínez-Echazábal, "Mestizaje and the Discourse of National/Cultural Identity in Latin America, 1845–1959," *Latin American Perspectives* 25, no. 3 (1998): 21–42.

52 Martí, *José Martí: Selected Writings*, 290.

53 W. E. B. Du Bois, "Criteria of Negro Art," *The Crisis* 32 (October 1926): 290.

CHAPTER 1

1 See Bernard Boxill, "Two Traditions in African-American Political Philosophy," *Philosophical Forum* 24, nos. 1–3 (1992–93): 119–35; Nicholas Buccola, *The Political Thought of Frederick Douglass: In Pursuit of American Liberty* (New York: New York University Press, 2012); Sharon R. Krause, *Liberalism with Honor* (Cambridge, MA: Harvard University Press, 2002); Peter C. Myers, *Frederick Douglass: Race and the Rebirth of American Liberalism* (Lawrence: University Press of Kansas, 2008); Jack Turner, *Awakening to Race: Individualism and Social Consciousness in America* (Chicago: University of Chicago Press, 2012).

2 See Robert S. Levine, *Dislocating Race and Nation: Episodes in Nineteenth-Century American Literary Nationalism* (Chapel Hill: University of North Carolina Press, 2008); Ifeoma K. Nwankwo, *Black Cosmopolitanism: Racial Consciousness and Transnational Identity in the Nineteenth-Century Americas* (Philadelphia: University of Pennsylvania Press, 2005); Millery Polyné, *From Douglass to Duvalier: U.S. African Americans, Haiti and Pan Americanism, 1870–1964* (Gainesville: University Press of Florida, 2010).

3 I include Haiti and the Caribbean coast of Central America within Latin America, despite the fact that their complex geopolitical histories and linguistic differences do not align with dominant ideas of the region as Indo-Hispanic and Spanish-speaking, in part because Douglass viewed them as such. More generally, I favor precisely such an expansive understanding of Latin America. On the origins and implications of the term, see Walter Mignolo, *The Idea of Latin America* (New York: Wiley-Blackwell, 2006).

4 For a succinct account of the position of black and indigenous peoples in Latin American racial orders, see Peter Wade, *Race and Ethnicity in Latin America* (London: Pluto Press, 1997). For a comprehensive analysis of the position of blacks, in particular, in Latin American societies, see George Reid Andrews, *Afro-Latin America, 1800–2000* (New York: Oxford University Press, 2004).

5 George M. Fredrickson, *The Black Image in the White Mind: The Debate on Afro-American Character and Destiny, 1817–1914* (Middletown, CT: Wesleyan University Press, 1987), 147. Douglass's use of the term "race" in his writings reflects these two usages: it refers to both human groupings identified in terms of phenotype (such as blacks, whites, etc.) and to distinctions between "Latins" and "Saxons."

6 Frederick Douglass, *The Claims of the Negro Ethnologically Considered: An Address before the Literary Societies of Western Reserve College at Commencement, July 12, 1854* (Rochester, NY: Lee, Mann, 1854), 6. The members of the American school

of ethnology were Prof. Louis Agassiz (a biologist), Dr. Samuel Morton (a craniologist), George Gliddon (an Egyptologist), and Dr. Josiah Nott (a physician).

7 Ibid., 15.

8 Ibid., 16.

9 This strand of scientific racism identified race as "the central factor in history"
and claimed that Anglo-Saxons had reached the highest level of civilization and
as a result were destined to rule over all other racial groups across the globe.
See Thomas E. Skidmore, *Black into White: Race and Nationality in Brazilian
Thought*, 2d ed. (Durham, NC: Duke University Press, 1993), 50–51.

10 Indeed, Douglass's own body was a site for debates about the validity of the new
racial science, as his extraordinary accomplishments were often attributed to
his mixed parentage. Rebutting the notions of black inferiority that pervaded
strictures against mixing, Douglass observed: "I am happy to attribute any love
of letters I may have, not to my presumed Anglo-Saxon paternity, but to the
native genius of my sable, unprotected, and uncultivated mother—a woman
who belonged to a race whose mental endowments are still disparaged and
despised." Frederick Douglass, *The Life and Times of Frederick Douglass*, 1892 ed.
(Mineola, NY: Dover Publications, 2003), 156.

11 As Stephen Marshall observes, the genre of the slave narrative "placed strictures
on which experiences former slaves could disclose, which emotional responses
they could reveal, and which private interpretations of these experiences slaves
could share with their white readers." Stephen H. Marshall, *The City on the Hill
from Below: The Crisis of Prophetic Black Politics* (Philadelphia: Temple University
Press, 2011), 62–63.

12 Douglass's only novel, *The Heroic Slave*, might also be considered a hemispheric
text because its US protagonist Madison Washington and his co-conspirators
aboard the ship the *Creole* gain their freedom in the British West Indies. Yet the
vast majority of the action takes place on US soil. For an insightful analysis of
The Heroic Slave as a brief depiction of diasporic transnational blackness, see Ivy
G. Wilson, "On Native Ground: Transnationalism, Frederick Douglass, and 'the
Heroic Slave,'" *PMLA* 121, no. 2 (2006): 453–68.

13 Sheldon S. Wolin, "Fugitive Democracy," *Constellations* 1, no. 1 (1994): 11.

14 Ibid., 23.

15 Ibid., 18.

16 Ibid., 24.

17 By liminal citizens, I mean persons who are not yet legal citizens but who act as
(and could become) such, and those who are citizens according to the law but
are not treated thus in practice.

18 Frederick Douglass, "What to the Slave Is the Fourth of July," in *The Oxford
Frederick Douglass Reader*, ed. William L. Andrews (New York: Oxford University
Press, 1996), 116.

19 There are important differences between his three autobiographies in how Douglass recalls and presents certain key moments in his life. His description of his life in the North as a fugitive is much more developed and less positive in the second and third autobiographies, but his claims about the slave's relationship to the law are consistent. The final edition of the third autobiography contains an account of his engagement with Haiti in the 1890s, and thus presents the most complete picture of Douglass's hemispheric investments.

20 Douglass, *The Life and Times of Frederick Douglass*, 69.

21 Ibid., 130.

22 Ibid., 110.

23 "What to the Slave Is the Fourth of July," 113.

24 Douglass also rejected the idea that elites were better able to interpret the law than ordinary citizens, such as when he exhorted his audience to reach their own conclusions about whether the US Constitution was an anti-slavery text. He argued that "every American citizen has a right to form an opinion of the Constitution. . . . I take it, therefore, that it is not presumption in a private citizen to form an opinion of that instrument." Ibid., 128.

25 *Autobiographies* (New York: Library of America, 1994), 90.

26 *The Life and Times of Frederick Douglass*, 146.

27 Ibid., 147.

28 Ibid., 154.

29 *Autobiographies*, 339–40.

30 Ibid., 340.

31 See Danielle S. Allen, *Talking to Strangers: Anxieties of Citizenship after Brown v. Board of Education* (Chicago: University of Chicago Press, 2004).

32 See Angela Y. Davis, *Lectures on Liberation* (Los Angeles: National United Committee to Free Angela Davis, 1971).

33 Contemporary theorists have drawn upon black fugitive thought to rethink freedom, justice, and democracy from the perspective of the enslaved. See Stephen Best and Saidiya Hartman, "Fugitive Justice," *Representations* 92, no. 1 (Fall 2005): 1–5; Anthony Bogues, *Empire of Liberty: Power, Desire, and Freedom* (Lebanon, NH: University Press of New England, 2010); Barnor Hesse, "Escaping Liberty: Western Hegemony, Black Fugitivity," *Political Theory* 42, no. 3 (2014): 288–313.

34 See, e.g., Boxill, "Two Traditions in African-American Political Philosophy."

35 Douglass, *The Life and Times of Frederick Douglass*, 349.

36 Du Bois's formulation of the term "abolition-democracy" in *Black Reconstruction* also links black fugitivity and democracy, as does Angela Davis's theorization of the prison as the bulwark of undemocratic practices in contemporary polities. Lawrie Balfour and Robert Gooding-Williams have also analyzed African American political thought and democracy. See Lawrie Balfour, *Democracy's Reconstruction: Thinking Politically with W.E.B. Du Bois* (New York: Oxford

University Press, 2011); Angela Y. Davis, *Abolition Democracy: Beyond Empire, Prisons, and Torture/Interviews with Angela Y. Davis* (New York: Seven Stories Press, 2005); Robert Gooding-Williams, *In the Shadow of Du Bois: Afro-Modern Political Thought in America* (Cambridge, MA: Harvard University Press, 2009).

37 See Marshall, *The City on the Hill from Below: The Crisis of Prophetic Black Politics*, 57–90.

38 Neil Roberts, *Freedom as Marronage* (Chicago: University of Chicago Press, 2015), 57.

39 Ibid., 74–78.

40 Anthony Bogues, "And What about the Human? Freedom, Human Emancipation, and the Radical Imagination," *boundary 2* 39, no. 3 (2012): 29–46.

41 See Angela Y. Davis, ed., "Introduction," in *Narrative of the Life of Frederick Douglass, an American Slave, Written by Himself: A New Critical Edition* (San Francisco: City Lights Publishers, 2010).

42 Harriet A. Jacobs, *Incidents in the Life of a Slave Girl: Written by Herself*, ed. Lydia Maria Child and Jean Fagan Yellin (Cambridge, MA: Harvard University Press, 1987).

43 See Shatema Threadcraft, *Intimate Justice: The Black Female Body and the Body Politic* (New York: Oxford University Press, 2016).

44 See Jenny Franchot, "The Punishment of Esther: Frederick Douglass and the Construction of the Feminine," in *Frederick Douglass: New Literary and Historical Essays*, ed. Eric J. Sundquist (Cambridge: Cambridge University Press, 1990).

45 Pleasure represented a form of resistance for enslaved men and women who had limited control over their own bodies, for example. See Stephanie M. H. Camp, "The Pleasures of Resistance: Enslaved Women and Body Politics in the Plantation South, 1830–1861," *Journal of Southern History* 68, no. 3 (2002): 533–72.

46 See Gooding-Williams, *In the Shadow of Du Bois: Afro-Modern Political Thought in America*, 172–74, 84–89.

47 On the shifting depictions of Caroline's role in the fight with Covey, see Roberts, *Freedom as Marronage*, 198–99n93.

48 Douglass, *The Life and Times of Frederick Douglass*, 14–15. Both of these sentences appear almost verbatim in *Bondage*, but in the third autobiography cited here slight alterations in sentence structure heighten their emotional impact.

49 *Autobiographies*, 150. Describing meeting his siblings for the first time, he wrote: "I really did not understand what they were to me, or I to them. We were brothers and sisters, but what of that? Why should they be attached to me, or I to them? Brothers and sisters we were by blood; but *slavery* had made us strangers. I heard the words brothers and sisters, and knew they must mean something; but slavery had robbed these terms of their true meaning." Ibid., 149.

50 Ibid., 152–53.

51 *The Life and Times of Frederick Douglass*, 17. In *Bondage* Douglass wrote that he found himself "in the ... arms of a mother." *Autobiographies*, 154. In the later version, he changed the wording to *his* mother.

52 Saidiya V. Hartman, *Scenes of Subjection: Terror, Slavery, and Self-Making in Nineteenth-Century America* (New York: Oxford University Press, 1997).

53 See Charles W. Mills, "Whose Fourth of July? Frederick Douglass and Original Intent," in *Blackness Visible: Essays on Philosophy and Race*, by Charles W. Mills (Ithaca, NY: Cornell University Press, 1998).

54 Douglass, *The Life and Times of Frederick Douglass*, 274, 368.

55 Douglass also famously argued that separate black political institutions should not be permanent, but were rather pragmatic, temporary accommodations to white supremacy.

56 Fredrickson, *The Black Image in the White Mind*, 147–51.

57 Robert S. Levine, *Martin Delany, Frederick Douglass, and the Politics of Representative Identity* (Chapel Hill: University of North Carolina Press, 1997), 229.

58 Frederick Douglass, "A Trip to Haiti," in *The Life and Writings of Frederick Douglass*, vol. 3, *The Civil War, 1861–1865*, ed. Philip S. Foner (New York: International Publishers, 1952), 87–88.

59 Ibid., 88.

60 Ibid., 86.

61 Ibid., 87.

62 Ibid., 85.

63 "West India Emancipation," in *Two Speeches by Frederick Douglass, One on West India Emancipation and the Other on the Dred Scott Decision* (Rochester, NY: C. P. Dewey, 1857), 23.

64 Levine, *Dislocating Race and Nation*, 191.

65 Douglass, "West India Emancipation," 19.

66 Ibid., 22.

67 Ibid., 22–23.

68 On the difficulties of interpreting Garner's actions, see Mark Reinhardt, "Who Speaks for Margaret Garner? Slavery, Silence, and the Politics of Ventriloquism," *Critical Inquiry* 29, no. 1 (2002): 81–119.

69 Martin R. Delany, *The Condition, Elevation, Emigration, and Destiny of the Colored People of the United States* (New York: Arno Press, 1968).

70 Because of its strategic importance as the Atlantic entrance to a possible inter-oceanic canal, San Juan was claimed by both the Mosquito Kingdom and Nicaragua, in a dispute that also involved Great Britain and the United States. The town's racial and geopolitical topography were complex. During the colonial era, black Creoles and indigenous Miskitus exercised significant autonomy on the Mosquito Coast, in which the port was located, but they were increasingly subject to Anglo hegemony after Britain officially re-established its protectorate over the Mosquito Kingdom in 1843. The discovery of gold in California in 1848

71 Communipaw, "Nicaragua," *Frederick Douglass's Paper*, January 8, 1852.

72 Squier reported that the Nicaraguan population was 6% black, 10% white, 32% Indian, and 52% mixed. McCune Smith revised these numbers by adding half of those originally counted as white to the mixed-race category and counting all of the mixed as black. He therefore concluded that Nicaragua was 64% black and 4% white.

73 The term *criollo* refers to Spaniards born in the Americas, which is how most of Nicaragua's political elite tended to imagine itself at this time. Nicaragua was hardly exempt from racism. In their dispute with the Mosquito Kingdom over ownership of San Juan, for example, Nicaraguan officials deployed a racially coded discourse of civilization and savagery to delegitimize the political capacities of the region's black and indigenous inhabitants. See Juliet Hooker, "Race and the Space of Citizenship: The Mosquito Coast and the Place of Blackness and Indigeneity in Nicaragua," in *Blacks & Blackness in Central America: Between Race and Place*, ed. Lowell Gudmundson and Justin Wolfe (Durham, NC: Duke University Press, 2010).

74 Communipaw, "Nicaragua."

75 "Nicaragua—No. II," *Frederick Douglass's Paper*, January 15. For an in-depth discussion of the participation of Salinas and other Afro-Nicaraguans from the Pacific coast in nineteenth-century Nicaraguan politics, see Justin Wolfe, "'The Cruel Whip': Race and Place in Nineteenth Century Nicaragua," in *Blacks and Blackness in Central America: Between Race and Place*, ed. Lowell Gudmundson and Justin Wolfe (Durham, NC: Duke University Press, 2010).

76 Frederick Douglass, "The President and His Speeches," in *The Life and Writings of Frederick Douglass*, vol. 3, *The Civil War, 1861–1865*, ed. Philip S. Foner (New York: International Publishers, 1952), 268.

77 James R. Starkey, "Letter," *Frederick Douglass's Paper*, May 27, 1852.

78 Ibid. Mattox reads this incident as referring to local residents enforcing US-style segregation, but throughout the letter the phrase "colored persons from the American States" refers to African Americans. Jake Mattox, "The Mayor of San Juan Del Norte? Nicaragua, Martin Delany, and the 'Cotton' Americans," *American Literature* 81, no. 3 (2009): 540.

79 Starkey, "Letter."

80 Mattox, "The Mayor of San Juan Del Norte? Nicaragua, Martin Delany, and the 'Cotton' Americans," 532–33.

81 Carolina, "San Juan de Nicaragua," *Frederick Douglass's Paper*, May 6.

82 On the link between notions of Anglo-Saxon racial superiority and US expansion during the nineteenth century, see Reginald Horsman, *Race and Manifest Destiny: The Origins of American Racial Anglo-Saxonism* (Cambridge, MA: Harvard University Press, 1981).

83 Polyné, *From Douglass to Duvalier*, 29.

84 See Farah Godrej, *Cosmopolitan Political Thought: Method, Practice, Discipline* (New York: Oxford University Press, 2011).

85 See, e.g., Joseph H. Carens, "Aliens and Citizens: The Case for Open Borders," *The Review of Politics* 49, no. 2 (1987): 251–73.

86 Douglass's vision of nonwhite immigration as a tool to dismantle white supremacy is in direct contrast to what Aziz Rana has argued is the intrinsic connection between "settlerism and [European] immigration" in US history. He writes: "Settlers recognized that in order to sustain a project of republican freedom and territorial conquest, they would necessarily need new migrants beyond the initial flows of English colonists. As a result, they created remarkably open immigration policies for Europeans deemed co-ethnics and thus co-participants in the republican project." Aziz Rana, *The Two Faces of American Freedom* (Cambridge, MA: Harvard University Press, 2010), 12–13.

87 Douglass became involved in the debate over annexation after President Grant appointed him assistant secretary to the Commission of Inquiry for the Annexation of Santo Domingo in 1871. Douglass viewed his appointment to the commission as an endorsement of multiracial democracy at the federal level, as is clear from his description of the event. See Douglass, *The Life and Times of Frederick Douglass*, 297–99.

88 See Philip S. Foner, ed., *The Life and Writings of Frederick Douglass*, vol. 4, *Reconstruction and After* (New York: International Publishers, 1955), 70. Slavery was not abolished until 1873 in Puerto Rico and 1886 in Cuba.

89 Frederick Douglass, "Annexion of San Domingo," *New National Era*, January 12, 1871.

90 Levine, *Dislocating Race and Nation*, 207.

91 Ibid., 209.

92 Ibid., 207, emphasis added.

93 Douglass, "Annexion of San Domingo," emphasis added.

94 "Our Composite Nationality: An Address Delivered in Boston, Massachusetts, on 7 December 1869," in *The Frederick Douglass Papers*, Series One, *Speeches, Debates and Interviews*, vol. 4, *1864–80*, ed. John W. Blassingame and John R. McKivigan (New Haven: Yale University Press, 1979), 245–46.

95 Ibid., 252.

96 "Santo Domingo," in Frederick Douglass Papers, Schomburg Center for Research in Black Culture, n.d., 3.

97 Ibid., 1.

98 Ibid., 5–6.

99 See Domingo Faustino Sarmiento, *Facundo: Civilization and Barbarism*, trans. Kathleen Ross (Los Angeles: University of California Press, 2004). Sarmiento was not the first Latin American thinker to formulate a critique of Spain. The region's most prominent founding father, Simón Bolívar, argued in 1819 that

Spain had deprived Latin American *criollos* of any education in politics by giving them no say in how they were governed. See Simón Bolívar, "The Angostura Address," in *El Libertador: Writings of Simón Bolívar*, trans. Frederick Fornoff and ed. David Bushnell (New York: Oxford University Press, 2003).

100 Domingo Faustino Sarmiento, *North and South America: A Discourse Delivered before the Rhode Island Historical Society, December 27, 1865* (Providence, RI: Knowles, Anthony, 1866), 27, 35.

101 Douglass, "Santo Domingo," 13.

102 Ibid., 15.

103 Ibid., 21.

104 For US debates about slavery's purported "civilizing" effects, see Fredrickson, *The Black Image in the White Mind*, 53–54, 69. Pro-slavery apologists drew support from the American ethnologist Morton's claim that blacks had never achieved a high degree of civilization. They also pointed to Haiti as an example of how blacks would relapse into their natural savagery and slaughter their white masters if they attained freedom.

105 Douglass, "Santo Domingo," 22–23.

106 Ibid., 26–27.

107 "Reminiscences of the Anti-Slavery Conflict (as Delivered during the Lecture Season of 1872–1873)," in Frederick Douglass Papers, Library of Congress, 1872–1873, 8–9.

108 The Latin Americanization of US racial politics is not necessarily positive. According to Eduardo Bonilla-Silva, for example, the United States became more like Latin America in the late twentieth century as it abandoned the use of race in public policy and adopted a form of color-blind racism that denied the existence of race even as it functioned to maintain white supremacy and racial inequality. See Eduardo Bonilla-Silva, *Racism without Racists: Color-Blind Racism and the Persistence of Racial Inequality in America*, 4th ed. (Lanham, MD: Rowman & Littlefield, 2013).

109 Douglass, "Annexion of San Domingo."

110 "Our Composite Nationality," 259.

111 "Composite," in *Oxford English Dictionary Online* (Oxford University Press, 2014).

112 "Our Composite Nationality," 249–50.

113 Ibid., 253.

114 Ibid., 256.

115 Caribbean intellectuals did not share Douglass's enthusiasm for annexation, nor his apparently sincere, if convenient, belief that it would benefit the Dominican Republic and the region as a whole. The Puerto Rican nationalist and proponent of an Antillean Confederation Ramón Betances, for example, along with other Caribbean intellectuals in the United States, defended Dominican sovereignty and mobilized support against annexation in the US

Congress. See letter from Betances reproduced in Manuel Rodriguez Objio, *Gregorio Luperón e historia de la restauración*, vol. 2 (Santiago, Republica Dominicana: Editorial El Diario, 1939), 323.

116 Douglass, "Reminiscences of the Anti-Slavery Conflict," 4, 13.

117 *The Life and Times of Frederick Douglass*, 453.

118 Douglass's primary interlocutor during his diplomatic mission in Haiti was the Haitian intellectual Anténor Firmin, who served as Foreign Relations Minister at the time. Firmin was the author of a radical text challenging Count Joseph Arthur de Gobineau's *Essay on the Inequality of the Races*, which coupled a historically determinist account of Aryan supremacy with a condemnation of miscegenation. Firmin argued that race was not biological, that all men were equal, and that racial mixing did not lead to degeneration. He mentions Douglass multiple times in the text, as an example of a "remarkable" mulatto. Firmin cited Douglass's *Narrative* directly, particularly Douglass's claim that he had inherited his abilities from his enslaved black mother. It is unclear whether Douglass read Firmin's book. It was originally published in 1885, a few years before Douglass's arrival in Haiti, but was only available in French until a recent English translation. See Anténor Firmin, *The Equality of the Human Races*, trans. Asselin Charles (Chicago: University of Illinois Press, 2002).

119 Frederick Douglass, "Haiti and the United States. Inside History of the Negotiations for the Môle St. Nicholas. I," *North American Review* 153, no. 418 (1891): 343–44.

120 Ibid., 339.

121 Ibid., 339–40.

122 José Martí, "Carta al Señor Director de *La Nación*, 30 de Octubre de 1889," in *Obras completas*, by José Martí (La Habana: Editorial Nacional de Cuba, 1964), 351–52. Martí's critique of Douglass was also driven in part by a strategic interest: securing Haitian support for the Cuban war of independence.

123 Jossianna Arroyo, "Revolution in the Caribbean: Betances, Haiti and the Antillean Confederation," *La Habana Elegante* 49 (Spring/Summer 2011).

124 On the idea of the Haitian revolution as "the unspeakable as trauma, utopia," which led to its disavowal, see Sibylle Fischer, *Modernity Disavowed: Haiti and the Cultures of Slavery in the Age of Revolution* (Durham, NC: Duke University Press, 2004), 2.

125 Colin L. Westerbeck, "Frederick Douglass Chooses His Moment," *Art Institute of Chicago Museum Studies* 24, no. 2 (1999): 146. According to Westerbeck, the person in charge of the Exposition's ethnological displays was Harvard professor F. W. Putnam, who was a mentee of Agassiz's and intellectual heir to the American school of ethnology.

126 This is evident from letters that various Haitians wrote to Douglass after 1891. See Foner, *The Life and Writings of Frederick Douglass*, 4:138–39.

127 Frederick Douglass, "Introduction to the Reason Why the Colored American Is Not in the World's Columbian Exposition," in *The Life and Writings of Frederick Douglass*, vol. 4, *Reconstruction and After*, ed. Philip S. Foner (New York: International Publishers, 1955), 470–71.

128 Ibid., 477.

129 "The Lessons of the Hour," 492–93.

130 Ibid., 496.

131 Ibid., 508.

132 Ibid., 511.

133 Ibid., 520.

134 One member of the audience at Douglass's lecture was the 27-year-old W. E. B. Du Bois, recently returned from obtaining his PhD in Germany. Du Bois recalled the moment (the only time the two men met), in a eulogy he delivered at Wilberforce upon Douglass's death in 1895. See Herbert Aptheker, "Du Bois on Douglass: 1895," *Journal of Negro History* 49, no. 4 (October 1964): 264–68.

135 Frederick Douglass, *Lecture on Haiti* (Chicago: Violet Agents Supply Co., 1893), 21–22.

136 Ibid., 15–16. Douglass's references to Haitian "manhood" and "men of the negro race" here are belied by his statements elsewhere in the speech in praise of Haitian women, of whom he said: "I thought the women quite superior to the men. They are elastic, vigorous and comely. They move with the step of a blooded horse. The industry, wealth and prosperity of the country depends largely upon them ... the men did not strike me as equal to the women." Ibid., 13–14.

137 Ibid., 16.

138 Ibid., 10.

139 Indeed, in a chapter on the impact of the Haitian revolution on US history, Du Bois suggested that one of the reasons the international slave trade was abolished in the United States in 1807 was because southern slave-owners feared the revolutionary ideas brought by free Haitians and West Indian slaves imported from the Caribbean. See W. E. B. Du Bois, *The Suppression of the African Slave Trade to the United States of America, 1638–1870* (New York: Oxford University Press, 2007), 50–66.

140 Douglass, *Lecture on Haiti*, 7.

141 Ibid., 11.

142 Ibid., 14.

CHAPTER 2

1 Domingo Faustino Sarmiento, "Introducción," in *Vida de Abran Lincoln* (New York: D. Appleton, 1866), xiv, xlvii. Sarmiento's correspondence dates the writing and original publication of the book to 1865.

2 An authoritative reconsideration of Sarmiento's oeuvre, for example, contains only one essay that deals with his writings on the United States. See Tulio Halperín Donghi et al., eds., *Sarmiento: Author of a Nation* (Berkeley: University of California Press, 1994). Readings of Sarmiento's work as an example of the travel narrative have also focused on *Facundo* and the European portions of *Viajes*, not his writings on the United States. See chapter 8 in Mary Louise Pratt, *Imperial Eyes: Travel Writing and Transculturation* (London: Routledge, 1992).

3 Katherine A. Gordy, "No Better Way to Be Latin American: European Science and Thought, Latin American Theory?," *Postcolonial Studies* 16, no. 4 (2014): 358–73.

4 If Sarmiento is read as an Argentinean nationalist and Argentina's political problems are seen as sui generis within the region, his status as a "representative" Latin American thinker is debatable. I do not think this is the case, however. Many of the themes Sarmiento articulated were also central concerns of other Latin American intellectuals, such as the problem of *caudillismo*, the question of how to adapt foreign models and ideas, and the fear of US hegemony in the Americas.

5 Nevertheless, this concern did not impel Sarmiento to call for the political unification of Latin America, in contrast to later anti-imperial Latin American thinkers.

6 Sarmiento was a strong proponent of secularism and the separation between church and state; in a Latin American context, he is thus classified as a liberal because of his anti-clericalism, defense of the rule of law, and promotion of public education. Martí was a fierce critic of the United States and advocate of Latin American Pan-Americanism who advocated a de-racialized liberalism. Mariátegui, meanwhile, was one of the forefathers of Latin American Marxism, which he nationalized by incorporating elements of *indigenismo*. Vasconcelos shared Sarmiento's critique of *caudillismo*, but he advocated Latin American unity on the basis of a shared mestizo identity deeply indebted to the Spanish colonial legacy. On the links between Sarmiento and Mariátegui, see Gordy, "No Better Way to Be Latin American."

7 Sarmiento, "Introducción," xv, emphasis added.

8 Gordy also argues that "the local overwhelms the universal" in *Facundo*, but she does not discuss Sarmiento's later writings, such as his concrete engagement with and critique of Europe in *Viajes*. See Gordy, "No Better Way to Be Latin American," 368.

9 This is probably especially true for those interested in recuperating a normatively appealing conception of race from within Latin American political thought, which is not my primary aim here. Diego Von Vacano, for example, has argued that Latin American thinkers developed a "synthetic" paradigm of race that still has useful implications today. See Diego A. Von Vacano, *The Color of Citizenship: Race, Modernity and Latin American/Hispanic Political Thought* (New York: Oxford University Press, 2012).

10 Echoes of Sarmiento's notion of indigenous people as barbarous and in need of civilization are evident in contemporary elite discourses and press depictions of Mapuche activists as "terrorists" who threaten the rule of law and economic development. See Patricia Richards, *Race and the Chilean Miracle: Neoliberalism, Democracy, and Indigenous Rights* (Pittsburgh, PA: University of Pittsburgh Press, 2013); Héctor Nahuelpan Moreno, "Formación colonial del Estado y desposesión en Ngulumapu," in *Ta iñ fijke xipa rakizuameluwün: historia, colonialismo y resistencia desde el país Mapuche*, by Héctor Nahuelpan Moreno et al. (Temuco, Chile: Ediciones Comunidad de Historia Mapuche, 2012), 123–56.

11 See Aline Helg, "Race in Argentina and Cuba, 1880–1930: Theory, Policies, and Popular Reaction," in *The Idea of Race in Latin America, 1870–1940*, by Richard Graham, Thomas E. Skidmore, Aline Helg, and Alan Knight (Austin: University of Texas Press, 1990); Lourdes Martínez-Echazábal, "Mestizaje and the Discourse of National/Cultural Identity in Latin America, 1845–1959," *Latin American Perspectives* 25, no. 3 (1998): 21–42.

12 Elizabeth Garrels, "Sobre indios, Afroamericanos y los racismos de Sarmiento," *Revista Iberoamericana* 63, nos. 178–179 (1997): 103.

13 Mary Tyler Peabody Mann was the wife and later widow of the famous educational reformer Horace Mann, whom Sarmiento greatly admired. She was a teacher and advocate of education in her own right, a committed abolitionist, and supporter of women's suffrage. During Sarmiento's stay in the United States in the 1860s, they established what became a lifelong correspondence. She gained him entrée into US intellectual circles and translated a number of his works into English for publication in the United States, most notably *Facundo*.

14 Social Darwinists applied biological concepts of natural selection and survival of the fittest to human societies; they argued that different races exhibited different levels of aptitude, including the ability to survive and become dominant. As a result, Anglo-Saxons or Europeans were destined to rule over nonwhite races. See Helg, "Race in Argentina and Cuba, 1880–1930."

15 George M. Fredrickson, *The Black Image in the White Mind: The Debate on Afro-American Character and Destiny, 1817–1914* (Middletown, CT: Wesleyan University Press, 1987), 2.

16 Thomas E. Skidmore, *Black into White: Race and Nationality in Brazilian Thought*, 2d ed. (Durham, NC: Duke University Press, 1993), 48–49, 52.

17 *Criollos* were Spaniards born in the Americas.

18 Helg, "Race in Argentina and Cuba, 1880–1930," 38.

19 Ibid., 62n6.

20 Fredrickson, *The Black Image in the White Mind*, 74–76.

21 Skidmore, *Black into White*, 50.

22 Cited in Brian Wallis, "Black Bodies, White Science: Louis Agassiz's Slave Daguerreotypes," *American Art* 9, no. 2 (1995): 44.

220 Notes

23 Cited in Louis Menand, "Morton, Agassiz, and the Origins of Scientific Racism in the United States," *Journal of Blacks in Higher Education* 34 (Winter 2001–2002): 112.

24 Wallis, "Black Bodies, White Science," 40, 44–46. See also Molly Rogers, *Delia's Tears: Race, Science, and Photography in Nineteenth-Century America* (New Haven, CT: Yale University Press, 2010).

25 Wallis, "Black Bodies, White Science," 52–54.

26 Agassiz assembled a similar photographic archive of different racial types during his trip to Brazil in 1865, which was also never published. See Maria Helena P. T. Machado and Sasha Huber, *(T)races of Louis Agassiz: Photography, Body and Science, Yesterday and Today* (São Paulo: Capacete, 2010).

27 Frederick Douglass, *The Claims of the Negro Ethnologically Considered: An Address before the Literary Societies of Western Reserve College at Commencement, July 12, 1854* (Rochester, NY: Lee, Mann, 1854), 20.

28 Ibid., 20–21.

29 Douglass argued that the visual playing field needed to be leveled: "if the very best type of the European is always presented . . . the very best type of the negro should also be taken." Why, he wondered, were the portraits used by the ethnologists never of black luminaries such as Henry Highland Garnet, Alexander Crummell, Martin Delany, and hundreds of others that would "indicate the presence of intellect." Ibid., 21. Douglass's wish was fulfilled by a lithograph of "distinguished colored men" produced in 1883 in which he is prominently featured in the center. See Menand, "Morton, Agassiz, and the Origins of Scientific Racism in the United States," 113.

30 Domingo Faustino Sarmiento, "El poeta Longfellow," in *Obras de D. F. Sarmiento*, vol. 55, ed. Augusto Belin Sarmiento (Buenos Aires: Imprenta Mariano Moreno, 1900), 372. Sarmiento used the phrase in an obituary of Longfellow published in 1882 in which he reported meeting Agassiz and the poet. The astronomer Benjamin Gould also mentioned meeting Sarmiento alongside Ralph Waldo Emerson, Longfellow, and Agassiz in the company of Mary Mann. See Benjamin Gould, "Letter to D. F. Sarmiento, March 26, 1872," Buenos Aires, Argentina, Museo Histórico Sarmiento, documento #4808.

31 July 22 and September 25, 1865, letters from Mary Mann to Sarmiento, in *"My Dear Sir": Mary Mann's Letters to Sarmiento (1865–1881)*, by Mary Tyler Peabody Mann and Barry L. Velleman (Buenos Aires: ICANA: Instituto Cultural Argentino Norteamericano, 2001), 38, 45.

32 Letter to Mrs. Mann, dated January 24, 1868, Domingo Faustino Sarmiento, *Cartas de Sarmiento a la señora María Mann* (Buenos Aires: Academia Argentina de Letras, 1936), 51.

33 Louis Agassiz, "Letter to D. F. Sarmiento, March 6th, 1867," Buenos Aires, Argentina, Museo Histórico Sarmiento, documento #4449, 2.

34 See Mary Mann's April 5, 1867, letter to Sarmiento, in Mann and Velleman, *"My Dear Sir": Mary Mann's Letters*, 138.

35 Domingo Faustino Sarmiento, *North and South America: A Discourse Delivered before the Rhode Island Historical Society, December 27, 1865* (Providence, RI: Knowles, Anthony, 1866), 26.

36 *Conflicto y armonías de las razas en América* (Buenos Aires: La Cultura Argentina, 1915), 113, 116–17.

37 Ibid., 116.

38 Louis Agassiz and Elizabeth Cabot Cary Agassiz, *A Journey in Brazil* (Boston: Ticknor and Fields, 1868), 293. The book was jointly written by Agassiz and his wife, but this particular passage appears in a footnote signed by Agassiz. On the context and impact of Agassiz's visit to Brazil, see Maria Helena P. T. Machado, "A ciência Norte-Americana visita a Amazônia: entre o criacionismo cristão e o poligenismo 'degeneracionista,'" *Revista USP*, no. 75 (2007): 68–75.

39 Domingo Faustino Sarmiento, "Una carta a Mrs. Mann, Diciembre 6 de 1882," in *Obras de D. F. Sarmiento*, vol. 37, ed. Augusto Belin Sarmiento (Buenos Aires: Imprenta Mariano Moreno, 1900), 319–20.

40 In Argentina, the Free Womb Act of 1813 declared all children of enslaved women free. The country's first constitution abolished slavery in 1853, and once national unification was achieved in 1861 slavery was abolished throughout the country. Gradual and contested emancipation was the pattern in most of Latin America. A few countries abolished slavery at the same time as they declared independence from Spain in the 1820s (i.e., Central America, Chile, and Mexico). The majority followed a program of gradual emancipation that began with "Free Womb Laws" and culminated with the abolition of slavery in the 1850s (i.e., Argentina, Bolivia, Colombia, Ecuador, Peru, and Venezuela). Cuba (1886) and Brazil (1888) were the last countries in the region to outlaw slavery.

41 Gordy, "No Better Way to Be Latin American," 368.

42 Emilio Carilla, *El embajador Sarmiento: Sarmiento y los Estados Unidos* (Rosario, Argentina: Universidad Nacional del Litoral, Facultad de Filosofía y Letras, 1961), 60.

43 Letter from Sarmiento to Mary Mann dated October 3, 1865, in Sarmiento, *Cartas de Sarmiento a la señora María Mann*, 10.

44 "El Norte Americanismo republicano," in *Obras de D. F. Sarmiento*, vol. 39, ed. Augusto Belin Sarmiento (Buenos Aires: Imprenta Mariano Moreno, 1900), 69.

45 "Carta a Augusto Belin Sarmiento, Marzo de 1874," in *Sarmiento a través de su epistolario*, ed. Julia Ottolenghi (Buenos Aires: Libreria y Casa Editora Jesus Menendez, 1939), 109.

46 As a result of its location as a port city with access to river trade routes and the South Atlantic, Buenos Aires was the largest and wealthiest city in Argentina. In addition to being a thriving commercial center, it was also the cultural and

intellectual capital of the country and was continuously exposed to ideas and cultural trends from Europe. These economic and cultural differences caused tension between Buenos Aires and the land-locked regions of the country.

47 John Lynch, *Caudillos in Spanish America, 1800–1850* (Oxford: Clarendon Press, 1992).

48 Domingo Faustino Sarmiento, *Facundo: Civilization and Barbarism*, trans. Kathleen Ross (Los Angeles: University of California Press, 2004), 32.

49 Ibid., 45–46. The term *"gaucho"* was used in certain South American countries to refer to rural populations of skilled horsemen that worked primarily in cattle herding. A *gaucho* is similar to a North American cowboy.

50 Ibid., 49. Sarmiento's arguments recall Montesquieu's on the geographical determination of character in *The Spirit of the Laws*. Sarmiento had certainly read Montesquieu, but he does not cite him by name in this passage. When he does specifically reference Montesquieu's ideas elsewhere in *Facundo*, it is to cite the adoption of his theory of the separation of powers in Latin America. See ibid., 123.

51 Sarmiento, *Facundo*, 50.

52 Ibid., 59.

53 See González Echevarría, "Introduction," in ibid., 12.

54 Sarmiento, *Facundo*, 51.

55 Arguments about civilization and savagery were also deployed in US debates about slavery. In the 1840s, defenders of slavery used Morton's argument that blacks had failed to reach an advanced state of civilization in Africa to claim that slavery had a "civilizing" effect on blacks. They claimed that emancipation would lead blacks to relapse into barbarism and to slaughter their white masters, as had occurred in Haiti. In the 1850s pro-slavery southerners continued to view Haiti as an example of degeneration, where blacks had relapsed into their "natural" savagery. Fredrickson, *The Black Image in the White Mind*, 53–54, 69.

56 Sarmiento, *Facundo*, 50–51.

57 Ibid., 152.

58 Lea Geler, ""¡Pobres negros!": algunos apuntes sobre la desaparición de los negros Argentinos," in *Estado, región y poder local en América Latina, siglos XIX–XX: algunas miradas sobre el estado, el poder y la participación política*, ed. Pilar Garcia Jordán (Barcelona: Universitat de Barcelona, 2007), 122.

59 Amaranto A. Abeledo, *Ambas Américas: en torno al discurso pronunciado por Domingo Faustino Sarmiento ante la Sociedad Histórica de Rhode Island, Providence 27 Diciembre 1865* (Buenos Aires: Talleres Luz, 1967), 25.

60 Sarmiento, *Facundo*, 126.

61 Independence-era thinkers such as Bolívar argued that Spain's colonial regime had been especially despotic and had left Latin Americans unprepared to govern themselves. See Simón Bolívar, "The Angostura Address," in *El Libertador: Writings of Simón Bolívar*, trans. Frederick Fornoff and ed. David Bushnell (New York: Oxford University Press, 2003).

62 Abeledo, *Ambas Américas*, 25–26.

63 Ibid., 248–49.

64 Allison Williams Bunkley, *The Life of Sarmiento* (New York: Greenwood Press, 1969), 303–4.

65 Carilla makes a similar point, arguing that the shift to the United States was accompanied by the adoption of more fixed ideas about race, a claim that is true for *Conflicto* but not for Sarmiento's writings in the 1860s. See Carilla, *El embajador Sarmiento*, 146–47.

66 In Sarmiento's words: "Tocqueville revealed to us, for the first time, the secret of North America." Sarmiento, *Facundo*, 126.

67 Domingo Faustino Sarmiento, *Viajes en Europa, Africa y América 1845–1847*, vol. 2 (Santiago, Chile: Imprenta de Julio Belin y Compañia, 1851), 76.

68 Ibid., 58.

69 Ibid., 59.

70 Ibid., 60.

71 Ibid., 75.

72 Ibid., 84.

73 Douglass's *Narrative* was published two years before Sarmiento's visit to the United States. It is not clear whether Sarmiento ever read this or any of Douglass's other works, although it seems unlikely that he would have been unaware of who he was given Douglass's prominence in abolitionist circles. In the introduction of *Vida de Lincoln* Sarmiento includes a list of great US statesmen: "Franklin, Webster, Clay, Chase, Grant, *Douglass*, Jackson, Lincoln, Johnson." See "Introducción," xliv, emphasis added. This is probably a typographical error, however, as Sarmiento likely meant to refer to Stephen Douglas, the Illinois senator. I have not been able to locate the original manuscript.

74 *Viajes en Europa*, 75.

75 Ibid., 159.

76 See Frederick Douglass, "What to the Slave Is the Fourth of July," in *The Oxford Frederick Douglass Reader*, ed. William L. Andrews (New York: Oxford University Press, 1996).

77 Domingo Faustino Sarmiento, "Carta al señor D. Luis Montt," in *Obras de D. F. Sarmiento*, vol. 29, ed. Augusto Belin Sarmiento (Buenos Aires: Imprenta Mariano Moreno, 1899), 6.

78 Letter from Sarmiento to his grandson, cited in "El año nuevo: a 'El Zonda' de San Juan, Nueva York, Enero 6 de 1866," in *Obras de D. F. Sarmiento*, vol. 29, ed. Augusto Belin Sarmiento (Buenos Aires: Imprenta de Mariano Moreno, 1899), 88, editor's note.

79 This is a paraphrase of the title of Martí's famous 1894 essay. See José Martí, "The Truth about the United States," in *José Martí: Selected Writings*, trans. Esther Allen (New York: Penguin Classics, 2002), 329–33.

80 On US expansion, see Reginald Horsman, *Race and Manifest Destiny: The Origins of American Racial Anglo-Saxonism* (Cambridge, MA: Harvard University Press, 1981).

81 Domingo Faustino Sarmiento, *Las escuelas: base de la prosperidad y de la república en los Estados Unidos* (New York: D. Appleton, 1866), 184.

82 Domingo Faustino Sarmiento, *Ambas Américas: revista de educación, bibliografía y agricultura*, 4 vols. (Nueva York: Imprenta de Hallet y Breen, 1867), 1:7.

83 Carilla, *El embajador Sarmiento*, 53.

84 Sarmiento, *North and South America*, 25.

85 Ibid., 19, 21.

86 Ibid., 17–18.

87 Ibid., 32.

88 Ibid., 35, emphasis added.

89 Ibid., 35–36.

90 Ibid., 15, emphasis added.

91 In 1863, Spain attempted to regain the Dominican Republic and the French led an expedition to Mexico that resulted in the creation of the Mexican empire under Maximilian of Austria in 1864. These events led to a continental congress to consider mutual defense, in which Sarmiento participated as Argentina's representative.

92 Sarmiento, *North and South America*, 44.

93 "Introducción," xxix–xxx.

94 Ibid., xxxiii.

95 Ibid., xxxiv.

96 Ibid., xxxv.

97 July 22, 1865, letter from Mary Mann to Sarmiento, in Mann and Velleman, *"My Dear Sir": Mary Mann's Letters*, 38–39.

98 Babcock's interest in emigration apparently continued, as he was part of a delegation of African Americans sent to British Honduras (now Belize) in August 1863 by the US Emigration Office to investigate its potential for colonization. Babcock and J. Willis Menard (a free black newspaperman who was the leader of the delegation) presented the British Honduras project to Rev. Henry Highland Garnet's African Civilization Society in New York City, and Babcock published a brief report on the trip entitled *British Honduras, Central America: A Plain Statement to the Colored People of the U.S. who Contemplate Emigration* (Salem, MA: C. Babcock, 1863).

99 Sarmiento, *Cartas de Sarmiento a la señora María Mann*, 165.

100 Mann and Velleman, *"My Dear Sir": Mary Mann's Letters*, 28n8. According to Velleman, Sarmiento's stay in the United States coincided with the most active years of the AFUC (1865–1869), and Sarmiento mentioned attending a meeting of the Freedmen's Aid Society in New York City in 1866 in an October 24, 1866, letter to Mrs. Mann. Sarmiento, *Cartas de Sarmiento a la señora María Mann*, 235.

101 Sarmiento, *Las escuelas*, 165.

102 Mann and Velleman, *"My Dear Sir": Mary Mann's Letters*, 25.

103 See Saidiya V. Hartman, *Scenes of Subjection: Terror, Slavery, and Self-Making in Nineteenth-Century America* (New York: Oxford University Press, 1997).

104 Sarmiento, *Las escuelas*, 166.

105 Mann and Velleman, *"My Dear Sir": Mary Mann's Letters*, 29n14.

106 Sarmiento, "Una carta a Mrs. Mann, Diciembre 6 de 1882," 318.

107 Sarmiento, *Cartas de Sarmiento a la señora María Mann*, 100.

108 Sarmiento, "En Estados Unidos," in *Obras completas de Sarmiento*, vol. 21, *Discursos populares, primer volumen*, by Domingo Faustino Sarmiento (Buenos Aires: Editorial Luz del Día, 1951), 231.

109 Sarmiento, *Las escuelas*, 13.

110 Ibid.

111 Ibid., 166. Sarmiento presumably inserted the italics when he reprinted the letter.

112 Ibid., 26.

113 Ibid., 27.

114 "Introducción," xxv.

115 Sarmiento, *Las escuelas*, 27.

116 Ibid., 168.

117 Ibid., 187.

118 Ibid., 182.

119 Ibid., 164. Sarmiento's reservations about uneducated voters also extended to white European immigrants.

120 Sarmiento, *Cartas de Sarmiento a la señora María Mann*, 98.

121 Ibid., 100.

122 June 8, 1866, letter from Sarmiento to Mary Mann, "Cartas de Sarmiento: III. Autobiográficas (Cont.)," *Boletin de la Academia Argentina de Letras* 4 (1936): 310.

123 Mann and Velleman, *"My Dear Sir": Mary Mann's Letters*, 77.

124 Ibid., 130.

125 Sarmiento, "Introducción," xxv.

126 Sarmiento, *Cartas de Sarmiento a la señora María Mann*, 255.

127 Sarmiento, "Introducción," xviii–xix.

128 Ibid., xxiii–xxiv.

129 Ibid., xlii.

130 Ibid., xlvi–xlvii.

131 "Review of Life in the Argentine Republic in the Days of the Tyrants," *New Englander and Yale Review* (October 1868): 678. *Facundo* was also reviewed in *The Atlantic Monthly, The New York Daily Tribune*, and *Putnam's Monthly Magazine*.

132 "Review of Vida de Abran Lincoln," *The Atlantic Monthly* (February 1866): 253.

133 "Review of Life in the Argentine Republic in the Days of the Tyrants," 679.

134 Sarmiento, *Cartas de Sarmiento a la señora María Mann*, 12.

135 Diana Sorensen Goodrich, *Facundo and the Construction of Argentine Culture* (Austin: University of Texas Press, 1996), 112.

136 Social Darwinism applied biological theories of natural selection and the survival of the fittest to societies and racial groups. According to social Darwinists, while humans had a common origin, different races had different levels of aptitude, and as a result whites were destined to prevail in the worldwide struggle between the races.

137 Sarmiento, *Conflicto y armonías de las razas en América*, 63.

138 Ibid., 449.

139 Ibid., 310.

140 Ibid., 449.

141 Ibid., 55.

142 Ibid., 449.

143 Ibid., 454.

144 Ibid., 110.

145 See, e.g., Gilberto Freyre, *The Masters and the Slaves (Casa-Grande & Senzala): A Study in the Development of Brazilian Civilization*, 2d English-language ed. (New York: Knopf, 1956).

146 As president of Argentina (1868–1874), Sarmiento doubled the rate of European immigration by offering immigrants the opportunity to acquire land and settle in the interior of the country. Under Sarmiento, military campaigns were undertaken to occupy frontier territories and displace indigenous peoples from their traditional lands. This policy, which was continued by later Argentinean presidents, culminated in the late 1870s and 1880s in a war of extermination against indigenous peoples in Patagonia known as the "Conquest of the Desert," which some scholars now describe as genocide. See Walter Delrio et al., "Discussing Indigenous Genocide in Argentina: Past, Present, and Consequences of Argentinean State Policies toward Native Peoples," *Genocide Studies and Prevention* 5, no. 2 (2010): 138–59.

147 These efforts echoed US policies of westward expansion and Indian removal fueled by notions of Anglo-Saxon racial superiority. As Horsman has shown, over the course of the nineteenth century, US opinion shifted from the Enlightenment's romantic idea of Indians as "noble savages" to the view that they were innately inferior, doomed to extinction, and beastly when they resisted the appropriation of their lands. See Reginald Horsman, "Racial Destiny and the Indians," in *Race and Manifest Destiny*, 189–207. Paternalistic notions of indigenous communal landholding as an impediment to progress also permeated the rhetoric of even so-called progressive reformers who saw themselves as advocates for Native Americans. This is clear from Martí's reporting on one of the Lake Mohonk Conferences on US Indian policy in 1885. His endorsement of these views also shows that he and Sarmiento were less

far apart on indigenous policy than is usually acknowledged. See Martí, "The Indians in the United States," in *José Martí: Selected Writings*, 157–64.

148 See Aníbal Quijano, "Coloniality of Power, Eurocentrism, and Latin America," *Neplanta* 1, no. 3 (2000): 533–80.

149 Sarmiento, *Conflicto y armonías de las razas en América*, 120.

150 Ibid., 122. On Argentina's black population, see George Reid Andrews, *The Afro-Argentines of Buenos Aires, 1800–1900* (Madison: University of Wisconsin Press, 1980).

151 Sarmiento, *Conflicto y armonías de las razas en América*, 124. Sarmiento's knowledge of African Americans in the United States is also evident in these passages. He observed that in the US blacks had amassed savings and become entrepreneurs, and cited Harriet Beecher Stowe's *Uncle Tom's Cabin*.

152 Sarmiento, *Conflicto y armonías de las razas en América*, 454.

153 David Solodkow, "Racismo y nación: conflictos y (des)armonías identitarias en el proyecto nacional Sarmientino," *Decimonónica* 2, no. 1 (Summer 2005): 95–121.

CHAPTER 3

1 The secondary literature on Du Bois spans multiple disciplines, but political theorists have tended to focus on the influential formulations he developed to limn the existential dilemmas of black identity and his conception of black politics. Recent examples include: Lawrie Balfour, *Democracy's Reconstruction: Thinking Politically with W. E. B. Du Bois* (New York: Oxford University Press, 2011); Robert Gooding-Williams, *In the Shadow of Du Bois: Afro-Modern Political Thought in America* (Cambridge, MA: Harvard University Press, 2009); chapter 3 in Stephen H. Marshall, *The City on the Hill from Below: The Crisis of Prophetic Black Politics* (Philadelphia: Temple University Press, 2011).

2 See Greg Carter, *The United States of the United Races: A Utopian History of Racial Mixing* (New York: New York University Press, 2013); Diego A. Von Vacano, *The Color of Citizenship: Race, Modernity and Latin American/Hispanic Political Thought* (New York: Oxford University Press, 2012).

3 I am indebted to the pioneering queer and feminist scholarship on Du Bois, which has drawn attention to the centrality of gender and sexuality in his work and expanded the relevant archive of Du Bois studies by focusing attention on his fiction. See Susan Kay Gillman and Alys Eve Weinbaum, "Introduction," in *Next to the Color Line: Gender, Sexuality, and W. E. B. Du Bois* (Minneapolis: University of Minnesota Press, 2007), Kindle locations 22, 369.

4 I use the term post-racist to differentiate it from post-racial, with its connotations of color-blindness and the elimination of all use of, or reference to, race. Instead, post-racist is meant to designate political projects to eliminate racial hierarchy and dismantle global white supremacy.

5 The "nadir" era is widely understood by scholars as the period after 1890 (when northern Republicans ceased supporting the rights of southern blacks) through the early twentieth century, extending until around 1940. It was characterized by open adherence to white supremacy, heightened racial terror (including lynching and other forms of racist violence), and the codification of racial segregation, including anti-miscegenation legislation. The term was initially coined by the historian Rayford W. Logan, *The Negro in American Life and Thought: The Nadir, 1877–1901* (New York: Dial Press, 1954).

6 Nancy Stepan, *The Hour of Eugenics: Race, Gender, and Nation in Latin America* (Ithaca, NY: Cornell University Press, 1991), 1–2, 31.

7 This is true of Latin America's most famous twentieth-century proponents of mestizaje, José Vasconcelos and Gilberto Freyre.

8 This chapter provides an intersectional reading of Du Bois on the specific topic of racial mixture. There is a much larger debate about Du Bois's gender politics. Some black feminists have argued that despite his public support for women's rights, Du Bois's masculinist presuppositions mar the portrayal of black women in his work. He has also been critiqued for his consistent failure to cite and give sufficient credit to black female intellectuals and activists who were his contemporaries (as well as the way he carried out intimate relationships in his personal life). Two of the key texts in the debate about Du Bois and feminism are the essays by Hazel Carby and Joy James in Gillman and Weinbaum, *Next to the Color Line*. Meanwhile, recent queer readings of Du Bois find examples of nonnormative masculinities in his work, such as: Monica L. Miller, "W. E. B. Du Bois and the Dandy as Diasporic Race Man," *Callaloo* 26, no. 3 (2003): 738–65.

9 Peggy Pascoe, "Between a Rock and a Hard Place," in *What Comes Naturally: Miscegenation Law and the Making of Race in America*, by Peggy Pascoe (Oxford: Oxford University Press, 2009), 172.

10 Reginald Horsman, *Race and Manifest Destiny: The Origins of American Racial Anglo-Saxonism* (Cambridge, MA: Harvard University Press, 1981), 157.

11 W. E. B. Du Bois, *Dusk of Dawn: An Essay toward an Autobiography of a Race Concept*, in *Writings*, ed. Nathan I. Huggins (New York: Library of America, 1986), 603.

12 Lawrie Balfour, "Darkwater's Democratic Vision," *Political Theory* 38, no. 4 (2010): 539.

13 Gillman and Weinbaum persuasively suggest that focusing on Du Bois's use of juxtaposition in his multi-genre works reveals the centrality of gender and sexuality in his work. See Gillman and Weinbaum, "Introduction," in *Next to the Color Line: Gender, Sexuality, and W. E. B. Du Bois*, Kindle locations 41, 350.

14 Balfour, "Darkwater's Democratic Vision," 541.

15 Lourdes Martínez-Echazábal, "Mestizaje and the Discourse of National/Cultural Identity in Latin America, 1845–1959," *Latin American Perspectives* 25, no. 3 (1998): 23–24.

16 Du Bois, *Dusk of Dawn*, 651.

17 My use of the term "futurism" to describe Du Bois and Vasconcelos's writings about mixture is meant to convey the importance of questions of temporality and political imagination in the texts analyzed in Part II. It is not a reference to the early twentieth-century avant-garde Italian artistic movement, whose involvement with Italian fascism nevertheless serves as an important reminder of the dangers of intellectual and political projects aimed at postulating possible or preferable futures. The Italian futurists prized technological innovations (such as the car, the airplane, the industrial city, etc.) that embodied human mastery over nature; they were also passionate nationalists who endorsed violence and glorified the hygienic properties of war.

18 Claudia Tate, "Introduction," in *Dark Princess: A Romance* (Jackson, MS: Banner Books/University Press of Mississippi, 1995), xxi.

19 Arnold Rampersad, "Du Bois's Passage to India: Dark Princess," in *W. E. B. Du Bois on Race and Culture: Philosophy, Politics, and Poetics*, ed. Bernard W. Bell, Emily Grosholz, and James B. Stewart (New York: Routledge, 1996), 161.

20 Dohra Ahmad, "'More Than Romance': Genre and Geography in Dark Princess," *ELH* 69, no. 3 (2002): 776.

21 Alondra Nelson, "Introduction: Future Texts," *Social Text* 20, no. 2 (Summer 2002): 1.

22 For instance, Du Bois's notion of double consciousness is an exploration of fractured subjectivity, and the concept of social death used to analyze enslavement is also reminiscent of the not-quite human condition of cyborgs and aliens.

23 Kodwo Eshun, "Further Considerations on Afrofuturism," *CR: The New Centennial Review* 3, no. 2 (2003): 293.

24 Lisa Yaszek, "An Afrofuturist Reading of Ralph Ellison's *Invisible Man*," *Rethinking History* 9, nos. 2–3 (2005): 299.

25 On Du Bois and the uses of the past, see Balfour, *Democracy's Reconstruction*, especially chapters 1 and 2.

26 A recently discovered (and previously unpublished) short story written between 1908 and 1910, which has been described as a work of speculative fantasy romance, shows that Du Bois was experimenting with science fiction at least a decade before *Darkwater*. See W. E. B. Du Bois, Adrienne Brown, and Britt Rusert, "The Princess Steel," *PMLA* 130, no. 3 (2015): 819–29.

27 Du Bois, *Dusk of Dawn*, 551, 55. There is a rich existing scholarship on the prophetic tradition in African American political thought specifically, and on prophecy as a dominant language in US politics. See Marshall, *The City on the Hill from Below*; George M. Shulman, *American Prophecy: Race and Redemption in American Political Culture* (Minneapolis: University of Minnesota Press, 2008); Cornel West, *Prophesy Deliverance!: An Afro-American Revolutionary Christianity* (Louisville, KY: Westminster John Knox Press, 2002).

28 W. E. B. Du Bois, "Criteria of Negro Art," *The Crisis* 32 (October 1926): 290, 96.

29 Ahmad, "'More Than Romance,'" 775.

30 Rampersad, "Du Bois's Passage to India: Dark Princess," 166.

31 Ahmad, "'More Than Romance,'" 781–82.

32 Du Bois was not the only African American intellectual in the 1920s to incorporate locales outside the United States in his texts. Black internationalism was a feature of the literature of the "New Negro" Movement, which, despite its putative location in Harlem, also encompassed black intellectuals outside the United States. See Brent Hayes Edwards, *The Practice of Diaspora: Literature, Translation, and the Rise of Black Internationalism* (Cambridge, MA: Harvard University Press, 2003).

33 Nicole Waligora-Davis, "W. E. B. Du Bois and the Fourth Dimension," *CR: The New Centennial Review* 6, no. 3 (2006): 61–63. "Transcaucasia" was coined by Herbert Aptheker, Du Bois's literary executor, and affixed to a letter by Du Bois describing the publication history of his essay, "My Evolving Program for Negro Freedom."

34 Ibid., 82.

35 On the great migration and other transformations in black life in the United States after the publication of *Souls*, see Evelyn Brooks Higginbotham's "Introduction," in W. E. B. Du Bois, *Darkwater: Voices from within the Veil*, The Oxford W. E. B. Du Bois (New York: Oxford University Press, 2007), xxv–xxxix.

36 According to Bill Mullen, *Dark Princess* reflects "Du Bois's political engagement with three central movements and events of the interwar era: the Indian home rule and national movements, the emergence of black radicalism in the United States, and the role of black and Asian radicals in revising Soviet policy on both 'Negro' and Asian liberation during the formation of the Third International after 1919 and the crucial 1922 and 1928 Cominterns in Moscow." Bill V. Mullen, "Du Bois, *Dark Princess*, and the Afro-Asian International," *positions* 11, no. 1 (2003): 218. The novel also anticipates the seminal 1955 Bandung conference of Afro-Asian internationalists to further decolonization that eventually resulted in the Non-Aligned Movement.

37 Herbert Aptheker, "Introduction," in W. E. B. Du Bois, *Dark Princess: A Romance* (Millwood, NY: Kraus-Thompson, 1974), 7.

38 Herbert Aptheker, "Introduction," in *Darkwater: Voices from within the Veil* (Millwood, NY: Kraus-Thomson, 1975), 7.

39 As Duncan Bell has shown, white supremacist racial utopias that envisioned imperial Anglo-Saxon domination over the globe as a means of securing peace and order constituted a significant (and entirely respectable) current in international relations thinking in the late nineteenth and early twentieth century. See Duncan Bell, "Before the Democratic Peace: Racial Utopianism, Empire and the Abolition of War," *European Journal of International Relations* 20, no. 3 (2014): 647–70.

40 Du Bois, *Dusk of Dawn*, 626.

41 As Higginbotham has observed; this was an era when "racial boundaries were adamantly defended." This was true of nonfiction works of racial science that purported to prove Anglo-Saxon racial superiority, such as those of Madison Grant and Lothrop Stoddard. It was also the case in the popular novels of Thomas Dixon Jr. (*The Leopard's Spots: A Romance of the White Man's Burden, 1865–1900*, published in 1902, and *The Clansman: An Historical Romance of the Ku Klux Klan*, published in 1905) that were the basis for the film *Birth of a Nation*. These romances of white supremacy were enormously popular and culturally influential, at precisely the moment when the Great Migration was occurring. See Higginbotham, "Introduction," in *Darkwater: Voices from within the Veil*, xxvii.

42 Du Bois, "Criteria of Negro Art," 296.

43 According to Aptheker, Du Bois's "sense of optimism ... [his] insistence upon the possibility of bringing about a decent global society" was at odds with the negative tenor of works published by the most popular white writers in the United States in the 1920s. Aptheker, "Introduction," in *Dark Princess: A Romance*, 17.

44 Paul Gilroy, *The Black Atlantic: Modernity and Double Consciousness* (Cambridge, MA: Harvard University Press, 1993), 144.

45 Aptheker, "Introduction," in Du Bois, *Dark Princess: A Romance*, 19.

46 Du Bois's "Conservation of Races" was published only four years after Douglass's "Lecture on Haiti."

47 K. Anthony Appiah, "Illusions of Race," in *In My Father's House: Africa in the Philosophy of Culture* (New York: Oxford University Press, 1992), 36. As Taylor has argued, Appiah's critique of Du Bois is motivated by an unstated commitment to "racial eliminativism," the position that anti-racism is best served by dispensing with any notion of race altogether. See Paul C. Taylor, "Appiah's Uncompleted Argument: W. E. B. Du Bois and the Reality of Race," *Social Theory & Practice* 26, no. 1 (Spring 2000): 103–28.

48 W. E. B. Du Bois, "The Conservation of Races," in *The Oxford W. E. B. Du Bois Reader*, ed. Eric J. Sundquist (New York: Oxford University Press, 1996), 41.

49 Ibid., 40.

50 This is the notion that black politics is a form of leadership and rule that should express the collective spiritual identity that antecedently unites the group. See Gooding-Williams, *In the Shadow of Du Bois: Afro-Modern Political Thought in America*, 4–15.

51 Du Bois, "The Conservation of Races," 43.

52 Ibid., 44. Du Bois's prescriptions for African American progress also included a rigid adherence to black respectability. He argued that African Americans "must be united ... to stop the ravages of consumption among the Negro people, united to keep black boys from loafing, gambling and crime; united to guard the purity of black women and to reduce that vast army of black prostitutes that is today marching to hell." Ibid., 44–45.

53 Ibid., 46, emphasis added.

54 Carter, *The United States of the United Races*, 111, 14. Carter provides a thought-provoking genealogy of an understudied US "optimist tradition" that valorized racial mixing and multiracial identity. Drawing mainly on "Conservation" he reads Du Bois as a foil to this tradition, who acknowledged mixture but nevertheless emphasized a resulting mono-racial identity. In my view this reading is mistaken. As this chapter demonstrates, mixture was an important element of Du Bois's political thought.

55 Jennifer L. Hochschild and Brenna Marea Powell, "Racial Reorganization and the United States Census 1850–1930: Mulattoes, Half-Breeds, Mixed Parentage, Hindoos, and the Mexican Race," *Studies in American Political Development* 22, no. 1 (2008): 67.

56 Most sources point variously to Booker T. Washington, Du Bois, the sociologist Kelly Miller, or the statistician Charles E. Hall (who was employed by the census bureau). Ibid., 70–71.

57 W. E. B. Du Bois, "The Twelfth Census and the Negro Problems," *Southern Workman* 29, no. 5 (May 1900): 307.

58 "Miscegenation," in *Against Racism: Unpublished Essays, Papers, Addresses*, ed. Herbert Aptheker (Amherst: University of Massachusetts Press, 1985), 97. Du Bois is referring to the fact that according to the census the mulatto population fluctuated from 15% of the total US population in 1890, to 21% in 1910, and back down to 16% in 1920, which represented a difference of about 400,000 individuals. The census bureau attributed the rise in the mulatto population in 1910 (and its subsequent decrease in 1920) to having employed a larger number of black enumerators that year. Hochschild and Powell, "Racial Reorganization and the United States Census 1850–1930," 70.

59 Du Bois, "Miscegenation," 96.

60 Cited in Pascoe, "Between a Rock and a Hard Place," 175, emphasis added. Du Bois satirized white paranoia about mixture and the absurdity of racial segregation in the name of preventing "social equality" in the short story, "On Being Crazy," in *Writings*.

61 W. E. B. Du Bois, "Sex Equality," *The Crisis* 19, no. 3 (January 1920): 106.

62 "Marrying of Black Folk," *The Independent*, October 30, 1910, 812–13.

63 Pascoe, "Between a Rock and a Hard Place," 169.

64 Ibid., 173.

65 W. E. B. Du Bois, "Intermarriage," *The Crisis* 5, no. 4 (February 1913): 180.

66 W. E. B. Du Bois, "President Harding and Social Equality," *The Crisis* 23, no. 2 (December 1921): 55.

67 Cited in Pascoe, "Between a Rock and a Hard Place," 183–84.

68 W. E. B. Du Bois, "Social Equality and Racial Intermarriage," *The World Tomorrow* 5, no. 3 (March 1922): 82.

69 "Miscegenation," 90–93, 100.

70 Micol Seigel, "Beyond Compare: Comparative Method after the Transnational Turn," *Radical History Review* 2005, no. 91 (2005): 69–70. According to Siegel, Roosevelt's account was later translated and reprinted on the front page of a Brazilian newspaper, further cementing the terms of the comparison.

71 Ibid., 71.

72 As editor, Du Bois also published a number of other articles on Brazil in *The Crisis*, including an African American journalist's extremely rosy account of his trip to Brazil. Echoing nineteenth-century black emigrationists, R. W. Merguson told his readers that "there is no color prejudice" in Brazil because "the mixture is so general that color ostracism does not exist." He also suggested that "for the ambitious and intelligent colored man . . . it might be well to turn his attention in the direction of Brazil." R. W. Merguson, "Glimpses of Brazil," *The Crisis* 11, no. 1 (1915): 40–41. On African American views of Brazil more generally, see David J. Hellwig, "Racial Paradise or Run-Around? Afro-North American Views of Race Relations in Brazil," *American Studies* 31, no. 2 (1990): 43–60.

73 W. E. B. Du Bois, "Brazil," *The Crisis* 7, no. 6 (April 1914): 287.

74 Du Bois, "President Harding and Social Equality," 56.

75 Carter, *The United States of the United Races*, 133.

76 Du Bois, "Marrying of Black Folk," 813.

77 Pascoe, "Between a Rock and a Hard Place," 178–79.

78 Du Bois, "Intermarriage," 180–81, emphasis added.

79 Pascoe, "Between a Rock and a Hard Place," 190.

80 See Alys Eve Weinbaum, "Interracial Romance and Black Internationalism," in *Next to the Color Line: Gender, Sexuality, and W. E. B. Du Bois*, ed. Susan Kay Gillman and Alys Eve Weinbaum (Minneapolis: University of Minnesota Press, 2007); Alys Eve Weinbaum, "Reproducing Racial Globality: W. E. B. Du Bois and the Sexual Politics of Black Nationalism," *Social Text* 19, no. 2 (Summer 2001): 15–41.

81 See Claudia Tate, "Race and Desire: *Dark Princess*: A Romance," and Michelle Elam and Paul C. Taylor, "Du Bois's Erotics," in *Next to the Color Line*.

82 Kenneth Robert Janken, "Introduction," in *What the Negro Wants*, ed. Rayford Logan (South Bend, IN: University of Notre Dame Press, 2001), xv, xvi.

83 Weinbaum, "Interracial Romance and Black Internationalism," Kindle location 1245.

84 The first two stories are from "Criteria." In addition to "The Comet," the other story of (foreclosed) mixing in *Darkwater* is "The Princess of the Hither Isles."

85 Balfour, "Darkwater's Democratic Vision," 548.

86 Du Bois's shift toward Marxism is evident in the novel's depiction of the ennobling effects of manual labor, and its capacity, when combined with leisure and the opportunity to appreciate beauty and art, to develop universal human political and aesthetic capacities. For example, Matthew's ultimate political development occurs while he is working digging tracks for a new railroad.

In a letter to Kautilya, Matthew explained his resulting realization that their joint mission involved not just an anti-racist, anti-imperial uprising but also economic transformation: "What are you and I trying to do in this world? Not merely to transpose colors. . . . But . . . to reunite thought and physical work." Du Bois's utopian vision in *Dark Princess* thus combined global racial justice (which required an end to colonialism), and the reorientation of African American politics toward black internationalism and economic justice. In Matthew's words: "Here in America black folk must help overthrow the rule of the rich by distributing wealth more evenly first among themselves and then in alliance with white labor, to establish democratic control of industry. During this process they must keep step and hold tight hands with the other struggling darker peoples." Du Bois, *Dark Princess*, 256, 66.

87 Mullen, "Du Bois, *Dark Princess*, and the Afro-Asian International," 219.

88 He also described meeting an Indian royal during the first Universal Races Congress in 1911, the Ranee of Sarawak, who may have been the model for Kautilya. See Du Bois, *Dusk of Dawn*, 722, 55.

89 Edwards, *The Practice of Diaspora*, 5.

90 Mullen, "Du Bois, *Dark Princess*, and the Afro-Asian International," 219, 23. Mullen's critique of Du Bois's Afro-Orientalism is accurate, even though one of the passages he cites as evidence of Du Bois's orientalist depiction of Kautilya is in fact a description of a white woman from the US, the companion of the Ku Klux Klan leader on the train.

91 Ahmad, "'More Than Romance,'" 777, 87–90.

92 Indeed, Weinbaum has argued that Du Bois's positive depiction of black maternity was a direct response to the reproductive politics of racial science, particularly fears of "race suicide." Writers such as Grant and Stoddard stoked fears of black and nonwhite fertility by juxtaposing them to a supposedly declining white birthrate that endangered the status of the United States as a white-majority country. See Weinbaum, "Reproducing Racial Globality."

93 Du Bois, "Criteria of Negro Art," 297.

94 Ibid.

95 Tate, "Introduction," *Dark Princess*, xxiii–xxv.

96 "Race Discrimination: Dark Princess, by W. E. Burghardt Dubois," *New York Times*, May 13, 1928.

97 *Dark Princess*, 49–50, 70.

98 Ibid., 152–53.

99 Ibid., 192.

100 Ibid., 112.

101 Ibid., 213. While Du Bois's portrayal of Sara is generally rather unsympathetic, at one point Matthew does acknowledge that: "Sara was in no sense evil. Her character had been hardened and sharpened by all that she had met and fought." Ibid., 200.

102 There are significant disagreements about Du Bois's gender politics, and about how to interpret these two texts specifically. For an especially even-handed reading of "Damnation," see Farah Jasmine Griffin, "Black Feminists and Du Bois: Respectability, Protection, and Beyond," *ANNALS of the American Academy of Political and Social Science* 568, no. 1 (March 2000): 28–40.

103 Du Bois, *Dark Princess*, 259–60.

104 Ibid., 19.

105 Weinbaum, "Interracial Romance and Black Internationalism," Kindle location 1387.

106 *Dark Princess*, 85–86.

107 These would no doubt have been exacerbated by Du Bois's preference for elitist forms of political rule, which were reiterated in *Dark Princess*. For example, Kautilya explained to Matthew that the Council of Darker Peoples viewed "democracy as a method of discovering real aristocracy. . . . Democracy is not an end, it is a method of aristocracy." Ironically, given her own position, Kautilya also suggested that leaders should be chosen on the basis of: "Talent . . . from the great Reservoir of All Men of All Races, of All Classes, of All Ages, of Both Sexes—this is real Aristocracy, real Democracy." Yet the members of the Council of Darker Peoples claimed that the superiority of the darker peoples was based on "the longer rule of natural aristocracy among us" compared to Europe. Matthew was forced to acknowledge that "we American blacks are very common people. My grandfather was a whipped and driven slave." But he also argued that "capacity for culture is not the hereditary monopoly of a few, but the widespread possibility for the majority of mankind if they only have a decent chance in life." *Dark Princess* thus combined a critique of inherited aristocracy with arguments about leadership and political rule reminiscent of Du Bois's notion of "The Talented Tenth." Ibid., 23, 26, 225, 85.

108 "Memorandum to the Secretary for the NAACP Staff Conference (10 October 1946)," in *Against Racism: Unpublished Essays, Papers, Addresses, 1887–1961*, ed. Herbert Aptheker (Amherst: University of Massachusetts Press, 1985), 257–58. This and other positions led to Du Bois's second dismissal from the NAACP in 1947.

109 *Dusk of Dawn*, 776.

110 *Dark Princess*, 102.

111 Ibid., 286, emphasis added.

112 "An Amazing Island," in *Writings*, 1167–68.

113 Edwards argues that black internationalism "necessarily involves a process of linking and connecting across gaps—a process we might term *articulation* . . . [which] offers a means to account for the diversity of black takes on *diaspora*." Edwards, *The Practice of Diaspora*, 11–12.

114 Du Bois, *Dusk of Dawn*, 551.

115 For example, he claimed to have recognized the scientific import of mixture as early as his famous study of the Philadelphia Negro, one of whose (ignored) recommendations was to study racial mixing in the United States: "here in America is the most remarkable opportunity ever offered of studying … the effect of amalgamating two of the most diverse races in the world—another subject which rests upon a cloud of ignorance." Ibid., 598.

116 Ibid., 629–30.

117 Ibid., 628.

118 Ibid., 560.

119 Ibid., 587.

120 Ibid., 631–32. Du Bois noted that upon *Darkwater*'s publication he was advised by his publisher that erroneously identifying a white person as mixed would be considered "libelous." In what appears to be a reference to Thomas Jefferson and Sally Hemmings's descendants, he added that "lately in Congress the true story in a WPA history, of miscegenation affecting a high historic personage raised a howl of protest."

121 Ibid., 569–70.

122 Ibid., 627–28.

123 Ibid., 636.

124 Ibid., 638, emphasis added.

125 See Benedict R. O'G Anderson, *Imagined Communities: Reflections on the Origin and Spread of Nationalism* (London: Verso, 1983); Eric Hobsbawm and Terence Ranger, eds., *The Invention of Tradition* (Cambridge: Cambridge University Press, 1983).

126 David Scott, *Refashioning Futures: Criticism after Postcoloniality* (Princeton, NJ: Princeton University Press, 1999), 107, 109.

127 Du Bois, *Dusk of Dawn*, 639.

128 Ibid., 640.

129 Ibid., 651.

130 Ibid., 654. See Charles W. Mills, "White Ignorance," in *Race and Epistemologies of Ignorance*, ed. Nancy Tuana and Shannon Sullivan (Albany: State University of New York Press, 2007).

131 Du Bois, *Dusk of Dawn*, 655.

132 Ibid., 665–66.

133 A particularly apt example of this is the discussion in the popular press about how growing rates of mixture in the United States are transforming its racial landscape, such as the *New York Times*'s "Race Remixed" series published in 2011. The articles take as their point of departure the demographic data in the census that show a marked increase in the number of US citizens opting for more than one racial category. According to the *Times*, the number of mixed-race Americans grew by 35% from 2000 to 2011. Most of the articles focused on the response of different government agencies and educational institutions to shifting racial categorizations, but they also highlighted how individuals

negotiated the construction of their own sense of identity. Ironically, despite the implied claim that multiracialism deconstructs racial essentialism, the very framing of the series assumed the existence of prior mono-racial identities that were treated as self-evident, socially obvious categories. See http://topics. nytimes.com/top/news/us/series/race_remixed/index.html.

134 Jared Sexton, *Amalgamation Schemes: Antiblackness and the Critique of Multiracialism* (Minneapolis: University of Minnesota Press, 2008), 1–2. Sexton also identifies the emergence of the academic field of mixed race studies as one of the contemporary manifestations of multiracialism. See Jayne O. Ifekwunigwe, *"Mixed Race" Studies: A Reader* (London: Routledge, 2004).

135 Sexton, *Amalgamation Schemes*, 13.

136 Seigel, "Beyond Compare," 73.

137 Hellwig, "Racial Paradise or Run-Around?," 49.

138 Ibid., 51.

CHAPTER 4

1 José Vasconcelos, *The Cosmic Race/la raza cósmica: A Bilingual Edition*, trans. Didier T. Jaén (Baltimore, MD: Johns Hopkins University Press, 1997), 19.

2 The other key account of Latin American mestizaje is Gilberto Freyre's notion of Brazilian racial democracy. Diego Von Vacano has identified Vasconcelos as part of a "synthetic paradigm" of race in Latin American political thought, in contrast to the "domination" and "dualistic" paradigms characteristic of European and US American political thought, respectively. While there are multiple strands of thinking about race in Latin American political thought, Von Vacano argues that the "synthetic paradigm" is the most distinctive. Diego A. Von Vacano, *The Color of Citizenship: Race, Modernity and Latin American/Hispanic Political Thought* (New York: Oxford University Press, 2012).

3 Henry Louis Gates Jr., for example, has noted the similarities between Jean Toomer's celebration of interracial intimacy and Vasconcelos's ideas in *The Cosmic Race*. See "Introduction," in Jean Toomer and Henry Louis Gates Jr., *Cane: Authoritative Text, Contexts, Criticism*, A Norton Critical Edition (New York: Norton, 2011).

4 I use the term "Latino/a" to refer to populations of Latin American descent living in the United States.

5 The literature on racism in Latin America is extensive, but recent empirical studies demonstrating the connection between race and inequality are especially noteworthy. See, e.g., Edward Telles and PERLA (Project on Ethnicity and Race in Latin America), *Pigmentocracies: Ethnicity, Race, and Color in Latin America* (Chapel Hill, NC: University of North Carolina Press, 2014).

6 See Peter Wade, *Blackness and Race Mixture: The Dynamics of Racial Identity in Colombia* (Baltimore, MD: Johns Hopkins University Press, 1993); Peter Wade, "Images of Latin American Mestizaje and the Politics of Comparison,"

Bulletin of Latin American Research 23, no. 3 (2004): 355–66; Lourdes Martínez-Echazábal, "Mestizaje and the Discourse of National/Cultural Identity in Latin America, 1845–1959," *Latin American Perspectives* 25, no. 3 (1998): 21–42.

7 See Paulina L. Alberto, *Terms of Inclusion: Black Intellectuals in Twentieth-Century Brazil* (Chapel Hill: University of North Carolina Press, 2011); Alejandro de la Fuente, *A Nation for All: Race, Inequality, and Politics in Twentieth-Century Cuba* (Chapel Hill: University of North Carolina Press, 2001).

8 See Tianna Paschel and Mark Sawyer, "Contesting Politics as Usual: Black Social Movements, Globalization and Race Policy in Latin America," in *New Social Movements in the African Diaspora: Challenging Global Apartheid*, ed. Leith Mullings (New York: Palgrave Macmillan Press, 2009); Deborah Yashar, *Contesting Citizenship in Latin America: The Rise of Indigenous Movements and the Postliberal Challenge* (Cambridge: Cambridge University Press, 2005).

9 Ilan Stavans and José Vasconcelos, *José Vasconcelos: The Prophet of Race* (New Brunswick, NJ: Rutgers University Press, 2011), xiii.

10 *Latinos: The Cosmic Race*, podcast audio, Latino USA, April 25, 2014, http://latinousa.org/2014/04/25/latinos-cosmic-race/.

11 For a more detailed analysis of how US Latino political theorists have selectively borrowed from Latin American sources, see Juliet Hooker, "Hybrid Subjectivities, Latin American Mestizaje, and Latino Political Thought on Race," *Politics, Groups, and Identities* 2, no. 2 (2014): 188–201.

12 Marilyn Grace Miller, *Rise and Fall of the Cosmic Race: The Cult of Mestizaje in Latin America* (Austin: University of Texas Press, 2004), 36.

13 See, e.g., Eduardo Mendieta, "The Making of New Peoples: Hispanicizing Race," in *Hispanics/Latinos in the United States*, ed. Jorge J. E. Gracia and Pablo de Greiff (New York: Routledge, 2000).

14 Vasconcelos was bilingual in Spanish and English. He lived in the US–Mexico border region as a child and attended elementary school in Texas. As a young man, he returned to live in the United States. In the 1910s, during his first period of exile during the Mexican Revolution, he lived for different periods in New York, Washington, DC, San Antonio, Texas, and California. In 1926–1927, he taught at the University of Chicago and lectured at other US universities. After losing his bid for the Mexican presidency in 1929, he again lived in the United States for short periods of time, principally in Texas in the 1930s. See Gabriella De Beer, *José Vasconcelos and His World* (New York: Las Americas, 1966), 90–125.

15 This is not to suggest that Vasconcelos did not also draw upon European ideas. On the influence of Nietzschean notions of aesthetics and synthesis on Vasconcelos's political thought, see chapter 4 in Von Vacano, *The Color of Citizenship*.

16 Luis Alberto Sanchez, "Bolivarismo, Monroísmo, y Aprismo," *La Nueva Democracia*, March 1, 1935.

17 Aníbal Quijano, "Coloniality of Power, Eurocentrism, and Latin America," *Neplanta* 1, no. 3 (2000): 533–80.

18 Catherine Walsh, "Shifting the Geopolitics of Critical Knowledge," *Cultural Studies* 21, no. 2–3 (2007): 224.

19 In fact, Ilan Stavans has argued that Vasconcelos is often referenced, but hardly ever read. See Stavans and Vasconcelos, *José Vasconcelos*, 4–5.

20 In his excellent analysis of racial ideas during the Mexican Revolution, Knight observes: "The heyday of European racist thought—dated from approximately 1850 to 1920—roughly coincided with Mexico's phase of liberal state-building and capitalist export-oriented economic development . . . which culminated in the neo-liberal or 'order and progress' dictatorship of Porfirio Díaz (1876–1911). . . . Porfirian thinkers were profoundly influenced by social Darwinism; Spenser's evolutionism, with its denigration of human hybrids exercised a strong appeal." Alan Knight, "Racism, Revolution, and *Indigenismo*: Mexico, 1910–1940," in *The Idea of Race in Latin America, 1870–1940*, ed. Richard Graham et al. (Austin: University of Texas Press, 1990), 78.

21 See José Enrique Rodó, *Ariel* (Austin: University of Texas Press, 1998). The essay was originally published in 1900.

22 Vijay Prashad, *The Darker Nations: A Biography of the Short-Lived Third World* (New York: New Press, 2007), 19–20, 22, 25–26. While the congress is believed to have been secretly funded in part by the Mexican government, Vasconcelos attended as one of Puerto Rico's delegates. The Brussels conference established the League Against Imperialism and was attended by other Third World luminaries such as Jawaharlal Nehru of the Indian National Congress, Sukarno from Indonesia, representatives of the South African Communist Party, etc. The other Latin American delegate was Peruvian nationalist and co-founder of the APRA party, Victor Raúl Haya de la Torre.

23 Between 1890 and 1925, there were thirty-five different instances of US military intervention (i.e., troops on the ground) in Latin America.

24 Nancy Stepan, *The Hour of Eugenics: Race, Gender, and Nation in Latin America* (Ithaca, NY: Cornell University Press, 1991), 45.

25 On the influence of scientific racism in Latin America, see Graham et al., *The Idea of Race in Latin America*.

26 Vasconcelos, *The Cosmic Race/la raza cósmica*, 34.

27 Ibid., 8.

28 Stepan, *The Hour of Eugenics*, 40, 145.

29 Natalia Priego, "Porfirio Díaz, Positivism and 'the Scientists': A Reconsideration of the Myth," *Journal of Iberian and Latin American Research* 18, no. 2 (2012): 138. Priego argues that while most of the historiography cites the influence of Herbert Spenser on Mexican positivism, "the scientists" rarely cited him directly, and instead derived many of their ideas from social Darwinism as it was formulated in the United States.

30 The literal translation of the lecture's title would be "Man." Given its subject, Vasconcelos probably intended it to be understood as "The Human," though women are hardly mentioned at all in the text.

31 José Vasconcelos, *Indología: una interpretación de la cultura Ibero-Americana* (Paris: Agencia Mundial de Librería, 1927), xx.

32 Stepan, *The Hour of Eugenics*, 138.

33 Vasconcelos, *The Cosmic Race/la raza cósmica*, 8.

34 Ibid., 33–34.

35 Ibid., 10.

36 Ibid., 19.

37 See Stepan, *The Hour of Eugenics*, 138–39.

38 Ibid., 148.

39 Vasconcelos, *The Cosmic Race/la raza cósmica*, 28–32.

40 Grant's book was originally published in English in 1916. He advocated restricting immigration to the United States and was a proponent of anti-miscegenation laws.

41 Vasconcelos, *Indología*, 102.

42 Ibid., 104.

43 Ibid., 107.

44 "La supremacia de los blancos," *La Prensa*, December 20, 1926, 3a.

45 Ibid., 7.

46 De Beer, *José Vasconcelos and His World*, 253.

47 José Vasconcelos, "Sarmiento estadista," *La Prensa*, December 23, 1938.

48 Vasconcelos, *Indología*, 18.

49 Vasconcelos lauded Sarmiento as a "victorious Quetzalcoatl" for his work as an educational reformer. Ibid., 147. The reference is to an Aztec myth about the struggle for primacy between two gods, one warlike and the other intellectual and dedicated to science and the arts (Quetzalcoatl). Vasconcelos and Sarmiento are credited with building the foundations of the public education systems in their respective countries. Vasconcelos held various government posts related to education after the triumph of the Mexican Revolution. He served as rector of the National University and Minister of Education (1921–1924). He is credited with the "complete revamping of the whole system of education in Mexico, beginning with the creation of the Ministry of Education itself, which controlled public schools, art, libraries and museums." Didier T. Jaén, "Introduction," in *The Cosmic Race/la raza cósmica*, xxiii.

50 Vasconcelos, *Indología*, 147–48, emphasis added.

51 José Vasconcelos, *Bolivarismo y Monroísmo: temas Iberoamericanos* (México, D.F.: Editorial Trillas, 2011), 76.

52 Vasconcelos, *The Cosmic Race/la raza cósmica*, 11.

53 Vasconcelos, "Sarmiento estadista."

54 Vasconcelos, *Bolivarismo y Monroísmo*, 23.

55 Ibid., 12.

56 Because of his famous essay of the same name, Martí is the thinker most directly associated with the phrase, but it was widely invoked in Latin America. Martí, like Vasconcelos, is part of the anti-colonial strand of Latin American political thought, but their ideas about race differed. Martí argued in favor of a deracialized liberalism that would transcend race and unite black and white Cubans in the struggle for independence. See "Our America," in José Martí, *José Martí: Selected Writings*, trans. Esther Allen (New York: Penguin Classics, 2002), 288–96.

57 Vasconcelos, *Indología*, 17.

58 Ibid., xxxiv.

59 José Vasconcelos, *La raza cosmica: misión de la raza Iberoamericana, Argentina y Brasil*, 5th ed., Colección Austral (México: Espasa-Calpe Mexicana, 1977), 62, 110. The travel sections of *The Cosmic Race* are very reminiscent of Sarmiento's *Viajes*.

60 Vasconcelos, *Indología*, 220–21.

61 Ibid., lv–lvi.

62 Jaén, "Introduction," in *The Cosmic Race/la raza cósmica*, ix, xi.

63 Miller, *Rise and Fall of the Cosmic Race*, 28.

64 Vasconcelos, *Indología*, xi.

65 Vasconcelos, *The Cosmic Race/la raza cósmica*, 32.

66 Ibid., 16.

67 Ibid., 18–19.

68 A rare exception appeared in the travel sections of the Spanish edition of *The Cosmic Race*. Vasconcelos observed that Latin Americans were ashamed of their blackness. He described how upon his visit to (predominantly black) Bahia, a Brazilian official sought to prevent the delegation of which he was a part, which also included representatives from the United States, from visiting areas where blacks were present. "I wanted to stop by the market to see the black women in their picturesque costumes … but I noticed that the government official did not want me to notice the presence of blacks; such a sight is suppressed from the itineraries of official tourism." Vasconcelos, *La raza cosmica*, 64.

69 *The Cosmic Race/la raza cósmica*, 32.

70 Ibid., 21–22.

71 I borrow the concept from Charles R. Hale, "Racial Eruptions: The Awkward Place of Blackness in Indian-centered Spaces of Mestizaje," paper presented at the Conference, Race and Politics in Central America, University of Texas at Austin, February 24–25, 2006. Hale defines the term as "bursts of signification," where particular understandings of race that reflect the dominant political imaginary are conveyed. Racial eruptions thus reveal underlying and often unspoken aspects of racial "common sense."

72 Vasconcelos, *The Cosmic Race/la raza cósmica*, 19.

73   Ibid., 20. Mexico adopted restrictions on Chinese immigration in 1921, and anti-Chinese sentiment was rampant at the time. For an analysis of anti-Chinese ethnic cleansing campaigns in Baja California as a result of a racial project of Mexicanization allied to a discourse of mestizaje, see Jason Oliver Chang, "Racial Alterity in the Mestizo Nation," *Journal of Asian American Studies* 14, no. 3 (2011): 331–59.

74   Vasconcelos, *La raza cosmica*, 98–99.

75   Vasconcelos, *Indología*, liii–liv.

76   See, e.g., Gilberto Freyre, *The Masters and the Slaves (Casa-Grande & Senzala): A Study in the Development of Brazilian Civilization*, 2d English-language ed. (New York: Knopf, 1956). For a discussion of the centrality of the body, and gender and sexuality in Freyre's work, see Jossianna Arroyo, *Travestismos culturales: literatura y etnografía en Cuba y Brasil* (Pittsburgh, PA: Universidad de Pittsburgh, Instituto Internacional de Literatura Iberoamericana, 2003).

77   Vasconcelos, *The Cosmic Race/la raza cósmica*, 31.

78   Ibid., 28–29.

79   See Michel-Rolph Trouillot, *Silencing the Past: Power and the Production of History* (Boston, MA: Beacon Press, 1995).

80   Vasconcelos, *Indología*, xxv.

81   Ibid., xxxi.

82   Ibid., xliv.

83   Vasconcelos visited the Dominican Republic during a relative period of calm following the end of the US military occupation in 1924, before the start of the Trujillo dictatorship in 1930, which explicitly fomented anti-black racism, primarily against Haitians, but also Dominicans. Vasconcelos's observation that his lecture rebutting condemnations of mixture in racial science, which were grounded in arguments about non-white racial inferiority, was most positively received by black Dominicans is thus extremely interesting. As Raj Chetty and Amaury Rodríguez observe, contemporary scholarship on race in the Dominican Republic tends to stress the country's unwillingness to identify as black and emphasizes its "self-hatred, negrophobia and anti-Haitianism." Raj Chetty and Amaury Rodríguez, "Introduction: The Challenge and Promise of Dominican Black Studies," *The Black Scholar* 45, no. 2 (2015): 2.

84   Vasconcelos, *Indología*, 116–17.

85   Ibid., 144.

86   *Indigenismo* became influential in various countries in Latin American during the first half of the twentieth century. A construct of mestizo elites, not indigenous people themselves, it glorified some aspects of indigenous cultural heritage, primarily as a relic of the past. It was thus characterized by nostalgia for an imagined, folklorized notion of indigeneity. *Indigenismo* became official state policy in Mexico after the Revolution of 1910–1920, but its aim was the integration of indigenous peoples, not their autonomous development. Alan

Knight has argued that *mestizaje* and *indigenismo* coexisted as official ideologies during the Mexican Revolution. See Knight, "Racism, Revolution, and Indigenismo."

87 Vasconcelos, *Indología*, 144.

88 Ibid., 145.

89 Ibid., 160.

90 Vasconcelos expressed his critique of *indigenismo* in even harsher terms in *Bolivarismo y Monroísmo*, where he argued that it was a Trojan horse for US imperialism that ultimately served to justify the idea of Anglo-Saxon racial superiority by vilifying the Spanish conquest. He also suggested that Protestant missionaries were responsible for propagating *indigenismo* in Latin America. *Bolivarismo y Monroísmo*, 32, 46–47, 68. At the time *Indología* was written, Vasconcelos was somewhat distanced from Catholicism. He was raised a devout Catholic, but became disillusioned with the church as a young man. By the 1930s, during his second period of exile, he vehemently attacked Protestantism and expressed significant anti-Semitism. Vasconcelos officially reconciled with the Catholic Church in the last two decades of his life. See De Beer, *José Vasconcelos and His World*, 142–47.

91 Vasconcelos, *Indología*, 81–82.

92 Ibid., 104–5, emphasis added.

93 Vasconcelos is often lauded as a proponent of multiracialism, but his theory of mestizaje in fact emphasized the achievement of a uniformly mixed and homogeneous mestizo subject in Latin America. On the basis of that misconception, he is seen as a foil to Du Bois's mono-racial conception of African American identity. See Greg Carter, *The United States of the United Races: A Utopian History of Racial Mixing* (New York: New York University Press, 2013).

94 Vasconcelos, *Indología*, 16, emphasis added.

95 Ibid., 26.

96 Ibid., lvii.

97 After his defeat in the 1929 Mexican presidential election, Vasconcelos became disillusioned with national politics and embarked on a period of self-imposed exile. He became more ideologically conservative later in life, but he continued to critique US imperialism. In fact, the more radical elements of his analysis of global white supremacy in *Bolivarismo y Monroísmo* suggest that he was able to become a more hemispheric thinker once he was less tethered to Mexican national politics. The title of the text echoes Sarmiento's discourse on "North and South America" (which in Spanish was retitled "La Doctrina Monroe" or the Monroe doctrine), suggesting that they shared a similar trajectory from the national to the hemispheric.

98 *Bolivarismo y Monroísmo*, 57.

99 See Richard Delgado, "The Law of the Noose: A History of Latino Lynching," *Harvard Civil Rights-Civil Liberties Law Review* 44 (Summer 2009): 297–312.

100 Vasconcelos, *Bolivarismo y Monroísmo*, 28.

101 Ibid., 92.

102 Ibid., 69.

103 Ibid., 65.

104 Ibid., 23.

105 Ibid., 61.

106 Ibid., 58.

107 Ibid., 59. Vasconcelos appears to be referencing the term "collective Bovarism" coined by the Haitian intellectual and politician Jean Price-Mars (1876–1969), an advocate of Négritude. Mars used it to describe the way the predominantly mixed Haitian elite embraced their European ancestry while denying any African legacy. It is a reference to the Gustave Flaubert character Emma Bovary.

108 Ibid., 52.

109 Ibid., 58.

110 Ibid., 62–63.

111 Ibid., 63–64.

112 For instance, many Brazilian intellectuals during the 1920s and 1930s continued to subscribe to a racial ideology of whitening, whereby the country's racial stock could (supposedly) be improved via European immigration. It was not until later in the twentieth century that elite discourses emerged that celebrated mixture and recognized the contributions of black and indigenous peoples to Brazilian national identity, as in the work of Gilbero Freyre. See Thomas E. Skidmore, *Black into White: Race and Nationality in Brazilian Thought*, 2d ed. (Durham, NC: Duke University Press, 1993).

113 In fact, Vasconcelos's adherence to the Spanish legacy almost leads him to renege on mestizaje at one point in in *Bolivarismo y Monroísmo*. Comparing the racial orders in the United States and Latin America, he observed: "Neither of the two systems can be lauded as successful. The United States has a caste war. . . . Among us, meanwhile, mixture tends to corrupt the primary values of culture. Even so, I see no other solution than to continue it. And to continue the work of absorbing the Indian into the system of the whites." Vasconcelos, *Bolivarismo y Monroísmo*, 46.

114 Sánchez, "Bolivarismo, Monroísmo, y Aprismo."

115 Laura E. Gómez, *Manifest Destinies: The Making of the Mexican American Race* (New York: New York University Press, 2007), 152.

116 Jennifer L. Hochschild and Brenna Marea Powell, "Racial Reorganization and the United States Census 1850–1930: Mulattoes, Half-Breeds, Mixed Parentage, Hindoos, and the Mexican Race," *Studies in American Political Development* 22, no. 1 (2008): 81. On the history of LULAC and the origins of its "reformist" brand of Mexican American politics, which stressed integration and Americanization but also struggled in favor of desegregation in

education and against housing and employment discrimination, see chapter 2 in Mario T. García, *Mexican Americans: Leadership, Ideology, and Identity, 1930–1960* (New Haven, CT: Yale University Press, 1989).

117 J. B., "La raza cósmica," *El Sol de Chicago*, March 21, 1960.

118 See http://www.nclr.org/index.php/about_us/faqs/general_faqs_and_requested_resources/.

119 See, e.g., the different positions on this question taken by Linda Martín Alcoff and Eduardo Mendieta in their essays in *Hispanics/Latinos in the United States*.

120 See, e.g., Clara E. Rodriguez, "Race, Culture, and Latino 'Otherness' in the 1980 Census," *Social Science Quarterly* 73, no. 4 (December 1992): 930–37. The literature on Latinos and the census is extensive, reflecting its centrality to debates about Latinos and US racial politics. See Clara E. Rodriguez, *Changing Race: Latinos, the Census, and the History of Ethnicity in the United States* (New York: NYU Press, 2000).

121 Nancy Lopez, "Killing Two Birds with One Stone? Why We Need Two Separate Questions on Race and Ethnicity in the 2020 Census and Beyond," *Latino Studies* 11, no. 3 (2013): 433. The scholarship on US Afro-Latinos, for example, emphasizes how they are rendered invisible in dominant accounts of Latinidad that equate Latino/a-ness with mixture or whiteness. See Miriam Jimenéz Román and Juan Flores, eds., *The Afro-Latino Reader: History and Culture in the United States* (Durham, NC: Duke University Press, 2010).

122 Nicandro F. Juárez, "José Vasconcelos and La Raza Cósmica," *Aztlán: A Journal of Chicano Studies* 3, no. 1 (1972): 70.

123 See Cristina Beltrán, "Patrolling Borders: Hybrids, Hierarchies and the Challenge of Mestizaje," *Political Research Quarterly* 57, no. 4 (2004): 595–607.

124 Pablo López Oro first suggested this formulation in my graduate seminar on Latin American political thought.

125 *Borderlands/La Frontera* is Anzaldúa's most widely cited work, particularly the chapter on mestiza consciousness. I focus on that chapter here because that is where she discusses the intellectual link between her version of Chicana futurism and Vasconcelos's theory of mestizaje. In keeping with this book's methodological call to read broadly beyond a thinker's most iconic texts, however, a full accounting of Anzaldúa's political thought would require going beyond *Borderlands/La Frontera*. For a representative compilation of Anzaldúa's published and unpublished writings, see Gloria Anzaldúa and Ana Louise Keating, *The Gloria Anzaldúa Reader* (Durham, NC: Duke University Press, 2009).

126 Gloria Anzaldúa, *Borderlands/La Frontera: The New Mestiza* (San Francisco, CA: Spinsters/Aunt Lute, 1987), 77.

127 Ibid., 97n1 of "La Conciencia de la mestiza" chapter.

128 Ibid., 79.

129 Ibid., 78.

130   Ibid., 80.

131   See Catherine S Ramírez, "Afrofuturism/Chicanafuturism: Fictive Kin," *Aztlán: A Journal of Chicano Studies* 33, no. 1 (2008): 185–94.

132   Anzaldúa, *Borderlands/La Frontera*, 80.

133   Ibid., 82.

134   Ibid., 85.

135   The artwork on the cover of the bilingual translation of *The Cosmic Race* reflects this shift in the center of gravity of mestizaje as it has traveled hemispherically. The original cover of the first 1979 UCLA Chicano Studies edition depicted the Mexican shield (an eagle holding a serpent), while the cover of the 1997 edition is an image of pre-Columbian art.

136   Anzaldúa, *Borderlands/La Frontera*, 91.

137   Ibid., 86.

138   See Abdias Do Nascimento, "Genocide: The Social Lynching of Africans and their Descendants in Brazil," in *Brazil, Mixture or Massacre? Essays in the Genocide of a Black People*, by Abdias Do Nascimento (Dover, MA: Majority Press, 1989), 59–93. Despite providing a valuable corrective to Freyre, Nascimento's critique of the sexual politics of mestizaje suffers from similar problems as Du Bois's critique of US anti-miscegenation discourses, as it presents black women not as agents, only as victims.

139   Anzaldúa, *Borderlands/La Frontera*, 82.

140   Cristina Beltrán, *The Trouble with Unity: Latino Politics and the Creation of Identity* (New York: Oxford University Press, 2010).

CONCLUSION

1   Vijay Prashad, *The Darker Nations: A Biography of the Short-Lived Third World* (New York: New Press, 2007), 16.

2   Domingo Faustino Sarmiento, *Ambas Américas: revista de educación, bibliografía y agricultura*, 4 vols. (New York: Imprenta de Hallet y Breen, 1867), 1:7.

3   Sheldon S. Wolin, "Fugitive Democracy," *Constellations* 1, no. 1 (1994): 11–25.

4   For a related argument, see Farah Godrej, *Cosmopolitan Political Thought: Method, Practice, Discipline* (New York: Oxford University Press, 2011).

5   See Leigh K. Jenco, ""What Does Heaven Ever Say?": A Methods-Centered Approach to Cross-Cultural Engagement," *American Political Science Review* 101, no. 04 (2007): 741–55.

6   See David Haekwon Kim, "José Mariátegui's East-South Decolonial Experiment," *Comparative and Continental Philosophy* 7, no. 2 (2015): 157–79.

7   Frederick Douglass, "Our Composite Nationality: An Address Delivered in Boston, Massachusetts, on 7 December 1869," in *The Frederick Douglass Papers*, Series One, *Speeches, Debates and Interviews*, vol. 4, *1864–80*, ed. John W. Blassingame and John R. McKivigan (New Haven, CT: Yale University Press, 1979), 251.

Bibliography

Abeledo, Amaranto A. *Ambas Américas: en torno al discurso pronunciado por Domingo Faustino Sarmiento ante la Sociedad Histórica de Rhode Island, Providence 27 Diciembre 1865*. Buenos Aires: Talleres Luz, 1967.

Agassiz, Louis. "Letter to D. F. Sarmiento, March 6th, 1867," 1–2. Buenos Aires, Argentina, Museo Histórico Sarmiento, documento #4449.

Agassiz, Louis, and Elizabeth Cabot Cary Agassiz. *A Journey in Brazil*. Boston, MA: Ticknor and Fields, 1868.

Ahmad, Dohra. "'More Than Romance': Genre and Geography in Dark Princess." *ELH* 69, no. 3 (2002): 775–803.

Alberto, Paulina L. *Terms of Inclusion: Black Intellectuals in Twentieth-Century Brazil*. Chapel Hill: University of North Carolina Press, 2011.

Alcoff, Linda Martín. *Visible Identities: Race, Gender, and the Self*. Oxford: Oxford University Press, 2006.

Allen, Chadwick. *Trans-Indigenous: Methodologies for Global Native Literary Studies*. Minneapolis: University of Minnesota Press, 2012.

Allen, Danielle S. *Talking to Strangers: Anxieties of Citizenship after* Brown v. Board of Education. Chicago: University of Chicago Press, 2004.

Anderson, Benedict R. O'G. *Imagined Communities: Reflections on the Origin and Spread of Nationalism*. London: Verso, 1983.

Andrews, George Reid. *The Afro-Argentines of Buenos Aires, 1800–1900*. Madison: University of Wisconsin Press, 1980.

Andrews, George Reid. *Afro-Latin America, 1800–2000*. New York: Oxford University Press, 2004.

Anzaldúa, Gloria. *Borderlands/La Frontera: The New Mestiza*. San Francisco, CA: Spinsters/Aunt Lute, 1987.

Anzaldúa, Gloria, and Ana Louise Keating. *The Gloria Anzaldúa Reader*. Durham, NC: Duke University Press, 2009.

Appiah, K. Anthony. "Illusions of Race." In *In My Father's House: Africa in the Philosophy of Culture*, by K. Anthony Appiah, 28–46. New York: Oxford University Press, 1992.

Appiah, K. Anthony. "The Uncompleted Argument: Dubois and the Illusion of Race." *Critical Inquiry* 12, no. 1 (Autumn 1985): 21–37.

Aptheker, Herbert. "Dubois on Douglass: 1895." *Journal of Negro History* 49, no. 4 (October 1964): 264–68.

Aptheker, Herbert. "Introduction." In W. E. B. Du Bois, *Dark Princess: A Romance*, p. 5–29. Millwood, NY: Kraus-Thomson, 1974.

Aptheker, Herbert. "Introduction." In W. E. B. Du Bois, *Darkwater: Voices from within the Veil*, p. 5–26. Millwood, NY: Kraus-Thomson, 1975.

Arroyo, Jossianna. "Revolution in the Caribbean: Betances, Haiti and the Antillean Confederation." *La Habana Elegante* 49 (Spring/Summer 2011). http://www.habanaelegante.com/Spring_Summer_2011/Invitation_Arroyo.html.

Arroyo, Jossianna. *Travestismos culturales: literatura y etnografía en Cuba y Brasil.* Pittsburgh, PA: Universidad de Pittsburgh, Instituto Internacional de Literatura Iberoamericana, 2003.

B., J. "La Raza Cosmica." *El Sol de Chicago*, March 21, 1960.

Balfour, Lawrie. "Darkwater's Democratic Vision." *Political Theory* 38, no. 4 (August 1, 2010): 537–63.

Balfour, Lawrie. *Democracy's Reconstruction: Thinking Politically with W. E. B. Du Bois.* New York: Oxford University Press, 2011.

Bell, Duncan. "Before the Democratic Peace: Racial Utopianism, Empire and the Abolition of War." *European Journal of International Relations* 20, no. 3 (2014): 647–70.

Beltrán, Cristina. "Patrolling Borders: Hybrids, Hierarchies and the Challenge of Mestizaje." *Political Research Quarterly* 57, no. 4 (2004): 595–607.

Beltrán, Cristina. *The Trouble with Unity: Latino Politics and the Creation of Identity.* New York: Oxford University Press, 2010.

Best, Stephen, and Saidiya Hartman. "Fugitive Justice." *Representations* 92, no. 1 (Fall 2005): 1–5.

Bogues, Anthony. "And What about the Human? Freedom, Human Emancipation, and the Radical Imagination." *boundary 2* 39, no. 3 (2012): 29–46.

Bogues, Anthony. *Empire of Liberty: Power, Desire, and Freedom.* Lebanon, NH: University Press of New England, 2010.

Bolívar, Simón. "The Angostura Address." In *El Libertador: Writings of Simón Bolívar*, trans. Frederick Fornoff and ed. David Bushnell, 31–53. New York: Oxford University Press, 2003.

Bonilla-Silva, Eduardo. *Racism without Racists Color-Blind Racism and the Persistence of Racial Inequality in America.* 4th ed. Lanham, MD: Rowman & Littlefield Publishers, 2013.

Boxill, Bernard. "Two Traditions in African-American Political Philosophy." *Philosophical Forum* 24, nos 1–3 (1992–93): 119–35.

Buccola, Nicholas. *The Political Thought of Frederick Douglass: In Pursuit of American Liberty.* New York: New York University Press, 2012.

Bunkley, Allison Williams. *The Life of Sarmiento*. New York: Greenwood Press, 1969.

Camp, Stephanie M. H. "The Pleasures of Resistance: Enslaved Women and Body Politics in the Plantation South, 1830–1861." *Journal of Southern History* 68, no. 3 (2002): 533–72.

Carens, Joseph H. "Aliens and Citizens: The Case for Open Borders." *Review of Politics* 49, no. 2 (1987): 251–73.

Carilla, Emilio. *El embajador Sarmiento: Sarmiento y los Estados Unidos*. Rosario, Argentina: Universidad Nacional del Litoral, Facultad de Filosofía y Letras, 1961.

Carolina. "San Juan de Nicaragua." *Frederick Douglass's Paper*, May 6, 1852.

Carter, Greg. *The United States of the United Races: A Utopian History of Racial Mixing*. New York: New York University Press, 2013.

Chang, Jason Oliver. "Racial Alterity in the Mestizo Nation." *Journal of Asian American Studies* 14, no. 3 (2011): 331–59.

Chetty, Raj, and Amaury Rodríguez. "Introduction: The Challenge and Promise of Dominican Black Studies." *The Black Scholar* 45, no. 2 (2015): 1–9.

Communipaw. "Nicaragua." *Frederick Douglass's Paper*, January 8, 1852.

Communipaw. "Nicaragua—No. II." *Frederick Douglass's Paper*, January 15, 1852.

Dallmayr, Fred, ed. *Border Crossings: Toward a Comparative Political Theory*. Lanham, MD: Lexington Books, 1999.

Davis, Angela Y. *Abolition Democracy: Beyond Empire, Prisons, and Torture/Interviews with Angela Y. Davis*. New York: Seven Stories Press, 2005.

Davis, Angela Y. "Introduction." In *Narrative of the Life of Frederick Douglass, an American Slave, Written by Himself: A New Critical Edition*, edited by Angela Davis, 21–37. San Francisco, CA: City Lights Publishers, 2010.

Davis, Angela Y. *Lectures on Liberation*. Los Angeles: National United Committee to Free Angela Davis, 1971.

Davis, Angela Y. *Women, Race, and Class*. New York: Vintage Books, 1983.

Dawson, Michael. *Black Visions: The Roots of Contemporary African-American Political Ideologies*. Chicago: University of Chicago Press, 2001.

De Beer, Gabriella. *José Vasconcelos and His World*. New York: Las Americas, 1966.

de la Fuente, Alejandro. *A Nation for All: Race, Inequality, and Politics in Twentieth-Century Cuba*. Chapel Hill: University of North Carolina Press, 2001.

Delany, Martin R. *The Condition, Elevation, Emigration, and Destiny of the Colored People of the United States*. New York: Arno Press, 1968.

Delgado, Richard. "The Law of the Noose: A History of Latino Lynching." *Harvard Civil Rights-Civil Liberties Law Review* 44 (Summer 2009): 297–312.

Delrio, Walter, Diana Lenton, Marcelo Musante, Mariano Nagy, Alexis Papazian, and Pilar Pérez. "Discussing Indigenous Genocide in Argentina: Past, Present, and Consequences of Argentinean State Policies toward Native Peoples." *Genocide Studies and Prevention* 5, no. 2 (2010): 138–59.

Douglass, Frederick. "Annexion of San Domingo." *The New National Era*, January 12, 1871.

Douglass, Frederick. *Autobiographies*. New York: Library of America, 1994.

Douglass, Frederick. *The Claims of the Negro Ethnologically Considered: An Address before the Literary Societies of Western Reserve College at Commencement, July 12, 1854*. Rochester, NY: Lee, Mann, 1854.

Douglass, Frederick. "Haiti and the United States: Inside History of the Negotiations for the Môle St. Nicholas. I." *North American Review* 153, no. 418 (1891): 337–45.

Douglass, Frederick. "Introduction to the Reason Why the Colored American Is Not in the World's Columbian Exposition." In *The Life and Writings of Frederick Douglass, Vol. IV: Reconstruction and After*, edited by Philip S. Foner, 469–77. New York: International Publishers, 1955.

Douglass, Frederick. *Lecture on Haiti*. Chicago: Violet Agents Supply Co., 1893.

Douglass, Frederick. "The Lessons of the Hour." In *The Life and Writings of Frederick Douglass*, vol. 4, *Reconstruction and After*, edited by Philip S. Foner, 491–523. New York: International Publishers, 1955.

Douglass, Frederick. *The Life and Times of Frederick Douglass*. 1892 ed. Mineola, NY: Dover Publications, 2003.

Douglass, Frederick. "Our Composite Nationality: An Address Delivered in Boston, Massachusetts, on 7 December 1869." In *The Frederick Douglass Papers, Series One: Speeches, Debates and Interviews*, vol. 4, *1864–80*, edited by John W. Blassingame and John R. McKivigan, 240–59. New Haven, CT: Yale University Press, 1979.

Douglass, Frederick. "The President and His Speeches." In *The Life and Writings of Frederick Douglass*, vol. 3, *The Civil War, 1861–1865*, edited by Philip S. Foner, 266–70. New York: International Publishers, 1952.

Douglass, Frederick. "Reminiscences of the Anti-Slavery Conflict (as Delivered during the Lecture Season of 1872–1873)." In Frederick Douglass Papers, Library of Congress, 1872–1873.

Douglass, Frederick. "Santo Domingo." In Frederick Douglass Papers, Schomburg Center for Research in Black Culture, n.d.

Douglass, Frederick. "A Trip to Haiti." In *The Life and Writings of Frederick Douglass*, vol. 3, *The Civil War, 1861–1865*, edited by Philip S. Foner, 85–88. New York: International Publishers, 1952.

Douglass, Frederick. "West India Emancipation." In *Two Speeches by Frederick Douglass, One on West India Emancipation and the Other on the Dred Scott Decision*, by Frederick Douglass, 3–24. Rochester, NY: C. P. Dewey, 1857.

Douglass, Frederick. "What to the Slave Is the Fourth of July." In *The Oxford Frederick Douglass Reader*, edited by William L. Andrews, 108–30. New York: Oxford University Press, 1996.

Du Bois, W. E. B. "An Amazing Island." In *Writings*, edited by Nathan I. Huggins, 1167–68. New York: Library of America, 1986.

Du Bois, W. E. B. "Brazil." *The Crisis* 7, no. 6 (April 1914): 286–87.

Du Bois, W. E. B. "The Conservation of Races." In *The Oxford W. E. B. Du Bois Reader*, edited by Eric J. Sundquist, 38–54. New York: Oxford University Press, 1996.

Du Bois, W. E. B. "Criteria of Negro Art." *The Crisis* 32 (October 1926): 290–97.

Du Bois, W. E. B. *Dark Princess: A Romance.* Jackson: Banner Books/University Press of Mississippi, 1995.

Du Bois, W. E. B. *Darkwater: Voices from within the Veil.* New York: Oxford University Press, 2007.

Du Bois, W. E. B. *Dusk of Dawn: An Essay toward an Autobiography of a Race Concept.* In *Writings*, edited by Nathan I. Huggins, 549–802. New York: Library of America, 1986.

Du Bois, W. E. B. "Intermarriage." *The Crisis* 5, no. 4 (February 1913): 180–81.

Du Bois, W. E. B. "Marrying of Black Folk." *The Independent*, October 30, 1910, 812–13.

Du Bois, W. E. B. "Memorandum to the Secretary for the NAACP Staff Conference (10 October 1946)." In *Against Racism: Unpublished Essays, Papers, Addresses, 1887–1961*, edited by Herbert Aptheker, 256–61. Amherst: University of Massachusetts Press, 1985.

Du Bois, W. E. B. "Miscegenation." In *Against Racism: Unpublished Essays, Papers, Addresses, 1887–1961*, edited by Herbert Aptheker, 90–102. Amherst: University of Massachusetts Press, 1985.

Du Bois, W. E. B. "On Being Crazy." In *Writings*, edited by Nathan I. Huggins, 1199–1201. New York: Library of America, 1986.

Du Bois, W. E. B. "President Harding and Social Equality." *The Crisis* 23, no. 2 (December 1921): 53–56.

Du Bois, W. E. B. "Sex Equality." *The Crisis* 19, no. 3 (January 1920): 106.

Du Bois, W. E. B. "Social Equality and Racial Intermarriage." *The World Tomorrow* 5, no. 3 (March 1922): 83–84.

Du Bois, W. E. B. *The Suppression of the African Slave Trade to the United States of America, 1638–1870.* New York: Oxford University Press, 2007.

Du Bois, W. E. B. "The Twelfth Census and the Negro Problems." *Southern Workman* 29, no. 5 (May 1900): 305–9.

Du Bois, W. E. B., Adrienne Brown, and Britt Rusert. "The Princess Steel." *PMLA* 130, no. 3 (2015): 819–29.

Dzidzienyo, Anani, and Suzanne Oboler. *Neither Enemies nor Friends: Latinos, Blacks, Afro-Latinos.* New York: Palgrave Macmillan, 2005.

Edwards, Brent Hayes. *The Practice of Diaspora: Literature, Translation, and the Rise of Black Internationalism.* Cambridge, MA: Harvard University Press, 2003.

Eshun, Kodwo. "Further Considerations on Afrofuturism." *CR: The New Centennial Review* 3, no. 2 (2003): 287–302.

Euben, Roxanne L. *Enemy in the Mirror: Islamic Fundamentalism and the Limits of Modern Rationalism.* Princeton, NJ: Princeton University Press, 1999.

Euben, Roxanne L. *Journeys to the Other Shore: Muslim and Western Travelers in Search of Knowledge*. Princeton: Princeton University Press, 2006.

Firmin, Anténor. *The Equality of the Human Races*. Translated by Asselin Charles. Chicago: University of Illinois Press, 2002.

Fischer, Sibylle. *Modernity Disavowed: Haiti and the Cultures of Slavery in the Age of Revolution*. Durham, NC: Duke University Press, 2004.

Foner, Philip S., ed. *The Life and Writings of Frederick Douglass*. Vol. 4, *Reconstruction and After*. New York: International Publishers, 1955.

Franchot, Jenny. "The Punishment of Esther: Frederick Douglass and the Construction of the Feminine." In *Frederick Douglass: New Literary and Historical Essays*, edited by Eric J. Sundquist, 141–65. Cambridge: Cambridge University Press, 1990.

Fredrickson, George M. *The Black Image in the White Mind: The Debate on Afro-American Character and Destiny, 1817–1914*. Middletown, CT: Wesleyan University Press, 1987.

Freyre, Gilberto. *The Masters and the Slaves (Casa-Grande & Senzala): A Study in the Development of Brazilian Civilization*. 2d English-language ed. New York: Knopf, 1956.

García, Mario T. *Mexican Americans: Leadership, Ideology, and Identity, 1930–1960*. New Haven, CT: Yale University Press, 1989.

Gates Jr., Henry Louis. "Introduction." In *Cane: Authoritative Text, Contexts, Criticism*, edited by Jean Toomer and Henry Louis Gates Jr., A Norton Critical Edition. New York: Norton, 2011.

Garrels, Elizabeth. "Sobre indios, Afroamericanos y los racismos de Sarmiento." *Revista Iberoamericana* 63, nos 178–179 (1997): 99–113.

Geler, Lea. "'¡Pobres negros!': algunos apuntes sobre la desaparición de los negros Argentinos." In *Estado, región y poder local en América Latina, siglos XIX–XX: algunas miradas sobre el estado, el poder y la participación política*, edited by Pilar Garcia Jordán, 115–54. Barcelona: Universitat de Barcelona, 2007.

Gillman, Susan Kay, and Alys Eve Weinbaum, eds. *Next to the Color Line: Gender, Sexuality, and W. E. B. Du Bois*. Minneapolis: University of Minnesota Press, 2007.

Gilroy, Paul. *The Black Atlantic: Modernity and Double Consciousness*. Cambridge, MA: Harvard University Press, 1993.

Godrej, Farah. *Cosmopolitan Political Thought: Method, Practice, Discipline*. New York: Oxford University Press, 2011.

Gómez, Laura E. *Manifest Destinies: The Making of the Mexican American Race*. New York: New York University Press, 2007.

Gooding-Williams, Robert. *In the Shadow of Du Bois: Afro-Modern Political Thought in America*. Cambridge, MA: Harvard University Press, 2009.

Gordon, Jane Anna, and Neil Roberts. *Creolizing Rousseau*. London: Rowman & Littlefield International, 2015.

Gordon, Lewis R. "Douglass as an Existentialist." In *Frederick Douglass: A Critical Reader*, edited by Bill E. Lawson and Frank M. Kirkland, 207–26. Malden, MA: Blackwell Publishers, 1999.

Gordy, Katherine A. "No Better Way to Be Latin American: European Science and Thought, Latin American Theory?". *Postcolonial Studies* 16, no. 4 (2014): 358–73.

Gould, Benjamin. "Letter to D. F. Sarmiento, March 26, 1872." Buenos Aires, Argentina: Museo Histórico Sarmiento, documento #4808.

Gracia, Jorge J. E., ed. *Forging People: Race, Ethnicity, and Nationality in Hispanic American and Latino/a Thought*. Notre Dame, IN: University of Notre Dame Press, 2011.

Gracia, Jorge J. E. *Hispanic/Latino Identity: A Philosophical Perspective*. Malden, MA: Blackwell Publishers, 1999.

Gracia, Jorge J. E. *Latin American Philosophy in the Twentieth Century: Man, Values, and the Search for Philosophical Identity*. Buffalo, NY: Prometheus Books, 1986.

Graham, Richard, Thomas E. Skidmore, Aline Helg, and Alan Knight. *The Idea of Race in Latin America, 1870–1940*. Austin: University of Texas Press, 1990.

Griffin, Farah Jasmine. "Black Feminists and Du Bois: Respectability, Protection, and Beyond." *ANNALS of the American Academy of Political and Social Science* 568, no. 1 (March 2000): 28–40.

Gudmundson, Lowell, and Justin Wolfe, eds. *Blacks and Blackness in Central America: Between Race and Place*. Durham, NC: Duke University Press, 2010.

Halperín Donghi, Tulio, Iván Jaksic, Gwen Kirkpatrick, and Francine Masiello, eds. *Sarmiento: Author of a Nation*. Berkeley: University of California Press, 1994.

Hartman, Saidiya V. *Scenes of Subjection: Terror, Slavery, and Self-Making in Nineteenth-Century America*. New York: Oxford University Press, 1997.

Helg, Aline. "Race in Argentina and Cuba, 1880–1930: Theory, Policies, and Popular Reaction." In *The Idea of Race in Latin America, 1870–1940*, by Richard Graham, Thomas E. Skidmore, Aline Helg, and Alan Knight, 37–69. Austin: University of Texas Press, 1990.

Hellwig, David J. "Racial Paradise or Run-Around? Afro-North American Views of Race Relations in Brazil." *American Studies* 31, no. 2 (1990): 43–60.

Hesse, Barnor. "Escaping Liberty: Western Hegemony, Black Fugitivity." *Political Theory* 42, no. 3 (2014): 288–313.

Hobsbawm, Eric, and Terence Ranger, eds. *The Invention of Tradition*. Cambridge: Cambridge University Press, 1983.

Hochschild, Jennifer L., and Brenna Marea Powell. "Racial Reorganization and the United States Census 1850–1930: Mulattoes, Half-Breeds, Mixed Parentage, Hindoos, and the Mexican Race." *Studies in American Political Development* 22, no. 1 (2008): 59–96.

Hooker, Juliet. "'Beloved Enemies': Race and Official Mestizo Nationalism in Nicaragua." *Latin American Research Review* 40, no. 3 (2005): 14–39.

Hooker, Juliet. "Hybrid Subjectivities, Latin American Mestizaje, and Latino Political Thought on Race." *Politics, Groups, and Identities* 2, no. 2 (2014): 188–201.

Hooker, Juliet. "Race and the Space of Citizenship: The Mosquito Coast and the Place of Blackness and Indigeneity in Nicaragua." In *Blacks & Blackness in Central America: Between Race and Place*, edited by Lowell Gudmundson and Justin Wolfe, 246–77. Durham, NC: Duke University Press, 2010.

Horsman, Reginald. *Race and Manifest Destiny: The Origins of American Racial Anglo-Saxonism.* Cambridge, MA: Harvard University Press, 1981.

Ifekwunigwe, Jayne O. *"Mixed Race" Studies: A Reader.* London: Routledge, 2004.

Jimenéz Román, Miriam, and Juan Flores, eds. *The Afro-Latin@ Reader: History and Culture in the United States.* Durham, NC: Duke University Press, 2010.

Jacobs, Harriet A. *Incidents in the Life of a Slave Girl: Written by Herself.* Edited by Lydia Maria Child and Jean Fagan Yellin. Cambridge, MA: Harvard University Press, 1987.

Janken, Kenneth Robert. "Introduction." In *What the Negro Wants*, edited by Rayford Logan, vii–xxx. South Bend, IN: University of Notre Dame Press, 2001.

Jenco, Leigh K. "'What Does Heaven Ever Say?': A Methods-Centered Approach to Cross-Cultural Engagement." *American Political Science Review* 101, no. 4 (2007): 741–55.

Juárez, Nicandro F. "José Vasconcelos and La Raza Cósmica." *Aztlán: A Journal of Chicano Studies* 3, no. 1 (1972): 51–82.

Kim, David Haekwon. "José Mariátegui's East-South Decolonial Experiment." *Comparative and Continental Philosophy* 7, no. 2 (2015): 157–79.

Krause, Sharon R. *Liberalism with Honor.* Cambridge, MA: Harvard University Press, 2002.

Latinos: The Cosmic Race. Podcast audio. Latino USA, April 25, 2014. http://latinousa.org/2014/04/25/latinos-cosmic-race/.

Levine, Robert S. *Dislocating Race and Nation: Episodes in Nineteenth-Century American Literary Nationalism.* Chapel Hill: University of North Carolina Press, 2008.

Levine, Robert S. *Martin Delany, Frederick Douglass, and the Politics of Representative Identity.* Chapel Hill: University of North Carolina Press, 1997.

Logan, Rayford W. *The Negro in American Life and Thought: The Nadir, 1877–1901.* New York: Dial Press, 1954.

Lomnitz, Claudio. "Por mi raza hablará el nacionalismo revolucionario (arqueología de la unidad nacional)." *Nexos*, February 1, 2010. http://www.nexos.com.mx/?p=13506.

Lopez, Nancy. "Killing Two Birds with One Stone? Why We Need Two Separate Questions on Race and Ethnicity in the 2020 Census and Beyond." *Latino Studies* 11, no. 3 (2013): 428–38.

Lynch, John. *Caudillos in Spanish America, 1800–1850.* Oxford: Clarendon Press, 1992.

Machado, Maria Helena P. T. "A ciência Norte-Americana visita a Amazônia: entre o criacionismo cristão e o poligenismo 'degeneracionista.'" *Revista USP*, no. 75 (2007): 68–75.

Machado, Maria Helena P. T., and Sasha Huber. *(T)races of Louis Agassiz: Photography, Body and Science, Yesterday and Today.* São Paulo: Capacete, 2010.

Mann, Mary Tyler Peabody, and Barry L. Velleman. *"My Dear Sir": Mary Mann's Letters to Sarmiento (1865–1881).* Buenos Aires: ICANA: Instituto Cultural Argentino Norteamericano, 2001.

March, Andrew F. "What Is Comparative Political Theory?". *Review of Politics* 71, no. 4 (2009): 531–65.

Marshall, Stephen H. *The City on the Hill from Below: The Crisis of Prophetic Black Politics.* Philadelphia: Temple University Press, 2011.

Martí, José. "Carta al Señor Director de *La Nación*, 30 de Octubre de 1889." In *Obras completas*, Tomo 12: En los Estados Unidos, escenas norteamericanas, by José Martí, 347–55. La Habana: Editorial Nacional de Cuba, 1964.

Martí, José. *José Martí: Selected Writings.* Translated by Esther Allen. New York: Penguin Classics, 2002.

Martínez-Echazábal, Lourdes. "Mestizaje and the Discourse of National/Cultural Identity in Latin America, 1845–1959." *Latin American Perspectives* 25, no. 3 (1998): 21–42.

Mattox, Jake. "The Mayor of San Juan Del Norte? Nicaragua, Martin Delany, and the 'Cotton' Americans." *American Literature* 81, no. 3 (2009): 527–54.

Menand, Louis. "Morton, Agassiz, and the Origins of Scientific Racism in the United States." *Journal of Blacks in Higher Education* 34 (Winter 2001–2002): 110–13.

Mendieta, Eduardo. "The Making of New Peoples: Hispanicizing Race." In *Hispanics/Latinos in the United States*, edited by Jorge J. E. Gracia and Pablo de Greiff, 44–59. New York: Routledge, 2000.

Merguson, R. W. "Glimpses of Brazil." *The Crisis* 11, no. 1 (1915): 38–43.

Mignolo, Walter. *The Darker Side of the Renaissance: Literacy, Territoriality, and Colonization.* Ann Arbor: University of Michigan Press, 1995.

Mignolo, Walter. "Delinking." *Cultural Studies* 21, nos 2–3 (2007): 449–514.

Mignolo, Walter. *The Idea of Latin America.* New York: Wiley-Blackwell, 2006.

Miller, Marilyn Grace. *Rise and Fall of the Cosmic Race: The Cult of Mestizaje in Latin America.* Austin: University of Texas Press, 2004.

Miller, Monica L. "W. E. B. Du Bois and the Dandy as Diasporic Race Man." *Callaloo* 26, no. 3 (2003): 738–65.

Mills, Charles W. "White Ignorance." In *Race and Epistemologies of Ignorance*, edited by Nancy Tuana and Shannon Sullivan, 13–38. Albany: State University of New York Press, 2007.

Mills, Charles W. "Whose Fourth of July? Frederick Douglass and Original Intent." In *Blackness Visible: Essays on Philosophy and Race*, by Charles W. Mills, 167–200. Ithaca, NY: Cornell University Press, 1998.

Mullen, Bill V. "Du Bois, *Dark Princess*, and the Afro-Asian International." *positions* 11, no. 1 (2003): 217–39.

Myers, Peter C. *Frederick Douglass: Race and the Rebirth of American Liberalism.* Lawrence: University Press of Kansas, 2008.

Nahuelpan Moreno, Héctor. "Formación colonial del Estado y desposesión en Ngulumapu." In *Ta iñ fijke xipa rakizuameluwün: historia, colonialismo y resistencia desde el país Mapuche*, by Héctor Nahuelpan Moreno et al., 123–156. Temuco, Chile: Ediciones Comunidad de Historia Mapuche, 2012.

Nascimento, Abdias Do. *Brazil, Mixture or Massacre? Essays in the Genocide of a Black People*. Dover, MA: Majority Press, 1989.

Nelson, Alondra. "Introduction: Future Texts." *Social Text* 20, no. 2 (Summer 2002): 1–15.

Nwankwo, Ifeoma K. *Black Cosmopolitanism: Racial Consciousness and Transnational Identity in the Nineteenth-Century Americas*. Philadelphia: University of Pennsylvania Press, 2005.

Ortiz, Fernando, and Harriet De Onís. *Cuban Counterpoint: Tobacco and Sugar*. New York: A. A. Knopf, 1947.

Oxford English Dictionary Online. Oxford University Press, 2014.

Paschel, Tianna, and Mark Sawyer. "Contesting Politics as Usual: Black Social Movements, Globalization and Race Policy in Latin America." In *New Social Movements in the African Diaspora: Challenging Global Apartheid*, edited by Leith Mullings, 13–32. New York: Palgrave Macmillan Press, 2009.

Pascoe, Peggy. "Between a Rock and a Hard Place." In *What Comes Naturally: Miscegenation Law and the Making of Race in America*, by Peggy Pascoe, 163–204. Oxford: Oxford University Press, 2009.

Polyné, Millery. *From Douglass to Duvalier: U.S. African Americans, Haiti and Pan Americanism, 1870–1964*. Gainesville: University Press of Florida, 2010.

Prashad, Vijay. *The Darker Nations: A Biography of the Short-Lived Third World*. New York: New Press, 2007.

Pratt, Mary Louise. *Imperial Eyes: Travel Writing and Transculturation*. London: Routledge, 1992.

Priego, Natalia. "Porfirio Díaz, Positivism and 'the Scientists': A Reconsideration of the Myth." *Journal of Iberian and Latin American Research* 18, no. 2 (2012): 135–50.

Quijano, Aníbal. "Coloniality of Power, Eurocentrism, and Latin America." *Neplanta* 1, no. 3 (2000): 533–80.

"Race Discrimination: Dark Princess, by W. E. Burghardt Dubois." *New York Times*, May 13, 1928.

Ramírez, Catherine S. "Afrofuturism/Chicanafuturism: Fictive Kin." *Aztlán: A Journal of Chicano Studies* 33, no. 1 (2008): 185–94.

Rampersad, Arnold. "Du Bois's Passage to India: Dark Princess." In *W. E. B. Du Bois on Race and Culture: Philosophy, Politics, and Poetics*, edited by Bernard W. Bell, Emily Grosholz, and James B. Stewart, 161–76. New York: Routledge, 1996.

Rana, Aziz. *The Two Faces of American Freedom*. Cambridge, MA: Harvard University Press, 2010.

Reinhardt, Mark. "Who Speaks for Margaret Garner? Slavery, Silence, and the Politics of Ventriloquism." *Critical Inquiry* 29, no. 1 (2002): 81–119.

"Review of Life in the Argentine Republic in the Days of the Tyrants." *New Englander and Yale Review* (October 1868): 666–79.

"Review of Vida de Abran Lincoln." *The Atlantic Monthly* (February 1866): 252–53.

Richards, Patricia. *Race and the Chilean Miracle: Neoliberalism, Democracy, and Indigenous Rights.* Pittsburgh, PA: University of Pittsburgh Press, 2013.

Roberts, Neil. *Freedom as Marronage.* Chicago: University of Chicago Press, 2015.

Rodriguez, Clara E. *Changing Race: Latinos, the Census, and the History of Ethnicity in the United States.* New York: NYU Press, 2000.

Rodriguez, Clara E. "Race, Culture, and Latino 'Otherness' in the 1980 Census." *Social Science Quarterly* 73, no. 4 (December 1992): 930–37.

Rodriguez Objio, Manuel. *Gregorio Luperón e historia de la restauración.* Vol. 2. Santiago, Republica Dominicana: Editorial El Diario, 1939.

Rogers, Molly. *Delia's Tears: Race, Science, and Photography in Nineteenth-Century America.* New Haven, CT: Yale University Press, 2010.

Said, Edward W. *Orientalism.* New York: Vintage Books, 1994.

Sánchez, Luis Alberto. "Bolivarismo, Monroísmo, y Aprismo." *La Nueva Democracia,* March 1, 1935.

Sarmiento, Domingo Faustino. *Ambas Américas: revista de educación, bibliografía y agricultura.* 4 vols. Vol. 1. New York: Imprenta de Hallet y Breen, 1867.

Sarmiento, Domingo Faustino. "Carta a Augusto Belin Sarmiento, Marzo de 1874." In *Sarmiento a través de su epistolario,* edited by Julia Ottolenghi, 108–10. Buenos Aires: Libreria y Casa Editora Jesus Menendez, 1939.

Sarmiento, Domingo Faustino. "Carta Al Señor D. Luis Montt." In *Obras de D. F. Sarmiento,* vol. 29, edited by Augusto Belin Sarmiento, 6–8. Buenos Aires: Imprenta Mariano Moreno, 1899.

Sarmiento, Domingo Faustino. *Cartas de Sarmiento a la señora María Mann.* Buenos Aires: Academia Argentina de Letras, 1936.

Sarmiento, Domingo Faustino. "Cartas de Sarmiento: III. Autobiográficas (Cont.)." *Boletin de la Academia Argentina de Letras* 4 (1936): 295–362.

Sarmiento, Domingo Faustino. *Conflicto y armonías de las razas en América.* Buenos Aires: La Cultura Argentina, 1915.

Sarmiento, Domingo Faustino. "El año nuevo: a 'El Zonda' de San Juan, Nueva York, Enero 6 de 1866." In *Obras de D. F. Sarmiento,* vol. 29, edited by Augusto Belin Sarmiento, 86–93. Buenos Aires: Imprenta de Mariano Moreno, 1899.

Sarmiento, Domingo Faustino. "El Norte Americanismo republicano." In *Obras de D. F. Sarmiento,* vol. 39, edited by Augusto Belin Sarmiento, 67–73. Buenos Aires: Imprenta Mariano Moreno, 1900.

Sarmiento, Domingo Faustino. "El poeta Longfellow." In *Obras de D. F. Sarmiento,* vol. 45, edited by Augusto Belin Sarmiento, 371–74. Buenos Aires: Imprenta Mariano Moreno, 1900.

Sarmiento, Domingo Faustino. "En Estados Unidos." In *Obras completas de Sarmiento,* vol. 21, *Discursos populares, primer volumen,* by Domingo Faustino Sarmiento, 229–33. Buenos Aires: Editorial Luz del Día, 1951.

Sarmiento, Domingo Faustino. *Facundo: Civilization and Barbarism*. Translated by Kathleen Ross. Los Angeles: University of California Press, 2004.

Sarmiento, Domingo Faustino. "Introducción." In *Vida de Abran Lincoln*, by Domingo Faustino Sarmiento, xi–xlviii. New York: D. Appleton, 1866.

Sarmiento, Domingo Faustino. *Las escuelas: base de la prosperidad y de la república en los Estados Unidos.* New York: D. Appleton, 1866.

Sarmiento, Domingo Faustino. *North and South America: A Discourse Delivered before the Rhode Island Historical Society, December 27, 1865*. Providence, RI: Knowles, Anthony, 1866.

Sarmiento, Domingo Faustino. "Una carta a Mrs. Mann, Diciembre 6 de 1882." In *Obras de D. F. Sarmiento*, vol. 37, edited by Augusto Belin Sarmiento, 317–22. Buenos Aires: Imprenta Mariano Moreno, 1900.

Sarmiento, Domingo Faustino. *Viajes en Europa, Africa y América 1845–1847*. Vol. 2. Santiago, Chile: Imprenta de Julio Belin y Compañia, 1851.

Scott, David. *Conscripts of Modernity: The Tragedy of Colonial Enlightenment*. Durham, NC: Duke University Press, 2004.

Scott, David. *Refashioning Futures: Criticism after Postcoloniality*. Princeton, NJ: Princeton University Press, 1999.

Seigel, Micol. "Beyond Compare: Comparative Method after the Transnational Turn." *Radical History Review* 2005, no. 91 (2005): 62–90.

Sexton, Jared. *Amalgamation Schemes: Antiblackness and the Critique of Multiracialism*. Minneapolis: University of Minnesota Press, 2008.

Shulman, George M. *American Prophecy: Race and Redemption in American Political Culture*. Minneapolis: University of Minnesota Press, 2008.

Skidmore, Thomas E. *Black into White: Race and Nationality in Brazilian Thought*. 2d ed. Durham, NC: Duke University Press, 1993.

Solodkow, David. "Racismo y nación: conflictos y (des)armonías identitarias en el proyecto nacional Sarmientino." *Decimonónica* 2, no. 1 (Summer 2005): 95–121.

Sorensen Goodrich, Diana. *Facundo and the Construction of Argentine Culture*. Austin: University of Texas Press, 1996.

Starkey, James R. "Letter." Frederick Douglass's Paper, May 27, 1852.

Stavans, Ilan, and José Vasconcelos. *José Vasconcelos: The Prophet of Race*. New Brunswick, NJ: Rutgers University Press, 2011.

Stepan, Nancy. *The Hour of Eugenics: Race, Gender, and Nation in Latin America*. Ithaca, NY: Cornell University Press, 1991.

Taylor, Paul C. "Appiah's Uncompleted Argument: W. E. B. Du Bois and the Reality of Race." *Social Theory & Practice* 26, no. 1 (Spring 2000): 103–28.

Telles, Edward, and PERLA (Project on Ethnicity and Race in Latin America). *Pigmentocracies: Ethnicity, Race, and Color in Latin America*. Chapel Hill: University of North Carolina Press, 2014.

Threadcraft, Shatema. *Intimate Justice: The Black Female Body and the Body Politic*. New York: Oxford University Press, 2016.

Trouillot, Michel-Rolph. *Silencing the Past: Power and the Production of History.* Boston, MA: Beacon Press, 1995.

Turner, Jack. *Awakening to Race: Individualism and Social Consciousness in America.* Chicago: University of Chicago Press, 2012.

Vasconcelos, José. *Bolivarismo y Monroísmo: temas Iberoamericanos.* México, D.F.: Editorial Trillas, 2011.

Vasconcelos, José. *The Cosmic Race/la raza cósmica: A Bilingual Edition.* Translated by Didier T. Jaén. Baltimore, MD: Johns Hopkins University Press, 1997.

Vasconcelos, José. *Indología: una interpretación de la cultura Ibero-Americana.* Paris: Agencia Mundial de Librería, 1927.

Vasconcelos, José. *La raza cosmica: misión de la raza Iberoamericana, Argentina y Brasil.* Colección Austral. 5. ed. México: Espasa-Calpe Mexicana, 1977.

Vasconcelos, José. "La supremacia de los blancos." *La Prensa,* December 20, 1926.

Vasconcelos, José. "Sarmiento estadista." *La Prensa,* December 23, 1938.

Von Vacano, Diego A. *The Color of Citizenship: Race, Modernity and Latin American/ Hispanic Political Thought.* New York: Oxford University Press, 2012.

Wade, Peter. *Blackness and Race Mixture: The Dynamics of Racial Identity in Colombia.* Baltimore, MD: Johns Hopkins University Press, 1993.

Wade, Peter. "Images of Latin American Mestizaje and the Politics of Comparison." *Bulletin of Latin American Research* 23, no. 3 (2004): 355–66.

Wade, Peter. *Race and Ethnicity in Latin America.* London: Pluto Press, 1997.

Waligora-Davis, Nicole. "W. E. B. Du Bois and the Fourth Dimension." *CR: The New Centennial Review* 6, no. 3 (2006): 57–90.

Wallis, Brian. "Black Bodies, White Science: Louis Agassiz's Slave Daguerreotypes." *American Art* 9, no. 2 (1995): 39–61.

Walsh, Catherine. "Shifting the Geopolitics of Critical Knowledge." *Cultural Studies* 21, nos 2–3 (2007): 224–39.

Weinbaum, Alys Eve. "Reproducing Racial Globality: W. E. B. Du Bois and the Sexual Politics of Black Nationalism." *Social Text* 19, no. 2 (Summer 2001): 15–41.

West, Cornel. *Prophesy Deliverance!: An Afro-American Revolutionary Christianity.* Louisville, KY: Westminster John Knox Press, 2002.

Westerbeck, Colin L. "Frederick Douglass Chooses His Moment." *Art Institute of Chicago Museum Studies* 24, no. 2 (1999): 145–262.

Wilson, Ivy G. "On Native Ground: Transnationalism, Frederick Douglass, and 'the Heroic Slave.'" *PMLA* 121, no. 2 (2006): 453–68.

Wolin, Sheldon S. "Fugitive Democracy." *Constellations* 1, no. 1 (1994): 11–25.

Yashar, Deborah. *Contesting Citizenship in Latin America: The Rise of Indigenous Movements and the Postliberal Challenge.* Cambridge: Cambridge University Press, 2005.

Yaszek, Lisa. "An Afrofuturist Reading of Ralph Ellison's Invisible Man." *Rethinking History* 9, nos 2–3 (2005): 297–313.

Index

Page numbers followed by an "*f*" indicate figures.

CPSIA information can be obtained
at www.ICGtesting.com
Printed in the USA
BVHW052336100523
663962BV00001B/1